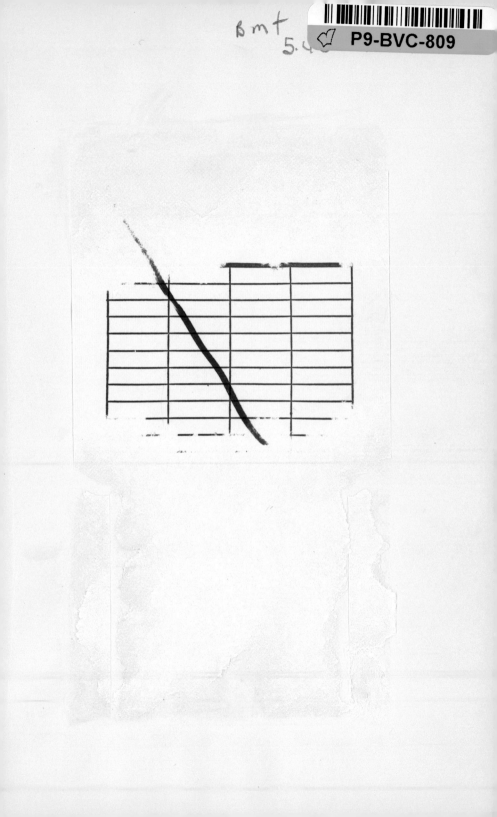

THE ORIGINS OF
THE GREAT SCHISM

VRBANVS . VI . PAPA . NEAPOLITANVS

Pope Urban VI

The
ORIGINS OF THE
GREAT SCHISM

A study in fourteenth-century
ecclesiastical history

by

WALTER ULLMANN

with a 1972 preface by the author

ARCHON BOOKS
1972

TO
RALPH

Library of Congress Cataloging in Publication Data

Ullmann, Walter, 1910–
   The origins of the Great Schism.

   Reprint of the 1948 ed.
   Includes bibliographical references.
   1. Schism, The Great Western, 1378-1417. I. Title.
[BX1301.U55 1972]   270.5   79-39365
ISBN 0-208-01277-X

First published 1938 by Burns Oates & Washburn Ltd.
Reprinted with permission 1967 as an Archon Book by The
Shoe String Press, Inc. Reprinted with permission 1972
with a new preface by the author as an Archon Book by
The Shoe String Press, Inc., Hamden, Connecticut. © 1972
by Walter Ullmann. *Printed in the United States of
America.*

PREFACE

MY AIM in writing this book was to give a brief representation of the main events of 1378 and the period immediately following it. I am fully aware of the deficiencies which are bound to result from the wealth of material at once profuse and contradictory. A very modest attempt has been made to combine juristic investigation with the purely historical analysis, because the neglect of medieval canon law and doctrine appeared to me detrimental to an adequate understanding of the situation. On the other hand, I have tried to avoid giving undue weight to purely legal technicalities. For those readers, however, who may be interested, I have appended a chapter dealing with the theory and canonistic background of Cardinal Francis Zabarella.

The period of the Schism is perhaps one of the most fascinating epochs in medieval history : it is a dramatic representation of the characteristic features of the fourteenth century. Right at the beginning of the century we witness the first heraldings of a profound ideological crisis that was to impress itself on the whole spiritual structure of the century. The ideological crisis is mirrored in the external events of the time : the quarrels between Boniface VIII and Philip the Fair, the contest between John XXII and Lewis of Bavaria, are merely symptoms of the underlying spiritual unrest. But whilst, in the first half of the century, the controversy was mainly focused on the vexed question of Church *versus* State (to use traditional terminology), in the second half, the full force of a crisis raged within the Church herself, culminating in the events of 1378. Whether the contest was Church *versus* State or cardinals *versus* pope, the crisis in both cases concerned the law. The law was considered to be in need of a drastic modification to suit the changed temper of the time. Before this need was fulfilled, events took their turn without the prudent guidance of legal force. This factor partially accounts for the repellent nature of certain actions occurring in this century. Men took the law into their own hands, until, instead of a new law, a fresh interpretation of the old was evolved. Consequently, the employment of extra-legal, meta-juristic ideas, such as the Aristotelian " epieikeia ", was a feature common to all " reformers ", precisely because these somewhat vague concepts offered a welcome opportunity to interpret the law in harmony with the changed times. In this, I believe, lies the real significance of the dogmatic, and sometimes antidogmatic, theories of such eminent writers as Conrad of Gelnhausen and Henry of Langenstein.

Men were torn by the tragedy which had befallen the Western Church—appeals to both popes had been unavailing. Is it then not understandable that there were many attempted solutions of the problem, although it is sometimes extremely difficult to consider the proposals as falling within the precincts of dogma and established Church teaching ? On the other hand, no small lack of imagination is shown by any sweeping condemnation of these protagonists who frequently acted from true sincerity of conviction. They all were typical children of an age in which the landmarks of the old and new, no less than those of right and wrong, were no longer clearly discernible. Under such circumstances men often lost a sense of proportion and perspective, and sometimes failed to see the true implications of their own thoughts. This applies not only to the writers, but also to the actual dramatis personae : whether popes, cardinals or lesser mortals—they all were in the fetters of the contemporary crisis, whose tools they unwittingly had become. The fourteenth century is a singular example of the truism that it is ideas which shape history, and not facts and events.

I would like to take this opportunity of expressing my most cordial thanks to the Reverend Philip Hughes for his generous counsel, particularly in the last stages of the production of the book : I am glad to say that the whole typescript went through the capable hands of this eminent historian of the Catholic Church ; his profound knowledge of everything connected with medieval Church life has preserved me from many pitfalls and blunders. My sincere thanks are also due to Mr. H. M. Adams for the customary and unsparing help he has rendered me so willingly in that treasury of the medieval historian which is accumulated in the Library of Trinity

College, Cambridge. My thanks are, furthermore, due to the librarians of St. John's College, Mr. H. P. W. Gatty, and of Caius College, Mr. Philip Grierson, for kindly putting at my disposal some of their manuscripts and lastly to the publishers for the great care which they have bestowed on the correction of the proofs.

Whitsun, 1947.   W. U.

PREFACE TO THE 1972 REPRINT

RESEARCH HAS not stood still since this book was published nearly twenty-five years ago. Yet the time for re-writing it has not yet come, because the results of recent research have not materially changed the picture as it is here presented, though the interpretation has in some respects been modified. It is especially gratifying to record that a number of my own pupils have had their share in the re-orientation and re-interpretation of the events and their aftermath. What I believe I can usefully do on this occasion is, by way of a short exposé, to draw attention to some new primary and secondary literature, a method which allows me to weave in at least part of the new material, and thereby avoids the expensive process of resetting the whole book.

There are two items which form the backbone of the book and are of particular interest to the student of the late Middle Ages and specifically of the Great Schism. The one is factual and related to the election of Urban VI in Rome,[1] and the other is constitutional and concerned with the position of the pope and his relation to the Church universal. Of these two items the latter has attracted—and perhaps rightly so—far greater attention than the former.

In regard to the first item—the events surrounding the election of Urban and its consequences—there is very little new material that would force us to alter the picture in any substantial way.[2] Urban's unsuitability can well be taken as an established fact, and the additional evidence proves that this was very well appraised by the cardinals. Moreover, it

[1] For the situation at Rome immediately prior to the eventful election, see R. G. Trexler, 'Rome on the eve of the Great Schism' in *Speculum*, xliii (1957), 489–509.
[2] The Calendar relating to all the persons and localities at least in Germany from Urban VI to Gregory XII has now been concluded: *Repertorium Germanicum*, vol. ii (ed. G. Tellenbach et al.) (Berlin 1933–61). For England *The Calendars of Papal Letters* are still indispensable.

was precisely in accord with this knowledge that they began
to act in the early summer of 1378. The situation as it presented itself in the late spring and early summer months
confronted the cardinals with a contingency for which neither
history nor the law provided any guidance, let alone solution. It should be borne in mind that what distinguished this
schism from its numerous predecessors, was that one and the
same body of electors chose two men as popes within a few
months. This step taken by the College of Cardinals reflected
clearly their view on the unsuitability of the man whom they
had first elected. But, and this was the real problem that
stared them in the face, what was to be done with a pope
who demonstrably had proved himself unfit for the papal
office? It is one of the extraordinary gaps in the otherwise
highly developed constitution of the Church evolved as it had
through something approaching a millenium, that there was
no provision for this contingency, although political writers
certainly from the early fourteenth century onwards had indeed envisaged the possibility of the pope's insanity, inepti-
tude or other grave inadequacy that prevented orderly government by him. The possibility of a pope governing in such
a manner that he turned upside down the very principle
which was the *raison d'être* of papal government, that is, that
he should govern for the good of the whole Church, was discussed at considerable length and depth in the very beginning
of the century by John of Paris.[3] It is one thing to put forward a suggestion which should be turned into the law, as
John of Paris and others had proposed, but it is an entirely
different thing to meet in reality this very contingency which
the proposal was to have eliminated and to apply a non-
existent law. The way out of this dilemma was the one recourse which the law had provided, that is to assert that the

[3]That is why John of Paris also maintained (though with hardly
any legal, literary or constitutional support) that the pope could,
if necessary, be deposed: *De potestate regia et papali*, ed. J.
Leclercq (Paris 1942), c. 24, p. 254. For John of Paris cf. W. Ullmann, *Principles of Government and Politics in the Middle Ages*,
2nd ed. (London 1966), 263ff.; M. J. Wilks, *The Problem of
Sovereignty in the later Middle Ages* (Cambridge 1963), 480, esp.
484f.

original election had been made under such pressure that it amounted to compulsion and was therefore invalid. That was exactly what the cardinals did when they elected Cardinal Robert of Geneva as Clement VII at Fondi in the early autumn of 1378.

What recent literature makes clear is that the dilemma was by the summer months of 1378 incapable of being solved. Factually the circumstances were by no means such as they would have made the election invalid. The cardinals—virtually all of them experienced, learned, mature and responsible men—did not need some five months to come to that conclusion, but could have done so immediately or very soon after the election. One of the newly discovered sources makes this perfectly plain. The *Consilium* by the most eminent Bolognese jurist, Bartholomaeus Salicetus, concluded after an exhaustive examination of the facts and their assessment that the plea of duress could not be upheld from the juristic standpoint.[4] In other words, the declaration by the cardinals that the election was invalid because of their fear resulting from the unruly conditions, was no more than a pretext that was perfectly understandable in these circumstances. In what other way, one should ask oneself if one wishes to face reality, should they have proceeded to neutralize the government of a man who as none knew better than they themselves (and as they actually were amply proved right subsequently by the pope's own deeds and words) was a megalomaniac and insane? It was the weakness of the ecclesiastical constitution which made the cardinals fall back on the unruly election. By this device of retrospectively and artificially inflating the circumstances of the election they hoped to achieve what the

[4]See Nicolo del Re, 'Il Consilium pro Urbano VI di Bartolomeo de Saliceto' in *Studi e Testi*, ccix (1962) (=Collectanea Vaticana *in honorem Anselmi Cardinalis Albareda*), 212–63. For the manuscript which contains very interesting material mainly relating to the Schism, see ibid., 223–33. Salicetus had some very famous pupils, such as Raphael Fulgosius, Jacobus Alvarottus (both civilians), Petrus de Ancharano and Franciscus Zabarella (both eminent canonists), see F. C. Savigny, *Geschichte des römischen Rechts im Mittelalter*, 2nd ed. (Heidelberg 1950), vi. 259ff., at 266.

law of the constitution had denied them. Their stratagem was designed to create an alibi in order to enable them to invoke the existing law. It is no doubt of some significance to note that the Clementine material in regard to the affidavits procured was incomparably bulkier than that assembled by the Urbanists.[5] However many witnesses the Clementines accumulated[6]—and there were, literally speaking, hundreds of testimonies and more are still coming to light[7]—the case for the cardinals did not thereby materially improve nor was that of Urban VI substantially impaired.

What must be borne in mind, and recent research once more supports this view, is that the Great Schism was not a problem of factual evidence, but purely and simply a matter of the law. There was a legal void where there should have been the unequivocal guide of the constitution.[8] The Schism

[5]And in parenthesis it might be remarked that a very similar stratagem was employed by the German opposition to Gregory VII in January 1076 when the ecclesiastical and secular princes declared that he was uncanonically elected pope—nearly three years after having been undisputed pope. Cf. *Monumenta Germaniae Historica: Constitutiones*, i. 108, no. 58=C. Erdmann, *Die Briefe Heinrichs IV*. (in *Mon. Germ. Hist., Scriptores Rerum Germanicarum* [1938] Appendix A, p. 68.) See also W. Ullmann, *Growth of Papal Government in the Middle Ages*, 4th ed. (London 1970), 349f.; W. Goez, 'Zur Erhebung und ersten Absetzung Papst Gregors VII.' in *Römische Quartalschrift*, lxiii (1968), 117–43 (an exhaustive examination of all the relevant points).

[6]For the exemplary collection of the *Libri de schismate* (in the Vatican Archives) containing some 170 depositions and affidavits assembled by order of the Spanish kings, see esp. M. Seidlmayer, *Die Anfänge des Grossen Abendländischen Schismas: Studien zur Kirchenpolitik insbesondere der spanischen Staaten und zu den geistigen Kämpfen der Zeit* (Münster 1940), 197ff., and details 206ff. This work was not available to me when I was engaged in the research for this book at the end of the last war.

[7]See K. A. Fink in *Handbuch der Kirchengeschichte*, ed. H. Jedin (Freiburg 1968), iii. 2, 493. For a further statement see that made by the Carmelite Procurator General: L. Saggi, 'Bartolomeo Peyroni, O. Carm., vescovo di Elne e la sua testimonianza circa il conclave del 1378' in *Archivum Historiae Pontificiae*, iv (1966), 59–77.

[8]K. A. Fink, op. cit., 491ff., seems to waver in his assessment, while a note of despair characterizes G. Mollat in his entry on

once it had become reality and once the main factors which gave rise to it had been assessed, brutally brought contemporaries face to face with the deficiency of the law. Hence the search for a formula not only of ending the Schism but also of preventing a similar occurrence in future. Both questions constituted the same problem looked at from different angles. From the historical as well as ideological point of view it is of some considerable concern to realize that the answer had to be sought within the framework of the law, because in its origins the Schism was a matter of the (defective) law and therefore its ending could reasonably be envisaged only within legal precincts. But the answer that emerged was by no means reconcilable with the traditional papal monarchic concept of rulership. For it was precisely this that was denied. What was advocated and broadcast was a kind of government in which the pope, formerly the master, became the servant of the Church. The searching historian is here confronted by one of the most fascinating features in the development of Western constitutionalism. Since the mid-fifth century the papacy was built on unadulterated monarchic foundations, according to which the pope as heir to St Peter embodied the apostle's fulness of power so that he was said to act vicariously as Christ would have acted. This so-called descending theme of government and law[9] maintained that since all power was concentrated in the pope as vicar of Christ (because he was the successor of St Peter), whatever power was

---

Clement VII in *Dictionnaire d'histoire et de géographie ecclésiastiques,* xii (1953), col. 1166: 'Tel est l'embarras que nous ressentions actuellement pour émettre un jugement équitable sur la légitimité d'Urban VI.' This is reminiscent of N. Valois' famous dictum 'La solution du grand problème posé au XIVe siècle échappe au jugement de l'histoire,' (*La France et le Grand Schisme* (Paris 1896), i. 82). It is most gratifying to record the strong support which the eminent Ed. de Moreau gave to the main theme of this book when he reviewed it under the title 'Une nouvelle théorie sur les origines du grand schisme d'Occident' in *Bulletin de l'Académie royale de Belgique,* 5th series, 1949), 182–90.

[9] See *Principles of Government* (above note 3), 21ff., 53ff.; further W. Ullmann, *A History of Political Ideas in the Middle Ages* (Pelican History of political ideas), 2nd ed. revised (1970). 31ff.

found in the lower placed officials was derived from the pope. These officers were delegates of the pope and responsible to him alone. Hence the exclusion of the synods and councils as law-creating organs on a universal scale unless they were approved by the pope. The hallmark of the descending theme was obedience of the 'inferior' (the sub/ject) to the 'superior' (the sovereign), that is obedience to the law as given by superior authority.

But as a result of a variety of factors, notably the influence of Aristotle's thought-patterns as well as of the prevailing practices in the lower non-ecclesiastical echelons of medieval society,[10] this descending theme came in the course of the thirteenth century to be replaced by its ascending counterpart, according to which supreme power was not located in one monarchic individual who distributed it downwards, but in the totality of the people who acted through their representative assemblies in councils, synods, and the like; and they in turn elected governors who remained always responsible to the assemblies, and thereby eventually to the people. Power rises, so to speak, from the base: it ascends from the broad base until it reaches its supreme head who therefore was said to have received his power 'from below'. He could, consequently, be deposed or his power be curtailed, enlarged or modified. Within the descending theme this was evidently not possible, because the people had not given any power to the Ruler, and could not understandably alter it in scope or take it away, because it was not theirs, but stemmed from divinity.

The ascending theme of government and law had gained considerable popularity in the course of the fourteenth century. It affected jurists as well as political writers, littérateurs as well as publicists and legislators. But as such the theme had not yet been advocated as a programme suitable also for adoption as a constitutional basis of Church government. The disaster of 1378 provided the opportunity of adopting the ascending theme, however antagonistic it might have

[10]For details see *Principles* (preceding note), 231ff.; *History* (preceding note), 159ff.; W. Ullmann, *Individual & Society in the Middle Ages* (Baltimore 1966), ch. 3 *passim*.

appeared to the writers on Church government of a generation earlier. What emerged was the so-called conciliar theme
of government which in its essence was a straightforward application of the ascending theme. Conciliarism had its roots
partly in the political ideology as propounded by the political
writers,[11] partly in the canonistic doctrines concerning the
structure of the ecclesiastical corporation,[12] and partly in the
civilian theses as they were modelled on the Italian city states
and set forth by the Post-glossators.[13] The conciliar theme
rapidly gained momentum. It was seen as a panacea to end
the Schism and to prevent similar contingencies from arising.
Supreme power was to be located in the General Council as
the organ that represented the whole of Christendom.[14]

The efforts of the various kingdoms, universities and
scholars to bring the Schism to a conclusion met with the
intransigence of the two contending popes.[15] This is not the

[11]As has been convincingly shown by my former pupil M. J.
Wilks, *The Problem of Sovereignty* (above note 3), 455ff.; cf.,
further, P. Sigmund, 'The influence of Marsilius on fifteenth-
century conciliarism' in *Journal of the History of Ideas*, xxiii
(1962) 392–402. Also L. Buisson, *Potestas und Caritas: die päpst-
liche Gewalt im Spätmittelalter* (Graz-Cologne 1958).

[12]Demonstrated by my former pupil B. Tierney, *Foundations
of Conciliar Theory* (repr. Cambridge 1969); id., 'Pope and Council: some new decretist texts' in *Medieval Studies*, xix (1957)
197–218.

[13]Cf. W. Ullmann, 'De Bartoli sententia: Concilium repraesen-
tat mentem populi' in *Bartolo di Sassoferrato: studi e documenti
per VI centenario* (Milan 1963), ii. 705–29.

[14]For some general assessment of conciliarism see K. A. Fink in
the paper cited below note 17; also H. Heimpel, ibid., pp. 179f.
Further, E. F. Jacob, *Essays in the conciliar epoch,* 3rd ed. (Man-
chester 1963).

[15]Of particular significance was the French withdrawal of
obedience from (the antipope) Benedick XII in 1397 (on this see
also the very interesting and not yet analysed discussion by Baldus de Ubaldis in his *Lectura in quinque libros decretalium*
(ed. Venice 1615) on I. iii. 25) and the French proposal to the
English king, Richard II, that he should follow suit. Richard II
consulted the University of Cambridge, on which see W. Ullmann, 'The University of Cambridge and the Great Schism' in
Journal of Theological Studies, new series, ix (1958) 53–77.

place to deal with the detailed proposals for terminating the
Schism, but mention should be made of the great number of
very well thought-out schemes proposed for the Council of
Pisa in 1409 to which cardinals of both obediences had re-
paired themselves to elect a new pope.[16] Not only is the invocation of the ascending theme of particular interest, but
also the appeal to history which, after the creation of the third
pope in this Pisan Council, was bound to fall on fertile soil
and actually led to the convocation of the Council of Constance. And in a number of its decrees this Constance Council
implemented the ascending theme faithfully. Two of these
deserve special mention. The one declared in classic form
the basic tenet of the ascending theme that every Christian
of whatever status or dignity, including the pope, was subjected to the rulings of the General Council in matters concerning the faith and the ending of the present Schism, the
reason being that the General Council was the organ which
represented the whole Church.[17] And since the General

[16]For the records of the Council of Pisa, see J. Vincke, 'Acta
concilii Pisani' in *Römische Quartalschrift* xlvi (1938) 81–331.
In parenthesis it should be pointed out that the so-called Capitu-
lations (i.e. the promises made under oath by the future pope)
played a considerable role before and at Pisa. On these Capitula-
tions cf. W. Ullmann, 'The legality of the papal electoral pacts'
in *Ephemerides Iuris Canonici* xii (1956) 312–36, and about their
role at Pisa some of the jurists had a great deal to say which too
has not yet been analysed. Cf., for instance, Paulus Castrensis,
Consilia (ed. Frankfurt 1582), *cons.* 419; Antonius de Butrio, ibid.,
cons. 420, and his *Commentaria ad decretales* (ed. Lyons 1556),
on I.ii.1,no.10; Petrus de Ancharano, *Consilia* (ed. Lyons 1539),
cons. 281; Dominicus de s. Geminiano, *Consilia* (ed. Lyons
1533), *cons.* 88. See further Baldus in his *Lectura* (above note 15),
ad loc. cit., and Panormitanus, *Super quinto libro decretalium*
(ed. Lyons 1512) on V.xxxix.44,no.5. For the latter cf. in general
K. Nörr, *Kirche und Konzil bei Nicolaus de Tudeschis* (Graz-
Cologne 1964).
[17]'Quod ipsa synodus in spiritu sancto legitime congregata
generale concilium faciens, ecclesiam catholicam repraesentans
potestatem a Christo immediate habeat, cui quilibet cuiuscumque
status vel dignitatis etiamsi papalis existat, obedire tenetur in
his, quae pertinent ad fidem et extirpationem dicti schismatis' in
Conciliorum oecumenicorum decreta, 2nd ed. (ed. by J. Alberigo
et al.) (Basle-Fribourg-Rome 1962), 384. For comments cf. W. Ull-

Council was the proper and sole legislative organ, the Council of Constance laid down in the other decree that General Councils must be held at certain stipulated intervals.[18] After all, if the General Council was to represent the whole of Christendom and was to control the pope, it had to meet frequently.

What seems clear is that it was originally the constitutional deficiency which galvanized contemporary opinion to adopt the radical conciliar theme. There is no need to emphasize again that this theme was the very antithesis of the traditional monarchic thesis. The explanation why this radical view found such ready response is not difficult—the extraordinary situation created by the election of Urban which painfully and dramatically made contemporaries aware of the deficient constitution. But what is less easily capable of an explanation is why the conciliarist theme which had gripped everyone in Europe during the schismatic age, within a short time petered out only to make room for a revived monarchic papacy, albeit shorn of some of its powers, but nevertheless standing on the traditional descending theme of government. For within two or three decades after the closure of the Council of Constance, the papacy had recouped a great deal of its powers, even though perhaps not of its customary authority.

Recent research has indicated the answer to the crucial question of how one can explain the rapid decline of conciliarism.[19] The question can also be put in a different way. How can one explain that so many of the staunch conciliarists

---

mann, *The medieval papacy, St Thomas and Beyond* (The Thomas Aquinas Lecture 1960), 23ff.; K. A. Fink, 'Die konziliare Idee im späten Mittelalter' in *Vorträge und Forschungen* vol. ix (1964): *Die Welt zur Zeit des Konstanzer Konzils*, 119–34 at 126; W. Brandmüller, 'Besitzt das Dekret "Haec sancta" dogmatischer Verbindlichkeit?' in *Römische Quartalschrift* lxii (1967), 1–17; B. Tierney, 'The Problem of "Haec sancta"' in *Essays presented to Bertie Wilkinson* (Toronto 1969), 354–70. K. A. Fink with good reasons suggests that the designation *Haec sancta* should be dropped, because it is misleading: more than a dozen decrees of Constance begin with these words, op. cit., iii.2,566 note 20.

[18]*Decreta* (preceding note), 414f.

[19]On this see my former pupil A. Black, *Monarchy and Community* (Cambridge 1970), part II.

left their own camp and returned 'to the old fold'? The answer can be given on several levels. In the first place, despite their vociferous assertions that original power rested with the whole Church, the *congregatio fidelium*, including as it did clergy as well as laity, the conciliarists saw in the General Council no more than an assembly of the higher clergy, notably the bishops, archbishops, abbots. The educated layman and the educated though lowly placed cleric had no standing in the General Councils and had no means of exercising influence. Of course, there were the delegates of the kings, but they were there as delegates of theocratic Rulers and not in their own right. Decision making and participation in the great assemblies was denied to the layman and the lowly cleric. Yet in the fourteenth and early fifteenth centuries there was a veritable proliferation of universities, colleges and schools producing precisely the kind of man who was knocking at the gate, but was refused admission, because he was 'merely' a layman or an ordinary parish priest, however well educated he might have been.[20]

Despite the pious assertions by the learned writers the members of the third estate—the newly arisen and dynamic bourgeoisie—were not considered fit enough to take an intelligent interest in the matters debated in the General Councils. It was as if the educational wheel had stood still. The popular forces included not only the educated layman and

[20]For the position of one of the most intelligent and perceptive conciliarists (that is, Cardinal Zabarella) cf. his revealing discussion in T. Sartori, 'Un discorso inedito di Francesco Zabarella a Bonifacio IX sull' aurorità del papa' in *Rivista di storia della chiesa in Italia*, xx (1966), 375–88. See now also the significant theory proposed by Heimerich of Kamp in A. Black, 'Heimericus de Campo: the Council and History' in *Concilium*, ii (1970), 78–87 (here also further literature). For the attitude of a man like Nicholas of Cusa, see W. Ullmann, 'The papacy and the faithful' in *Recueil de la société Jean Bodin*, xxv (1965), 7–45, esp. 34ff. In this context special attention ought to be drawn to the changes which ecclesiology itself underwent in this period, cf. F. Merzbacher, 'Wandlungen des Kirchenbegriffs im Spätmittelalter: Grundzüge der Ekklesiologie des 14. and 15. Jahrhunderts' in *Savigny Zeitschrift für Rechtsgeschichte, Kanonistische Abteilung* xxxix (1954), 274ff.

cleric, but also the cosmopolitan and prosperous merchant, the trader, the banker and the professional, men in other words whose mental horizon was frenquently far larger and whose vision no less frequently more acute than the somewhat encrusted, if not ossified mental framework of the scholar whose perspicacity and appreciation of vital social and political matters oftentimes was eclipsed by the men of practical wisdom and experience. But the latter had no representatives in the Great Councils and were 'represented' by the archbishops or bishops or abbots in whose making they had no share. It was hardly possible to say that the bishops, the abbots, and so on, had been chosen by those whose representatives they allegedly were. In other words, despite clamorous demands for the implementation of the idea of representation very little was in actual fact done to bring this idea nearer to practical realization.[21]

This consideration links up with a much more fundamental

---

[21]Cf. J. Gill, 'Representation in the conciliar period' in *Studies in Church History*, ed. D. Baker (Cambridge 1971), vii (1971), 177–95. For a general survey of Constance, Basle (and Florence) with translation of texts and decrees see now id., *Constance, Bâle-Florence* (Paris 1965); further A. Franzen (ed.), *Das Konzil von Konstanz: Beiträge zu seiner Geschichte und Theologie* (Freiburg 1964) (with copious literature and sources); K. A. Fink, 'Die weltgeschichtliche Bedeutung des Konstanzer Konzils' in *Savigny Zeitschrift für Rechtsgeschichte, Kanon.Abt.*, li (1965), 1–23; id., *Handbuch* (above note 7), iii.2,545ff. (with good bibliography); for Hus see M. Spinka, *John Hus at the Council of Constance* (New York 1965) (with translation of Latin and Czech texts), and for Wyclif (and Hus) see J. H. Dahmus, 'John Wyclif and the English government' in *Speculum*, xxxv (1960), 61ff.; Edith Tatnall, 'The condemnation of John Wyclif at the Council of Constance' in *Studies in Church History* (above), vii (1971), 209–18; M. J. Wilks, 'The early Oxford Wyclif: Papalist or Nominalist?' ibid., v (1969), 69–98 (with copious literature); J. Kejr, 'Zur Entstehungegeschichte des Hussitentums' in *Vorträge und Forschungen* (above note 17), 47ff.; for the Council of Basle see specifically J. Gill, *The Council of Basle* (Cambridge 1959), and for a very competent guide to the original material relative to this council, see A. P. J. Meijknecht, 'Le concile de Bâle: aperçu général sur les sources' in *Revue d'histoire ecclésiastique*, lxv (1970), 465–73.

one. What the conciliarist theme in reality postulated and proposed was a deadly threat to the existing social order hallowed as it was by tradition and ancient lore. For by its very essence the conciliarist theme as the ecclesiastical manifestation of the ascending theme had aimed at the release of popular forces, precisely because original power was allegedly located in the totality of the Christians. However useful this theme was during the schismatic period, it could well redound to the detriment of the whole established social order. As a matter of fact, at numerous diets and princely assemblies in the forties and fifties of the fifteenth century the plea was made by influential speakers that the adoption of the ascending theme of government would lead to utter disorder and chaos in the public field. The spectre of rebellion was raised in these speeches: kings and princes would be constantly exposed to the factions and whims and demagogues of the people who instead of being governed would soon become the real governors. Lurid language was employed to make gloomy predictions about sedition and the collapse of all orderly life. The diets held at Mainz, Nürnberg, Frankfurt, and other places, reverberated from the dire warnings if the ascending theme were to be implemented.[22] The result of this apocalyptic prophesy was the creation of real fear on the part of secular governments which saw themselves as much exposed to the new-fangled 'democratic' processes as the papacy was. The conciliarists became frightened of their own programme, of their own ideas, of their own scheme of government—and one by one they forsook their own camp and rejoined the papal-monarchic followers, the very men whom they had fought so bitterly only a few years before. The story of the Council of Basle 1437–1449 is an epilogue—at once

[22]Some of the councils in Germany held at this time (mid-fifteenth century) were almost wholly preoccupied with the effects which the conciliar theme, or rather the ascending theme of government in its ecclesiastical form, was to have on the established social order. 'Subversive,' 'overthrow of all human authority,' 'danger of revolt,' 'the deadly poison,' 'destruction of Christendom,' 'overthrow of kingdoms and provinces.' These were some of views expressed, see A. Black, op. cit. (above note 19), 54f., 85ff., 97f.

pitiful and contemptible—of a great movement the adherents
of which had not the courage of their own convictions. Indeed, fear is never a good counsellor.

I have gone into these matters at some length because I
think that this historical situation can serve as a very useful
starting point for discussions concerning the great divide
that was to engulf the whole of Europe in the next generation. The cataclysm which during the Reformation shook
Europe in its very foundations, cast its shadows back to the
first half of the fifteenth century. The gain which accrued
to the monarchic papacy was on a long-term view deceptive,
and lulled it and the established forces into a frame of mind
incapable of assessing the strength of the swelling tide of the
opposition forces. It was a very short-sighted policy to exclude
the new forces which were only too keen and ready to play
their part in the government of the Church and to make
available their talents and service in the interest of the common good. But they were rejected and labelled as mischief
makers, as troublesome, if not subversive, agents of 'dark'
forces. The insistent demand of the new forces for a share
in the government of the Church (as well as of the State)
did not indicate that they intended to attack the foundations
of society (which was as much theirs as of the Establishment).
On the contrary, the new forces intended to strengthen these
foundations, so as to provide more stable conditions. The
cold, uncompromising manner by which the papacy and the
other traditional organs—all of which were manifestations
of the descending theme of government—adamantly opposed
any co-operation could only produce an easily predictable
antagonism on the part of the new popular forces and help
to bring about their conviction that only a radical surgery
could effect a cure. The new forces had great potentialities,
and only a modicum of statesmanship and wisdom was necessary to harness them to a positive and constructive programme. A rigidly maintained negative and repressive attitude is hardly ever a sign of prudence, and coupled with the
fear that characterized the former stalwarts of conciliarism,
could only produce great harm to the very cause which both
the papacy and the conciliarists were anxious to serve. This

untapped reservoir of the uncontaminated youthful intelligentsia in the late fifteenth and early sixteenth centuries could have been harnessed to the service of the common good. And it was precisely to these sections of the populace that Luther and the other Reformers so successfully appealed shortly afterwards.[23]

Seen therefore from a wider perspective the factors which led to the outbreak of the Great Schism present themselves as the harbingers as well as the first distinctly audible rumblings of the events which were to culminate in the Reformation of the early sixteenth century. The period that lies between the outbreak of the Schism and the burning of the law books by Martin Luther manifestly demonstrated all the signs of the coming revolution, and yet it was a revolution which by a little foresight, sagacity and forward looking strategy could have been avoided. There can be few parallels in history which give so much food for thought as the period which was so dramatically and tragically inaugurated by the fateful election of the archbishop of Bari as Pope Urban VI.

Cambridge,   W.U.
Christmas 1971

[23]For the same theme looked at from a different angle, cf. W. Ullmann, 'Julius II and the schismatic cardinals' in *Studies in Church Hist.* (above n.21), iv (1972).

CONTENTS

ILLUSTRATIONS

*The Publishers gratefully acknowledge permission
to reproduce these illustrations.*

I

INTRODUCTION

"T H E S C H I S M," wrote a recent historian, " was the issue of the two contending forces of the later medieval world—the new spirit of nationalism and the spirit of international solidarity which formed the basis of old-time Catholicism."[1] This statement epitomizes one general view of the Schism : a clash between national and international forces. Historical evidence does not, however, bear out the truth of this generalization. The existence of these two opposed forces cannot be denied, but the assertion that they were causal for the outbreak of the Schism is both superficial and historically incorrect. Moreover, this general statement betrays a profound lack of understanding of the history of the Catholic Church, although, as we shall presently see, some Catholic writers have done little to question the truth of this statement. The most that can safely be maintained is that the sentiment of nationality contributed to the outbreak of the Schism. If, as it is said, these two forces alone were the causes of this disaster to the Church, the logical sequel would be that one of the rival parties was opposed in its international outlook by the nationalistic claims of the other. But it would be difficult to say with certainty which of the two sides represented the spirit of internationalism, and which fought for nationalism. Viewing the policies and actions of the two rival popes, especially in the beginning of their pontificates, one can hardly say that Urban VI was a pope imbued with the idea of a cosmopolitan mission any more than that Clement VII was a pope who had at heart the promotion of aims that were purely nationalistic. If Urban was cosmopolitan in his outlook and policy, so was Clement : if Clement was nationalistic, so too was Urban.

[1] Workman, *John Wyclif*, vol. ii, p. 58. See also L. Elliott, *History of the Decline and Fall of the Medieval Papacy*, p. 149 : " The spirit of nationalism was in the air."

French support of Clement's papacy and the overwhelmingly French composition of the Sacred College have given rise to another generalization concerning the cause of the Schism, the statement namely, that the Schism was a mere quarrel between the Italians and the French for the headship of medieval Christianity.[1] In support of this thesis historians refer to the national grouping of Europe which, it is true, had been at least partly carried out on nationalistic lines which, in their turn, were promoted by purely political motives. But as regards the Sacred College itself, there is nothing to suggest that this generalization is borne out by the facts : in none of the official documents, in neither the all-important *Factum Urbani* nor in the *Declaratio*, for example, is there even a hint at French and Italian antagonism. If any antagonism existed, it lay between the French cardinals themselves. That the Italian and French *nations* and their rulers would have preferred to have one of their own race as pope may well be taken for granted : but the likes and dislikes of nations and rulers should not be confused with the likes and dislikes which influenced popes and cardinals. This confusion of the policy of the State with the policy of the Church reveals a remarkable ignorance of the mentality of Churchmen and cardinals, who stood above the purely biological element of race and above nationalistic sentiments. We need to apply a different standard when judging the rulers of nations and the rulers of the Church. If we begin by declaring that the Schism was a national conflict we are judging the policy of the Church by criteria only applicable to the State—and this approach to the problem will mislead us just as surely as if we judged the State by criteria solely applicable to the Church. It is only by attempting to explain the policy of a particular institution from within, and according to its own peculiar standards, that we can hope to arrive at a correct interpretation of its aims and policies.

The story of the Schism shows indeed abundantly that national sentiments played but a very subordinate role in the minds of the cardinals, and of Clement and Urban.

[1]See, for instance, H. A. L. Fisher, *History of Europe*, p. 348 ; Belloc, *History of England*, vol. iii, *passim* ; A. W. Dunning, *History of Political Theories*, vol. i, p. 258.

Both popes sent emissaries to the same governments in Europe, totally disregarding the national and political ties of those governments and rulers ; Clement especially was by no means certain of eventual success. In other words, the break was not one caused by a conflict of Italian and French sentiments amongst the cardinals, but by a revolt of all the cardinals against the constitution of the Church.

The nations and rulers were of course mainly concerned with the political advantages to be derived from adherence to the one or the other pope, but this political grouping should not lead to the facile assumption, still less to the definite assertion, that the Schism was a contest between French and Italians : in so far as it was a contest of this kind, it was accidental, for the contest really concerned nothing less than the constitution of the Church herself and the supremacy in her of the pope. Moreover, the grouping of Europe was an effect of the Schism already established ; it became more pronounced and received a greater emotional impetus and force through the double headship of Christianity, but it was not in itself an element that caused the outbreak of the Schism. It is, of course, tempting to take the political constellation of Europe as a sure symptom of nationalistic tendencies within the Church, and then to go a step further and maintain that the Schism signified the break-up of the old universal Church and the beginning of a new era in Christendom based upon a nationally conceived Christianity—with the inevitable consequence that each nation sought its own spiritual head. But, however attractive this explanation of the Schism may be, it fails to offer a solution that is historically satisfactory. Nationalistic sentiments were undoubtedly employed in the furtherance of those constitutional and legal aims which at once make the Schism understandable and bring it into line with the general ideological trends of the fourteenth century. But in themselves these aims, far from being national or international, represented new ideological forces that had arisen within the Church herself. However vaguely conceived, they manifested themselves in the desire of cardinals and theological thinkers to base the government of the Church upon " broader foundations " than hitherto. The objective of these forces was the papal power : the pope's prerogatives were challenged by the members of the Sacred College, the cardinals. At first this particular aim showed itself only in a negative way, that is, in the cardinals' refusal to acknowledge Urban as true pope : the policy of the cardinals themselves was characterized by a singular lack of any constructive proposals. The cardinals had nothing positive to offer. It was only towards the end of the century, some twenty years after the break had occurred, that a constructive policy emerged ; which, eventually, culminated in the Council of Constance in 1414 —a body illegally convened, but legally disposing of three popes.

The character of the Schism as an ideological crisis within the ecclesiastical hierarchy can hardly be denied. It was a crisis, not caused by nationalistic sentiments, nor by the ever growing strength of national States, although these stimulated and assisted the outbreak, but caused by the influence of ideas directly upon the highest functionaries of the Church herself. The cardinals themselves came to be the protagonists of ideas inimical to Catholic dogma and doctrine—in all likelihood without consciously or intentionally knowing how far they had deviated from dogma and doctrine. It is, therefore, a strange phenomenon in the history of thought that cardinals no less than theologians became the exponents of views which were diametrically opposed to the ancient teaching of the Church on the supremacy of the pope as the vicar of Christ. Their views were a challenge to the pope's legal and constitutional position based as this was upon dogma and doctrine. The Schism brought to the fore the problem as to whether the pope should henceforth have unfettered, uncontrolled and unrestricted powers, or whether his power should be subjected to the control and supervision of a body. Monarchy versus oligarchy was the real issue of the Schism, or, seen from a different angle, absolute versus constitutional monarchy.

To this state of affairs the Avignonese adventure of the popes in the fourteenth century greatly contributed. The second factor which has to be borne in mind when assessing the causes of the Schism was the general trend of ideas current in fourteenth-century thought, a trend by no means confined to secular thinkers or anti-papalists. That there was a tendency on the part of the French monarchy to influence the papacy whilst at Avignon cannot be denied. That, furthermore, some papal actions, especially in the diplomatic field, might have lent some superficial support to the common (and facile) reproach that the papacy was a French appanage is also true. The uncritical amongst the devout may easily have been alienated by certain popes at Avignon whose political activities seemed strangely to coincide with French political designs. Nevertheless, this reproach against the Avignonese papacy which originated with some contemporary personalities, notably with Petrarch, and which was repeated since with greater or lesser ingenuity,[1] loses much of its substance if the actual aims of the papacy between 1305 and 1378 are examined in the light of objective, independent criteria of judgment. The aims of the Avignonese popes can be summarized, according to Professor Mollat, thus : the pacification of Europe, the recovery of the Holy Land, and the restoration of the papal States.[2] In fact, the last-mentioned historian has convincingly proved that the popes at Avignon pursued a policy independent of French influence,[3] and that only a biased and prejudiced view was able to re-assert and repeat the unfounded and unsubstantiated charges against the papacy. It should be borne in mind, moreover, that the popes at Avignon displayed a truly cosmopolitan mission, especially in the educational, cultural and artistic spheres. Nor must it be forgotten that both the popes

[1] According to H. Belloc, " the papacy had become a French thing " (loc. cit., pp. 16, 80)—a highly misleading statement. The most that can be said is that the popes at Avignon were readier to lend their help to the French than other popes, but this is still far from identifying the papacy with France. That the French rulers would have liked to see the papacy " a French thing " cannot be doubted, nor that the peoples came to hold this view, but all this still fails to prove that the papacy actually was " a French thing ". Considered under modern aspects, one could equally unjustly claim that the papacy was " an Italian thing ", because no other nationality but the Italian has succeeded to St. Peter's chair for more than 400 years, and because of the overwhelmingly Italian composition of the Sacred College until quite recent times.

[2] See G. Mollat, Les Papes d'Avignon, p. 401, and his article in Cambridge Medieval History, vol. vii, pp. 272–3.

[3] See Mollat, op. cit., pp. 229–72, 400–2.

who returned to Rome (Urban V and Gregory XI) were of
French origin proper, and that they took the majority of
the (French) cardinals with them to Rome. And at the
time of the outbreak of the Schism, France was ruled by
a king with whom a desire to enlarge his powers or his
kingdom was conspicuously absent. This king, Charles V,
was more concerned with consolidating the gains of his
predecessors than with further expansions. He remained
indeed lukewarm to the first overtures of the cardinals
when they asked his help and appealed to French sentiment.

The mere fact of the seventy years' residence of the popes at
Avignon—a stone's throw from French territory proper—the
overwhelmingly French composition of the Sacred College,
and the geographical nearness of their residence to France,
fail as an explanation of the Schism, resulting as it did from
the unanimous election of a Neapolitan archbishop to St.
Peter's throne. These factors are only of an external and
accidental character. They could never, alone, have sufficed
to array the whole of the Sacred College against the pope who
was left like a " sparrow on the house top ". Of far greater
consequences were the personalities of the popes themselves :
only few of the seven popes residing at Avignon showed the
true strength, force of character and firmness of mind that the
times called for, and which the best of their·illustrious predecessors possessed in centuries gone by. Far more than any
other factor, it was a certain " internal weakness " that made
itself felt in the critical year of 1378. The immorality, luxury,
and lascivity which had become proverbial at the Court of
Avignon was, to say the least, condoned by the popes. The
cancer of immorality, of which the Avignonese hierarchy
gave such a conspicuous example, also attacked the lower
strata of the clergy and did not fail to corrode their morals
also. " La cour pontificale brilla, entre toutes les cours euro-
péennes, par son luxe et l'éclat des fêtes."[1] " The papacy set
itself to extract all that heaped-up wealth could supply of
worldly renown and human delights. The pope's example
became contagious."[2] Religious feasts no less than their secular

[1]Mollat, *op. cit.*, p. 348.
[2]*Idem*, in *Cambridge Medieval History*, *loc. cit.*, pp. 282–3.

counterparts were performed without a parallel in magnificence, splendour and luxury,[1] so that people were able to talk, admittedly with some exaggeration, of " scenes of orgies " at Avignon. This " internal weakness " was fraught with evil and disastrous consequences, because it affected and infected the very personalities in whose hands lay the earthly fate of the Church.

It was precisely through this internal weakness that the cardinals gradually acquired over the pope unconstitutional and illegal powers, which they were resolved to retain. The pope, according to their schemes, was to be a ruler willingly governed by the advice of his counsellors. So long as policy, aims and interests of pope and cardinals were identical, there was no reason for resistance on the part of the latter. But as soon as their respective policies came into conflict, the real issue emerged, and the whole problem was declared : nothing less in fact than this, whether the pope was to be a ruler, as dogma and doctrine demanded, or one who must follow his counsellors. The clash was bound to come. And that it did come so soon after the departure from Avignon was largely due to the personality and character of Urban VI himself. It is this short interval between the departure from Avignon and the outbreak of the Schism which lends some superficial support to the generally entertained opinion. Urban VI dismally failed to grasp the trend of opinion within the Sacred College, and tried to maintain a position which he was unfitted to handle successfully and which was wholly out of harmony with the temper of the time. On the other hand, that the cardinals failed in their endeavour to change the constitution of the Church according to their own designs is largely due to their incapacity to formulate their own proposals clearly and constructively. Instead, the story of the Schism is unique

[1]Mollat, *op. cit.*, pp. 351–5. The private court of the popes consisted of some 300 to 400 individuals, sometimes even more ; some cardinals had rented more than 50 houses to provide accommodation for their households, whilst others again had to rent ten or more stables to place some 200 horses in them. " The cardinals, like the pope, led a life of pomp and magnificence," Mollat, *C.M.H.*, *loc. cit.*, p. 282. On the luxurious life of the clergy at Avignon, see E. Muntz, " L'argent et le luxe à la cour pontificale d'Avignon " in *Revue des Questions Historiques*, vol. lxvi, pp. 5–44, 378–406.

in its mutual showers of abuse and aspersions : each side lowered itself by vituperative and wholly undignified outbursts which only widened the gulf between them and made a rapprochement all the more difficult.

II

THE ELECTION OF URBAN VI

S O O N after the return of Gregory XI from Avignon to Rome, the cardinals entreated him to return to Avignon. He was not impervious to the supplications of his cardinals. His determination to remain in Rome wavered, and he yielded. He intended to be back at Avignon by the autumn of 1378. But fate decreed otherwise—on 27th March, 1378, Gregory was dead. The inevitable rumour had it that his early death was a sure indication of divine displeasure at his intention.

According to custom and law, nine days had to elapse before the cardinals retired into the conclave to elect a successor. The following cardinals resided in Rome at this time. Peter Corsini, Cardinal-bishop of Porto, called Cardinal of Florence ; Peter Tebaldeschi, Cardinal-priest of S. Sabina, and archpresbyter of St. Peter's, called Cardinal of St. Peter ; Simon de Bursano, Cardinal-priest of SS. John and Paul, called Cardinal of Milan ; Jacob de Ursinis (Orsini), Cardinal-deacon of S. Giorgio in Velabro (*velum aureum*)—were the Italian representatives. The following French cardinals were present : Jean de Cros, Cardinal-bishop of Palestrina, called Cardinal of Limoges ; William d'Aigrefeuille, Cardinal-priest of St. Stephen (*Stefano rotundo*) ; Bertrand de Lagery, Cardinal-priest of S. Cecilia, called Cardinal of Glandève ; Hugh de Montelais, Cardinal-priest of SS. Quatuor Coronati, called Cardinal of Brittany ; Robert Count of Geneva, Cardinal-priest of the XII Apostles, called Cardinal of Geneva ; Guido de Malesset, Cardinal-priest of S. Croce, called Cardinal of Poitiers ; Peter de Sortenac, Cardinal-priest of S. Lorenzo, called Cardinal of Viviers ; Gerard du Puy, Cardinal-priest of St. Clement, called Cardinal of Marmoutier ; Peter Flandrin, Cardinal-deacon of St. Eustace ; William Noellet, Cardinal-deacon of St. Angelo ; Peter de Vergne, Cardinal-deacon of S. Maria in Via Lata—and, finally, a Spaniard, Peter de Luna, Cardinal-deacon of S. Maria. There were altogether sixteen cardinals in Rome ; some members of the Sacred College had remained in Avignon, one other, the Cardinal of Amiens, was engaged on a special mission at the Congress of Sarzana.

The composition of the Sacred College leaves no room for doubt that the election of a Frenchman would have created no difficulties, the Italian minority being in no position to challenge the election of a Frenchman effectively. However, the French were divided amongst themselves and had split into two camps, the Limousins, comprising the Cardinals of Limoges, Aigrefeuille, Poitiers, Marmoutier and de Vergne, confronted by the Gallic Cardinals consisting of the Cardinals of Geneva, Glandève, Brittany and St. Eustace and reinforced by Peter de Luna, the Spaniard. The Limousins were resolved to continue with the practice so often observed in the Sacred College during the Avignon regime, i.e., to elect one of their own " nationality " : they had furnished the last four popes and now proposed the election of either Cardinal de Vergne or the Cardinal of Poitiers as their candidate.

But this proposal met with the determined resistance of the Gallic cardinals, whose spokesman was the thirty-six years old Robert of Geneva, a man of extraordinary zeal, ambition and fire. Obviously playing with the thought of becoming pope himself, even before Gregory XI was actually dead, he visited the four Italian cardinals and also Peter de Luna, as well as the Cardinals of Glandève and of Brittany. This fact is testified by one of the cardinal's closest friends, Marino, then Bishop of Cassano, and later Archbishop of Brindisi.[1] For understandable reasons Marino did not conceal his amazement at this canvassing campaign conducted at such an inopportune moment, and on one occasion he dropped a remark to this effect. Robert's reply was that he himself would not care for the pontificate, but that he was resolved to do everything in his power to forestall the election of a candidate proposed by those " Limousin conspirators ". On another occasion, after

[1]Raynaldus, *Annales Ecclesiastici*, tom. vii, p. 301, and Eubel, *Hierarchia Catholica*, tom. i, pp. 154, 176.

the death of Gregory but before the conclave, he declared to Marino that he had now made certain that the Limousins would not get their way. Laying his hand upon his breviary Robert exclaimed : "By the power of this Sacred Writ we shall have no other pope but the Archbishop of Bari." He asserted that out of sheer spite against the Limousins he had won over the four Italian cardinals, together with Peter de Luna and the Cardinals of Brittany and Glandève, so that the Limousins would now easily be outvoted.

In the end, the Archbishop of Bari, Bartolomeo Prignano, was elected and took the name of Urban VI. Prignano, who had long been in the service of the curia, where he held a number of official positions, was made Archbishop of Bari by Gregory XI, and appointed vice-chancellor of the curia in Rome. The cardinals later declared that they had elected Prignano under compulsion and for fear of the reactions of the Roman population : his election was declared by them null and void. They left Rome and later elected as pope Robert of Geneva, who took the name of Clement VII. Whether or not the cardinals had acted under compulsion is a question which can be answered only when relevant testimonies and reliable witnesses have been examined, analysed, and tested as to their trustworthiness. Needless to say, the events immediately preceding the election, as well as those during and after the election, were not always described with any particular regard for the truth. It will be our task to investigate on which of the divergent testimonies we may place the greater reliance. Urban VI, challenged by the cardinals' protestations, was compelled to declare himself in a papal memorandum, which came to be regarded as the official document of the curia concerning his election. In view of the importance of this document, called *Factum Urbani*, it appears advisable to give it in full.[1]

" Already before Gregory's death, when no hope of his recovery could be entertained, the cardinals, apart from the

[1]Raynaldus, *loc. cit.*, pp. 348 seq. An attempt at a reconstruction of the events on the basis of available data is to be found in Noel Valois, *La France et Le Grand Schisme*, vol. i, pp. 35–55.

sick and aged colleague of St. Peter's, had repeated meetings, but they could not agree about the election of an ultra-montane. Since the cardinals, especially the French, felt somewhat uneasy, they arranged for all their private goods, particularly money, books, jewels, and all other mobile possessions to be brought into the castle of St. Angelo, as soon as Gregory died.

" When it became known that Gregory's death was imminent, the officials of the city, i.e., Guido de Primis, a French knight, the city counsellors and the district governors, together with all those who were entrusted with the management of public affairs and many other citizens of repute, approached the cardinals in the church of the Holy Ghost and expressed their regret for the illness of Pope Gregory XI and declared themselves ready to help the cardinals in this grave hour and to obey all their wishes. At the same time, in case of Gregory's death, the deputation asked the cardinals to elect a man who would be suitable for the government of the Church in those days.[1] The cardinals replied that, without any undue influence being brought to bear upon them, they would elect one who was suitable for this post and whose choice was inspired by God. The cardinals requested the city authorities to do everything to take care of the maintenance of public order and discipline. This request was granted : guards and sentries were to be posted all over the city, in the Borgho and around the Conclave, thus protecting the cardinals against all violence and insults.

" On 27th March, 1378, Gregory died and the apostolic see was vacant. The cardinals sent for the Senator (Guido de Primis) and other officials of the city and requested them to take the oath according to the decretal *Ubi periculum*. The officials did so and repeated the above promise. On the following day, however, when all the cardinals were in the church of S. Maria Nova (in which the body of Gregory XI had been buried), the Senator and other officials approached them and humbly and civilly submitted the request that a worthy man of the Italian nation should be elected, adding that this would be in the interest of the

[1]Raynaldus, *loc. cit.*, p. 349, col. 2.

universal Church and of the whole of Christendom. This request was repeated by them on subsequent days when they gave their reasons : that the Roman see, which was and is apostolic, had suffered greatly through the long absence of the pope ; also that the state of the city of Rome itself was ruinous and near collapse ; that churches, monasteries, cloisters, palaces and many other buildings were in a lamentable and deplorable state ; that ecclesiastical goods and possessions in and around Rome were neglected, and that this bad example was now being followed in other parts of Italy, whereby enormous and almost irreparable damage was inflicted upon many churches, monasteries, etc. The only way to remedy this state of affairs was to elect a pope who was a Roman (*Romanus pontifex*) and, furthermore, for the cardinals themselves to reside at Rome and not, as hitherto, to despise the city. In the opinion of the officials, it was because of the French origin of the popes that they had treated Rome with so much contempt ; they felt themselves foreigners in the city. It is a notorious fact that during the long absence of the curia from Rome, wars and many other tribulations had afflicted nearly all the states, cities, towns, villages, even castles, and had torn them asunder ; moreover, French officials had oppressed the population and contributed greatly to the vexations of the people. The Roman Church therefore had suffered great financial loss through this disturbed state of affairs, and the revenues had shrunk to an almost negligible amount. The Church is ' notoriously exhausted and fallen everywhere into great contempt ' (' notorie exhausta et in magno contemptu ubique posita '). The presence of the pastor of the Roman Church at Rome itself is, therefore, strongly indicated : he would then rid himself of the pernicious influence exercised upon him by political intriguers, and he would succumb less easily to the supplications of his relatives, friends, etc., which influence was ' hurtful to the Church of God ' (' ecclesiae Dei nociva') ; nor would any favouritism be tolerated in ecclesiastical appointments, and the purely political elections made ' in favour of the said lay princes with these in view ' (' in favorem et contemplationem dictorum saecularium principum ') would be excluded. For hitherto only those were elevated to high functions who were ' looked upon with favour by the princes and were by nationality their subjects ' (' principibus favorabiles et de natione illis subditi '). Much lack of devotion and obedience had sprung from this practice. The papal states themselves had already revolted against the Church herself. Urban V was moved by those considerations and *visitavit* Rome only in order to re-transfer to Avignon ; and Gregory XI *venit cum magnis laboribus*, in spite of the protests of nearly all his cardinals, relatives, friends, brothers, and of the French monarch and nobles.

" After listening to this address of the officials, the cardinals consulted each other and replied to them *constanter et intrepide* that they did not favour any particular nation and that, eliminating all undue influence, they intended to elect a pope to the advantage of the Church of God and the world, as God and their consciences bid them do. At the same time they requested the officials and senators to protect them, the palace, the conclave and the Borgho of St. Peter as well as the bridges leading to the Borgho. The officials immediately appointed as guards certain Roman district governors and four other Roman citizens of repute. The cardinals trusted these guards and made them take the oath as above, to the effect that they would protect the cardinals and their households.

" Nevertheless, the cardinals ordered the remainder of their personal goods and property belonging to the Church to be brought immediately into the castle of St. Angelo ; moreover, the papal *camerlengo* (i.e., the head of the Treasury) was ordered to move into the castle with many strong soldiers and warlike nobles as well as with a good supply of foodstuffs. There he remained until the pope was elected. By order of the cardinals the *camerlengo* appointed William, Bishop of Marseilles, as his *locum tenens* to perform all those duties incumbent upon the *camerlengo*, especially the custody of the conclave and the palace. The cardinals appointed as assistants to this bishop the Bishops of Tivoli and Todi, who were Roman citizens. These three guarded the conclave and the palace until the election of the pope was performed. They executed their duties *bene fideliter et diligenter*, and protected the cardinals from all violence or injury throughout the time they were in the conclave, before the election was celebrated.

" One must bear in mind, however, that before the cardinals went into the conclave they had a meeting in which the person of the future pope was discussed. But no agreement was reached as to the personality of the candidate. For it became known that five of the cardinals, i.e., the Cardinals of Limoges, Aigrefeuille, Poitiers, de Vergne and Marmoutier, had nominated the Cardinal of Poitiers.[1] Upon being told that this was an impossible choice, they proposed the Cardinal of Viviers who was their *vicinus* (neighbour) and one of their party (*de sequela eorum*). Five other cardinals, all of whom are called the Gallic or French proper, i.e., Glandève, Brittany, Geneva and St. Eustace, and the Spanish Cardinal Peter de Luna, were equally anxious to have one of themselves ; they seemed to have

---

[1] The statement of the Bishop of Recanati contains interesting and supplementary remarks by Cardinal Orsini. This witness also says that the Cardinal of Brittany, jointly with Orsini, raised objections to Prignano's election, on the ground that he was not a member of the Sacred College, and that they could not inflict this humiliation on the Sacred College by electing an outsider, even though he was *sanctus et bonus homo*. The bishop remarked : " Audivi pluribus vicibus a domino de Vernejo et de Brittannia, quod Lemovicenses et de Agrifolio nominaverunt dictum nostrum modernum, qui erat de raubis suis, ipsis nimirum maxime addictus et deditus, cogitantes : ex quo nullus nostrum esse potest, habemus tamen istum ad voluntatem nostram : et tunc alii audientes eum nominari omnes consenserunt praeter dominum Jacobum et dominum de Brittannia, ut egomet audivi a domino de Brittannia in Anagnia : et causa quare contradixit fuit, dicens certe iste est sanctus homo et bonus homo, sed amore Dei non faciamus tantam verecundiam collegio nostro, quod eligamus de extra collegium . . ." see Raynaldus, p. 304, col. 2. The attempt to delay the election is also confirmed by Bishop Faventino before the King of Castile, see Raynaldus, p. 305, col. 1 : " (Dixit) dominus Cardinalis de Agrifolio aliis dominis haec verba : domini, sedeamus statim, quia pro certo credo, quod incontinenti eligemus et habebimus papam. Cardinalis de Ursinis (Deus scit ex quo fonte) tale dedit consilium: domini, differamus istam electionem et deludamus istos Romanos, qui vellent et petunt papam Romanum, et fingemus nos eligisse unum fratrem Minorem Romanum, quem ego nominabo, et induamus eum cappa et mitra, et postmodum loco et tempore faciemus veram electionem . . ."

been supported by Cardinal Orsini. The other three cardinals, the Italians, appeared desirous to have an Italian candidate. Nevertheless, the Limousins attempted *per varias inductionès* to persuade the French cardinals and also the Italians to elect a Limousin, i.e., the Cardinal of Poitiers. The French strongly declared that they would never consent to such an election : the Limousins must not think that they had rented the papacy because the last four popes had been of their nationality.

" Since these negotiations had broken down, the French cardinals approached their Italian colleagues and told them that they would prefer an Italian pope to a Limousin. The Limousins, on the other hand, declared that should they not have a sufficient number for their candidate, or at least for the Cardinal of Viviers, they would elect the Archbishop of Bari, hoping that the other cardinals also would agree with this choice, in view of the learning and experience of this candidate, who was well informed in all curial matters and known to all of them : he belonged to the household of the Cardinal of Pampeluna (himself a Limousin) and was his chaplain ; moreover, since this cardinal had stayed behind at Avignon, Gregory XI had appointed the Archbishop of Bari as vice-chancellor for the Italian lands. Until Gregory's death he had carried out that office efficiently and faithfully. The cardinals considered him as a Frenchman who conformed to their way of life, because he had lived for a long time in Avignon and had always been in their company. He was by birth of the kingdom of Naples which was now ruled by Queen Joanna, a princess very devout and loyal to the Church. It was common knowledge in Rome that, even before the cardinals had entered the conclave, they had in mind the Archbishop of Bari as future pope.

" The cardinals, sixteen altogether, entered the conclave on 7th April, 1378. As they entered, a crowd of Romans standing around the palace shouted : ' We want a Roman.' These words were also heard repeatedly during the conclave. The conclave itself was firmly locked on all sides. Then the Cardinals of Aigrefeuille and Poitiers approached the Cardinal of St. Peter and asked him whether, if they should give their votes to the Archbishop of Bari, he would support them. The Cardinal of St. Peter, who had already agreed to Prignano before their entry into the conclave, repeated his consent.

" On the morning of 8th April the sixteen cardinals were present at two masses, one *de Sancto Spiritu*, the other *de feria*. Afterwards they began the election proper in the chapel of the palace, where the Cardinal of Poitiers remarked to the party of the Cardinal of Milan : ' What do you think ? Does not the Archbishop of Bari appear to you a good pope ? ' The cardinal's answer was in the affirmative. The Cardinal of Poitiers now consulted the Cardinal of Aigrefeuille and all the other Limousins, and they found that they had already the necessary majority. Whereupon the same cardinal spoke to all others present thus : ' My Lords, let us sit down, for I am certain we will very soon have a pope.' After these words Cardinal Orsini, seeing the unanimity of the cardinals, rose and made the following speech, in order to delay the election (or, as was thought, to hinder it altogether) : ' My Lords, let us postpone this election, so that we can delude the Romans who want a Roman pope, and let us send for a Roman Friar Minor, put upon him the cope and mitre and pretend that we have elected him pope ; then we may retire to a safe place and elect another one.' The Limousins replied : ' Certainly not, my Lord Orsini, we shall not do as you say, because we do not want to deceive the Roman people nor to damn our souls : no, we intend to elect a real pope at this very moment, and we refuse to take notice of the clamourings and petitions of the people.'

" The Cardinal of Florence also had the intention of putting off the election in order to prevent the choice of the Archbishop of Bari, and he proposed that they should elect the Cardinal of St. Peter. The Cardinal of Limoges replied that the Cardinal of St. Peter was a good and saintly man, but firstly he was a Roman (and a Roman was asked for by the populace, therefore they could not have a Roman), and secondly, he was too infirm and decrepit, and, therefore, unsuitable for the office of supreme pontiff. Addressing the Cardinal of Florence, he said : ' You come from a city which is hostile to the Roman Church and, therefore, we shall not elect you. The same holds true of the Cardinal of Milan, and Cardinal Orsini is a Roman and too partial and too young, and therefore we shall not elect any of you Italians.'[1]

" Immediately after these words, whilst the conclave was still firmly locked and complete silence reigned both within and without the palace, the Cardinal of Limoges gave his vote for the Archbishop of Bari saying, so that all heard it, ' Ego pure et libere eligo et assumo in papam dominum Bartholomeum archiepiscopum Barensem et animo et voluntate, quod sit verus papa.'[2] The archbishop was freely elected by two-thirds of the cardinals, including even the Cardinal of Florence.

" After this election the cardinals discussed the advisability of making the result known to the public. They decided to postpone the announcement until after dinner, because the elect was not present in the palace ; if the candidate were to appear, the fact of his election would become known and might have unpleasant consequences for him (since he was no Roman and the population would have very much liked a Roman as pope). Another reason for the postpone-ment of the publication was that the cardinals wanted to remove some plate from the conclave *dubitantes, ne illa Romani raperent.* Soon after that, the rumour spread amongst the Roman crowd that the cardinals had already elected a pope, although no one knew his identity, or even his nationality. Therefore the crowd shouted and made it clear to the cardinals in the conclave that they wanted to hear the result of the election. Whereupon the Bishop of Marseilles, the *locum tenens* of the chamberlain, was sent out to the crowd, who told them in French : ' Allez à St. Pierre' ;

[1]This is completely identical with the statement of Bartolomeo, Bishop of Recanati, who heard it from a member of de Vergne's suite, see Raynaldus, p. 304, col. 1 : " Lemovicensis dixit: Certe, domine Jacobe, vos estis nimis juvenis et nimis partialis, certe non eritis. Aliqui autem volebant Mediolanensem, et Lemovicensis dixit : Certe non erit, quia de terra Bernabonis, et alii nominarunt Florentinum, et dictum fuit, quod certe non esset, quia Florentini erant inimici ecclesiae."

[2]Raynaldus, p. 353, col. 1.

Monument to Pope Gregory XI in
the Church of St. Francesca Romana, Rome

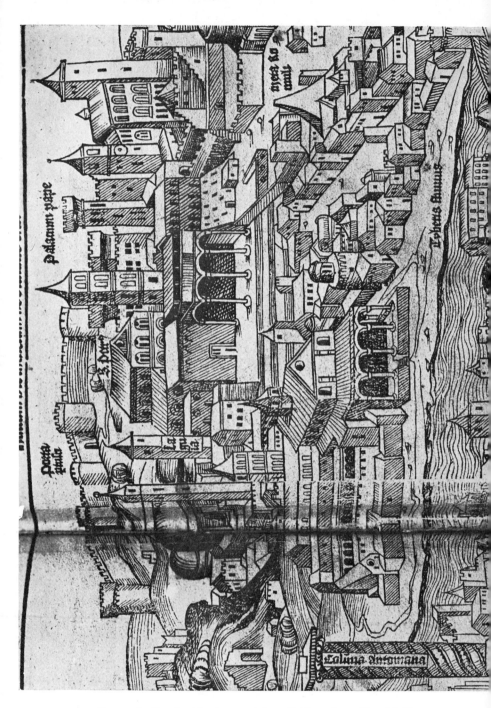

Rome: St. Peter's, about 1400 (*from* " *Nuremberg Chronicle* ")

he meant to say that they should go to St. Peter's (i.e., where they would hear more). Some of the crowd, however, understood that the Cardinal of St. Peter was elected, went to his quarters in the city, entered it and carried away a good deal of his belongings, justifying their action by saying that this was an old custom when the Roman pontiff was elected.[1] The rest of the Roman crowd stayed behind in the vicinity of the palace and exclaimed : ' We want a Roman, we have a Roman.' The cardinals sent for the Archbishop of Bari, the Patriarch of Constantinople and several more prelates and dignitaries of the Church, who were outside the city boundaries, and they were all requested to come to the palace to discuss important business concerning the Church. Most of the prelates arrived at the palace, where they dined, whilst the cardinals took their meal inside the conclave.

" After this meal, whilst all within and without the conclave kept silence, and whilst the conclave was still firmly locked, the cardinals retired to the chapel for greater safety as well as *ad majorem expressionem liberae voluntatis et consensus eorum* and re-elected the archbishop, expressly stating that they did this without external compulsion *concorditer et unanimiter* and with the intention *ut esset verus papa.*

" Since the announcement was still delayed, some of the crowd waiting outside suspected some fraud. In order to carry away the above-mentioned plate one door of the palace was opened and through this the mob surged into the palace to see whether a pope had been elected. The ultramontane cardinals presumed that the mob was indignant because no Roman had been elected, and they feigned that they had elected the Cardinal of St. Peter who, according to the above-reported misunderstanding, was rumoured to have been made pope. The cardinals implored the aged cardinal to pose as pope : moved by their supplications, he agreed to undertake this in order to prevent the cardinals being subjected to insult and to pacify the population. He was placed on the papal throne and arrayed with the papal

[1]*Dicentes esse de more antiquo, quando Romani pontifices praesentes in urbe eligebantur.*

mitre and cope. The door of the conclave was opened and
through this there entered *maxima multitudo hominum.* Believing
him to be the rightful pope, they paid homage to him. The
cardinals, however, taking advantage of this, disappeared
one by one from the palace under the cover of the general
commotion and went to their quarters, some of them
accompanied by Roman citizens of high standing. The
Archbishop of Bari, nevertheless, remained in the palace.
The Cardinal of St. Peter said to the multitude : ' I am not
the pope, nor do I want to be an anti-pope. A better one
has been elected, the Archbishop of Bari.'

" When the Cardinal Peter de Luna rode to his quarters
on horseback he was accompanied by many distinguished
Roman citizens. The guards of the castle of St. Angelo,
together with the camerlengo, were, however, under the
misapprehension that he was being taken away as prisoner.
They closed the bridge across which he was to ride with
his ' escort,' and threw stones and flung arrows at the
Romans. The rumour then spread that the sentries of St.
Angelo had opened an attack upon peaceful Roman citizens.
The tocsins of St. Peter were rung, but as soon as the misunderstanding was cleared up, the general commotion
subsided.

" In the meantime, whilst the Archbishop of Bari remained
in the palace, a rumour reached him that the people wanted
to kill him, because he was a non-Roman. Thereupon the
archbishop locked himself up in the most secret room of
the palace, where he lay hidden up to the very moment
when the election was made public. Some of the cardinals
began to fear popular revenge for their deceptive machinations with the old Cardinal of St. Peter, and, therefore,
they withdrew to the castle of St. Angelo. These cardinals
were : Limoges, Aigrefeuille, Poitiers, Brittany, Viviers
and de Vergne. Other cardinals fled into fortified places
far from the city proper. They were : the Cardinals of
Geneva, St. Eustace, and St. Angelo.[1] Others again, such
as the Cardinals of Florence, Marmoutier, Milan, Glandève

---

[1] The *Factum* gives the names of places the cardinals had fled to,
but they are not essential to the account and to give them would
merely lengthen the story.

and de Luna, remained in their own quarters quite unmolested.

"At a late hour on the same day the last mentioned cardinals went to the castle of St. Angelo, and the others, who had withdrawn from the city, sent messengers to the Archbishop of Bari, who was still in the palace, telling him that he was the true pope ; they besought him to remove his residence from the palace to a safe place ' pro securitate et salvatione honoris et personae suae et status universalis ecclesiae.' The Archbishop of Bari consulted with the only cardinal remaining at the palace, i.e., that of St. Peter, as to what was to be done : the advice he received was that under no circumstances should he leave the palace. He followed the cardinal's advice and remained in the palace throughout the night.

"On the following day, 9th April, the election was made known to the officials and governors of the city of Rome. They were pleased with the election and immediately entered the palace to pay homage to the newly-elected pope. But he did not allow this and said that he would not like to be addressed other than as Archbishop of Bari. On the same evening the above five cardinals who had remained in their quarters, came to the palace and to the elected pope and congratulated him upon his election saying : ' verba multa grata et humilia.' They earnestly begged him to accept the election which was harmoniously and canonically performed. They furthermore advised him to send for the cardinals in the castle of St. Angelo so that they could be present at the enthronement.

"In order to be completely certain as to his status, the Archbishop of Bari asked everyone of those present individually whether he had been elected *sincere, pure, et libere et canonice* by all the cardinals, adding that if the election had not been carried out canonically and without compulsion he would not consent to become pope. They answered, ' firmiter et constanter ', that the election was performed freely, canonically, and without compulsion. If he should refuse he would commit a grave sin : for his refusal could easily cause a long vacancy of the papal throne owing to the difficulties of assembling the majority of cardinals in one place.

" The cardinals who had stayed in the castle of St.
Angelo, instead of complying with his request to come to
the palace, sent a letter, signed by all of them, to the effect
that they would approve of everything that was being done
as regards the enthronement. When the Senator and the
officials heard that the cardinals were frightened to come to
the palace because they had not elected a Roman, they
themselves went to the castle and gave the cardinals the
assurance that they could come to the palace *audacter et
secure* : they would not have to fear any public reproach,
because the population was in fact satisfied with the election.
The cardinals were encouraged by this report and went
over to the palace in the afternoon. There they immediately
consented to the election and sent the Cardinal of Aigrefeuille to the new pope to ask him to come to the chapel.
He came to the cardinals by whom he was elected pope and
who received him as such. He and all the other cardinals
sat down. The Cardinal of Florence, as spokesman, asked
him on behalf of the others whether he accepted the election.
He arose from his seat, and being earnestly requested by the
cardinals to consent, accepted the election. Thereupon the
cardinals intoned the *Te Deum* ' cum magna laetitia ', robed
him with the papal vestments, whilst saying the usual
prayers, and performed the enthronement. The bells of
the palace were rung. He was asked what name he would
take, and he replied : ' Urban'. They paid homage to
him and with a profound obeisance kissed his pallium.[1]
" Immediately afterwards Cardinal de Vergne went

[1]The papal auditor, Robert Straton, testifies that there was no
disturbance during the ceremony, see Raynaldus, p. 309, col. 2.
The detailed description of the Bishop of Recanati, Bartolomeo of
Bologna, entirely confirms the statement of the *Factum*: " Supervenit
praefatus dominus noster (i.e. Urbanus) sanctissimus electus, cui in
assurgendo maximam reverentiam (cardinales) fecerunt, et ipsum,
me vidente, in capite inter eos sedere fecerunt, et electionem de ipso
factam sibi nuntiarunt, humiliter et devote supplicantes, ut huiusmodi electioni consentiret. Qui post praeces et rogamina finaliter
consensit, genuflectendo se versus altare in dicta capella, ac surgens
ad illud ascendit in sede se ponendo. Qui depositis vestibus quibus
induebatur, exiit papaliter inthronizatus ; cuius electionem dominus de Vernejo populo congregato solemniter publicavit, ipsum
dominum Urbanum Papam VI publice nominando . . ."

to the window and spoke to the multitude : ' I have to announce joyful tidings. We have a pope called Urban VI.' On the same day the Cardinals of Limoges, Aigrefeuille and Poitiers sought an interview with the pope, in which they told him that it was they who were mainly responsible for the election. They requested his favourable treatment of their friends and of others of the kin of his predecessor, Gregory. They also begged him to make efforts to obtain the release of the late pope's brother from captivity in England and, when creating new cardinals, to raise the late pope's nephew, Hugh de Rupe, to the cardinalate, since Gregory himself had intended to do so.

"On the following Sunday the pope and the twelve cardinals were present at the enthronement and, together with Cardinal Orsini, who had already returned to the city, went to St. Peter's and, seated in the papal chair, in front of the main altar, Urban received the homage of the canons of St. Peter's in the presence of these cardinals and of a large crowd. The canons sang the *Te Deum*. After celebrating low mass at this altar, Urban gave his blessing and returned to the palace with the cardinals, where he addressed them according to custom. As is usual with a new pope, the cardinals upon this occasion submitted several requests, and in particular asked him with humility for a complete absolution from their sins and for a dispensation from all irregularities which they might incidentally have incurred. All of which was granted by the new pope. Each of the cardinals then chose his confessor ' per quem in forma ecclesiae se absolvi fecerunt.'

"On Palm Sunday, 11th April, the above-mentioned cardinals went to the palace and then, together with the pope, to St. Peter's. After blessing the palms, he himself, clothed in the papal vestments and seated on his papal throne, distributed them to the cardinals, to many other ecclesiastical and secular dignitaries and to the great number of people who had gathered in the Church. After this he betook himself to the sanctuary in procession with the cardinals. The Cardinal of Florence sang solemn High Mass, whilst the cardinals assisted the pope, who performed all those functions which are solely papal prerogatives.

On all the following days until Easter Sunday Urban VI functioned as pope, granting indulgences, showing himself to the people and the like, wherein he was assisted by the cardinals. On 15th April—the day on which the Roman pontiffs traditionally published bulls of excommunication—Urban VI, standing on the steps leading to St. Peter's, clothed in the papal vestments, in full view of the people and with the candles lighted, proceeded to the publication of a bull against the Florentines, who were the enemies of the Church. And during all those ceremonies he was assisted by the cardinals, arrayed in their appropriate vestments and holding candles in their hands. The pope and, following him, the cardinals threw down the candles publicly, as was the old custom. On Holy Saturday, also, those cardinals who had left Rome, returned, and all the cardinals presented him with the ring and pallium. On the same day he celebrated High Mass at St. Peter's, where all the cardinals assisted him and where all the cardinal deacons publicly received communion from his hands.

" On the morning of Easter Sunday Urban was crowned by Cardinal Orsini in the presence of all the cardinals, who had also assisted at the ceremony. The coronation should have been performed by the Cardinal Bishop of Ostia, but since this cardinalate was vacant at the time, Cardinal Orsini officiated as the first amongst the cardinal deacons. He received the tiara with the usual ceremonies in the presence of the whole population of Rome and of innumerable people from outside. After giving his blessing to the whole people he and his cardinals mounted their magnificent horses, which were finely arrayed and covered with white linen. Followed by ecclesiastical and secular dignitaries on horse, and by a huge crowd on foot, the procession soon reached the Lateran. Here the Senator took the oath of fealty and the Canons of St. Peter's paid homage to him, after singing the litany and distributing certain sums of money to the cardinals according to the old custom. The whole congregation then returned to St. Peter's on horseback.

" During the following three months the cardinals were constantly in the papal presence ; they treated him as pope, obeyed his commands, assisted him, publicly as well as privately, in his papal functions, presented him with gifts, addressed him as ' dominus noster ' and said prayers for him as pope during their masses. And they treated him as pope even during their stay at Anagni, which, according to their own assertion, was a place where they were safe."

So runs the memorandum of the curia. Weighty testimonies and impressive witnesses can be adduced to support its main statements although there are some details which lack sufficient corroboration. The trustworthiness of this document is enhanced rather than diminished by its omission of certain, not negligible, events, such as the appearance of the city governors at the wicket of the conclave, precisely at the moment when the cardinals were about to begin their deliberations. There is every reason to assume that this memorandum was composed on the basis of statements made by witnesses (unknown to us) who were consulted some time after the events, probably more than three months afterwards. Anyone acquainted with judicial proceedings and with the varying degrees of correct observation and registration of events is aware of the fact that witnesses are not always reliable as to details, and the omission of details which were by no means unfavourable to Urban only increases our confidence in the trustworthiness of the memorandum. On the other hand, its over-emphasis on the " complete silence " i.e.—during the voting on the morning of 8th April (cf. *supra* p. 19) and during the afternoon session (*ib.* p. 20) is bound to arouse suspicion, not only because it is insufficiently supported by reliable witnesses, but also because it is highly improbable that there could have been " complete silence." But this over-emphasis is understandable in view of the exaggerated statements made by cardinals in their *Declaratio*. The Urbanists were anxious to present the election as an affair conducted in a perfectly calm and peaceful atmosphere, whilst the Clementines were equally anxious to present it as a farce conditioned by the tumult of the people.

Let us now turn to witnesses whose statements corroborate the curial memorandum. These witnesses are all the more trustworthy as most of their depositions were made immediately or very soon after the election. An especially illuminating account of some of the events, before, during, and after the election, is contained in the *Informationes* of Bishop Alphonso of Jaën.[1] This account supports the *Factum Urbani* in very many details and it deserves all the more credit as it comes from the pen of one who belonged to the suite of Cardinal Peter de Luna. Alphonso himself calls Peter de Luna " dominus meus familiarissimus ". The bishop reports that the cardinals, as soon as Gregory XI had closed his eyes, consulted each other about the future pope. These consultations were not, however, actuated by the holy desire to elect someone who was suitable to rule the Church, but were prompted by the " affectus carnalis et partialis," so that a friend, relative or partisan should be elected " secundum carnem et sanguinem." The split between the Limousins and the French cardinals is described by Alphonso in a manner not fundamentally different from that of the *Factum* ; and he goes on to speak of the difficulties each party encountered in making sure of the requisite number of votes. But in spite of some strenuous efforts, and despite a canvassing campaign conducted by some cardinals, the " Gallic " section amongst them was unable to secure the needed two-thirds majority.[2] In these circumstances it appeared obvious to the cardinals to look for someone from outside the Sacred College.[3] Alphonso gives now several reasons why the Archbishop of Bari came eventually to be proposed as the most suitable candidate. Firstly, he was, as vice-chancellor, well versed in curial business, style and affairs ; he had great experience in all curial matters, he was learned, scrupulously honest and reputedly just. Secondly,

---

[1]These *Informationes* of Bishop Alphonso of Jaën are printed in Raynaldus, *loc. cit.*, pp. 374–80.

[2]" Ideo propter defectum sufficientis numeri vocum quaelibet dictarum partium totis viribus conabatur supplantare aliam, et accumulare sibi et subtrahere voces alterius partis et etiam Italicorum cardinalium : sed cum toto hoc non potuerunt facere, quod aliquis cardinalis ultramontanus haberet sufficientem numerum duarum partium collegii, ut eligeretur ad cathedram piscatoris," *ibid.*, p. 377, col. 1.

[3]" Confracti igitur in mente de hoc ultramontani cardinales devenerunt ad tractandum de eligendo papam de extra collegium," *ibid.*

the Cardinal of Aigrefeuille, who belonged to the Limousin party, considered Prignano as his *familiaris* and table companion (*commensalis*) and, moreover, was very fond of him ; this cardinal, as the leader of the Limousin party, persuaded his followers then to vote for the archbishop. Thirdly, Cardinal Robert of Geneva, too, had reasons to vote for the archbishop. For the latter was once a member of the household of one of Robert's uncles, who had been a cardinal. And, remembering this connexion, Robert expected and hoped to be favoured by the proposed candidate : the Cardinal of Geneva as the spokesman of the " French " cardinals persuaded his party then to vote for Prignano, hoping in the case of an election through their votes " quod esset sibi et suis multum propitius."[1]

The election of the archbishop was thus taken for granted by this witness, the Bishop of Jaën. He was strengthened in this conviction by consultations which his own master, Peter de Luna, had with some of his intimate friends as well as with the witness himself. It was on the strength of this conviction that Alphonso took a step which leaves no room to doubt the veracity of his statements. It must be remembered that Alphonso was the legal adviser and agent of St. Catherine of Sweden, still resident in Rome and actively urging the canonization of her mother, St. Bridget. Four or five days before the conclave took place, Alphonso went to see St. Catherine in order to advise her to pay a humble visit to the Archbishop of Bari, and that without delay she should, he suggested, show him great reverence and urge upon him the canonization of her mother. " For I saw", says Alphonso, " that he would be elected pope." St. Catherine then visited Prignano, paid homage to him and strongly pleaded for the canonization. The archbishop, according to Alphonso's report, appeared greatly surprised by the attitude of his visitor who, hitherto, had not exceeded in respect and reverence for him.[2]

[1]Raynaldus, *loc. cit.*, p. 377, col. 2.

[2]" Et quia ego per quatuor vel quinque dies, antequam intrarent conclave, verisimiliter vidi, quod dictus archiepiscopus Barensis debebat eligi de communi consensu ambarum partium, ideo tunc ivi ad dominam Catharinam filiam beatae Brigittae, cuius negotium promoveo in curia, et persuasi sibi, quod iret ad dominum archiepiscopum et ei maximam reverentiam faceret et negotium canoniza-

Concerning the election itself, the Bishop of Jaën writes that Peter de Luna had told him that he himself (Peter) first approached the Cardinal of Limoges to make sure that the latter cast his vote for Prignano. The Limousins then suggested the same name to the Cardinals of Aigrefeuille and Poitiers. " These three called on other cardinals and then all of them sat down and voted *libere et sponte* for the archbishop."[1] In his account of the enthronement of the newly-elected Pope the bishop confirms that there was no protestation (*requisitio*) on the part of the Romans, and that the cardinals performed this ceremony *laeto animo et jucundo*.[2] This gives our witness an opportunity to touch briefly upon the reaction of the Romans. When they heard of the result of the election they were, for the next few days, very sad and perturbed.[3] They complained that " those ultramontane cardinals had cheated us, for we wanted a Roman pope, and now they have given us an alien in the person of a Neapolitan." These and similar

[1]Raynaldus, *loc. cit.*, p. 378, col. 1. As our witness was not present at the election, his report contains no reference to the events outside the conclave.

[2]Raynaldus, p. 378, col. 2.

[3]" Erant etiam eadem die et aliquibus diebus sequentibus cives Romani satis tristes et quasi consternati in suis gestibus"—*ibid.*, p. 378, col. 2.

---

tionis suae matris valde efficaciter recommendaret, ex eo, quod ego videbam, ut ipse eligeretur in papam. Ipsa vero hoc audiens statim illuc perrexit et in ecclesia S. Petri ipsum invenit, et tunc ei maximam reverentiam ultra solitum exhibuit et negotia sua illi humiliter recommendavit. De quo ipse tunc magnam admirationem concepit, eo quod dicta domina Catharina non consueverat ei facere tam profundam reverentiam," Raynaldus, p. 377, col. 2.

That the election of Prignano was a foregone conclusion follows also from the letter of Petrus Pileus, the Cardinal of Ravenna and a former chaplain of Charles V : in this letter the cardinal said that it was known " antequam intrassent conclave, quod eum in pastorem eligerent. Ista est purissima veritas, sicut Christus veritas est," Raynaldus, p. 399, col. 2. This cardinal, it should be pointed out, was elevated to his cardinalate by Urban in September, 1378 ; during the critical days in April, 1378, he was living in Flanders. The letter was written on 14th December, 1378 ; see also Lindner, *Geschichte des Deutschen Reiches unter Koenig Wenzel*, vol. i, p. 398, and d'Archery, *Spicilegium*, vol. iii, p. 743, and also Baluzius, tom. ii, cols. 811, 812.

utterances were made by the Romans " with angry faces "
(" vultu turbido ").[1]

The curial memorandum is, furthermore, supported by
various statements which the cardinals themselves made,
before they discovered the " irregularity " of the election, and
which, accordingly, deserve all the more credit. On 19th
April, on the very day following the coronation of Urban,
the cardinals sent a letter to their six colleagues at Avignon,
amongst whom was the Cardinal of Albano, notifying them
of the result of the election. This letter, signed by all sixteen
cardinals, contains not the slightest hint about any compulsion,
popular upheaval or subsequent intimidation of the electors.
On the contrary, it reveals their satisfaction at the choice :
" We have given our votes for Bartolomeo, the Archbishop of
Bari, who is conspicuous for his great merits and whose mani-
fold virtues make him a shining example ; we have *concorditer*
elevated him to the summit of apostolic excellency and have
announced our choice to the multitude of Christians. On the
9th April the elect assumed the name of Urban VI, and on
Easter Sunday he was crowned at St. Peter's *magnifice et
solemniter* in the presence of a huge and joyful crowd. We
have firm hope and confidence in our pope and believe that
under his guidance the orthodox faith will be strengthened and
that the state of the universal Church will begin to blossom
again. May our Saviour grant that he may serve for a very
long time."[2] In view of this explicit declaration of the
cardinals it was difficult for them later to deny what it contained : the only way open to try and reduce its value as
evidence against them was to assert that this letter—like all
their other actions during their stay in Rome subsequent to
the election—had been forced upon them, although none
of the cardinals revealed from what quarter the compulsion
had actually come.

There are two other documents which support the main

[1]" Satis malitiose deluserunt nos isti cardinales ultramontani :
nam nos volebamus papam Romanum, et ipsi dederunt nobis alieni-
genam Neapolitanum. Et similia verba proferrebant cum vultu
turbido "—*ibid.*

[2]This letter is printed by Bulaeus, *Historia Universitatis Parisiensis,*
tom. iv, p. 465, by Raynaldus, p. 312, cols. 1 and 2, and d'Archery,
Spicilegium, vol. i, p. 763.

points of the *Factum Urbani*. They are especially valuable because they are private letters, written in a familiar epistolary style, during the period between the election and the coronation, that is to say at a time when nobody had as yet cast any doubt upon the validity of Urban's election. The one is written on 11th April, two days after the proclamation of Urban as pope, when events were still fresh in the mind of the writer. Moreover, he belonged to a set which was to prove most antagonistic to Urban, for he was a member of Peter de Luna's household, and was present during the greater part of the election, as a companion of his master. In the letter, written to a friend at Avignon, he described the events from the moment the cardinals entered the conclave on 7th April. According to his description, the conclave was soon securely locked up, but from outside there arose a sound of tumult. The noise became so loud that the cardinals could hardly understand each other. After some discussion they elected the Archbishop of Bari, the vice-chancellor, " a man of wide knowledge and experience in spiritual and temporal affairs." The writer declares that the new pope was unable to enter the conclave, owing to the huge crowd assembled in front of the palace. But since the cry " We want a Roman " became more insistent and threatening, the cardinals hesitated to publish the result. The writer's descriptions of the faked enthronement of the Cardinal of St. Peter, of the flight of the cardinals and of the incident before the castle of St. Angelo, substantially agree with those in the *Factum Urbani*. It is, however, interesting to note the witness's statement that on the Friday (9th April) some officials came to the house of Cardinal Peter de Luna and asked him to go to the palace so that the ceremony of the election could be completed. On the same day the cardinals who had fled from Rome had also returned. The letter concludes : " The new pope calls himself Urban. The coronation will take place either on Easter Sunday or Easter Monday. Since these events may be reported in different regions differently, and may even be distorted, I intended to give you a description. Written at Rome, 11th April, 1378."[1]

[1]See Gayet, *Le Grand Schisme d'Occident*, vol. i, pièces justif., pp. 148–51.

The other letter was written by the Cardinal of Florence to his former teacher, John de Pistoris, a monk in Apulia.[1] His later attempt to deny having written this letter cannot command serious attention. It is in his own handwriting and it reveals an unmistakable personal tone. After some introductory remarks thanking John for a previous letter, the cardinal went on to speak of the election, saying that they had assembled on the evening of Wednesday, 7th April. " On Thursday we reassembled after mass, and ' Spiritus Sancti gratia inspirante ' we unanimously elected the Archbishop of Bari, the vice-chancellor." He then described the enthronement and gave reasons for the election. " We firmly believe and hope that, on account of his knowledge, his blameless life, his numerous great virtues, his wide experience, and with the help of Him whose vicar he is, he will rule the universal Church profitably, according to the will and justice of God, and that the whole Christian people will be comforted and consoled." The letter is dated 14th April, 1378.

A spontaneous statement made by Cardinal de Vergne to the Bishop of Reti and Macerata on the very day of the enthronement may serve as a typical example of the cardinals' attitude. However much they may have tried to pretend that they acted under compulsion—even the letter just summarized was written by a cardinal who stoutly maintained that all letters were dictated and censored by the pope—spontaneous statements like the following exclude the possibility of such compulsion precisely because of their informal character. " Throughout my whole life," the cardinal said, " I have not experienced such joy as I have to-day, because we have completed this business so peacefully. For I doubted whether the Romans would be satisfied." The bishop replied : " Sir, the Romans are not so bad as they are made out to be . . . but those men who were drunk yesterday did not know what they were saying, and everyone wanted to have his own pope." Then the bishop expressed his conviction that the Church would be reformed, " for I always considered him an upright and holy man, and certainly his election illustrates the miraculous working of the Holy Ghost." The

---

[1]Gayet, *op. cit.*, vol. ii, pp. 64 seq.

hope of a reformation was also expressed by the Cardinals of Florence and Milan and by Cardinal Orsini.[1]

It is alleged that the Cardinal of Geneva wrote a private letter to the Emperor in which he speaks of the free election of Urban. A Benedictine monk, Adam Easton, maintained that he had seen the actual letter.[2] This same witness also saw the letters written by the Cardinal of Aigrefeuille to certain German princes. Urban VI issued an encyclical, *Nuper felicis*, in which he informed all princes and bishops officially of the death of Gregory XI and of the result of the election. In this bull the pope stated that, by the inspiration of the Holy Ghost, he had been elected *rara concordia* and that the election itself was canonical and unanimous. Aware of the heavy burden which now rested upon his shoulders, he asked all to offer prayers for him and for his policy.[3]

A witness whose testimony should be of particular value is the Bishop of Todi who, in his capacity as a guardian of the conclave, was bound to have been an eye-witness of the crucial events. The statements of the Bishop of Marseilles, who was the chief guardian outside the conclave, are also preserved and coincide with the substance of the evidence given by his colleague.[4] No testimony is preserved from the third guardian, the Bishop of Tivoli. These statements corroborate the *Factum Urbani* in all essential points. Both witnesses report that the cardinals met repeatedly before the election. The Romans, too, held meetings and submitted their requests to the cardinals for the election of a Roman or an Italian, but the popular cry was for a Roman : " Vox communis erat in populo habere Romanum." The witnesses testify, in agreement with

[1] See the testimony of Canon Thomas Petra in Raynaldus, *loc. cit.*, p. 310, col. 2 : " Saepe audivi dominum Mediolanensem, Florentinum et de Ursinis, et diversis temporibus dicentes, dominum nostrum Urbanum praedictum fuisse verum papam concorditer electum, per quem sperabant ecclesiam Dei reformari."

[2] Raynaldus, p. 311, col. 2, where his name is spelled " Escon ".

[3] Raynaldus, p. 310–11. " Quia supra vires nostras esse conspicimus susceptum officium, illudque soli portare nequimus, orationum vestrarum suffragia humiliter imploranda, et vos in partem solicitudinis evocatos, ut collaborando nobiscum diligentius exequamini commissa nobis officia, decrevimus exhortandos . . ."

[4] Baluzius, *Vitae Paparum Avenionensium*, tom. i, cols. 1207 seq. (ed. Mollat, vol. ii, pp. 725 seq.).

the *Factum*, to their appointments as custodians of the conclave. As soon as the cardinals had entered the conclave on the Wednesday evening, they had locked it firmly, leaving only (according to custom) a small opening in the door. The Bishop of Marseilles says that the Romans would not allow the sealing up of the conclave, and that they had even taken his key from him, so that the conclave was open during part of the night. The Romans, screaming wildly in their rage, had inflicted much damage upon the papal food stores. The Bishop of Todi, too, reports that the crowd shouted furiously the now famous words. Both witnesses state that after mass and breakfast on Thursday, the Archbishop of Bari was elected : it was rumoured at the time that his election had been fixed by the cardinals before they had entered the conclave. About 9 o'clock officials had appeared and asked the witnesses to allow them to enter the conclave in order to request the cardinals to expedite the election and to elect a Roman, since both they themselves and the cardinals would otherwise be in danger. The clamouring, which had subsided for a while, now started again with increased ferocity : " Romano, Romano, o Italiano " ; but the majority screamed " Romano, Romano ". The Bishop of Marseilles then conducted the officials to the window of the conclave, opened it and asked for one of the cardinals, to whom he reported the request of the officials. In the meantime the deafening cries went on : " Romano lo volemo ", and only a few shouted " Italiano ".

At this point we may insert the testimony of the Abbot de Sistre, who reports details which could not be observed by the custodians. In a letter to the King of Aragon[1] the Abbot says the cardinals, when addressed through the window by one of the city governors, said that they had been asked on a previous occasion to elect one who would be acceptable to God and to the world, but had always given the reply that since a papal election was a divine act they could not commit themselves in advance, but that they would elect as pope a man who was just and pleasing and through whom the Church would be well governed. " But now, gentlemen," the official continued, " you know that when you entered the conclave,

[1]Raynaldus, *loc. cit.*, pp. 308 seq.

many clamoured for the election of an Italian or Roman. Now, however, I am sent to you on behalf of the whole population to notify you, most reverend Fathers, that the multitude wants a Román only—an Italian would not satisfy them. For they fear that under some secret agreement an Italian might again decide to transfer to Avignon . . . if you do not fulfil the wishes of the populace I fear that serious trouble will arise, which may have unpleasant consequences to you not less than to ourselves."

The Cardinal of Glandève appeared as the spokesman of the Sacred College and in unmistakable terms gave the governor a dignified reply : " We are amazed," the cardinal said to the officials, " how much you vex us with this request, for we have already given you the answer which we will always give you and which should be satisfactory to you and the people." Withdrawing from the window the governor muttered in an intentionally audible tone : " Please God that you will give us a Roman, otherwise you will be certain to feel something more than mere words."

This incident was reported to the cardinals who were waiting within the conclave, whereupon the Cardinal of Limoges strongly condemned this attempt at intimidation on the part of the city officials, rightly pointing out how quick the Romans or governors had been to change their minds : first they wanted a just and righteous man, irrespective of nationality, then they restricted their demand to a pope of Italian or Roman origin, and lastly they would consent only to the election of a Roman pope. " I cannot see," the cardinal said, " how we can elect a Roman, since his election would, to all intents and purposes, have been carried out under compulsion." But supposing they did consider the election of a Roman, who would be the likely man ? The candidate would be either a member of the Sacred College or an outsider. " Now," the cardinal continued, " there are only two Romans in our midst, the Cardinal of St. Peter and Cardinal Orsini. Neither is acceptable : the first because he is too old, infirm and decrepit ; the second because he is too young and inexperienced. I do not know any Roman outside the College who is worthy of the dignity. But I propose that we elect one to whom the people can have no serious objection and who would in all likelihood prove favourably disposed towards us."[1]

In the cardinal's opinion six requirements should be fulfilled by a candidate : mature age ; blameless life ; great learning ; experience in the administration of papal matters ; Italian origin, to ensure that the Roman curia could be reformed, because a foreigner appeared incapable for this task ; and a friendly disposition towards the cardinals. " These six conditions I can see fulfilled by one and one only, and that is the Archbishop of Bari. Well over 50 years of age, for more than 14 years in the service of the curia, a despiser of underhand intrigues and acts of favouritism, of upright and honest character, a man of wide talents and learning and great administrative experience. Moreover, he is well known to us ; by birth he is an Italian, but politically devoted to the French—a fact which will certainly be gratifying to the King of France and his brethren."

So spoke the Cardinal of Limoges. " On the strength of all these considerations," he continued, " I elect in the name of the Father, the Son and the Holy Ghost the Archbishop of Bari to be pontiff of the holy and universal Church *sponte et libere*." The first vote for the archbishop was cast. According to our witness, the second to vote for him was the Cardinal of Aigrefeuille, followed by the Cardinals of Poitiers, Viviers, Brittany, Marmoutier, de Vergne, St. Angelo, St. Eustace, de Luna, and Geneva. The Italians—three of whom had aspired to the throne, as the abbot drily remarked—elected Prignano " concorditer ", when they saw that the ultramontanes had given their votes for him ; except Cardinal Orsini, who abstained from voting and declared, somewhat mysteriously : " I elect the one who is elected by the majority."[2]

We may now resume the story as reported by the guardians of the conclave. After the incident at the window, the Bishop

[1]Raynaldus, *loc. cit.*, p. 303, col. 2 : " De extra collegium neminem scio aptum ad papatum, unde nec primo capite nec secundo apparet mihi quod Romanum eligere debeamus. Sed faciamus sic, quod provideamus ecclesiae Dei, et talem eligamus, quod huic populo debeat merito complacere, et nobis omnibus se verisimiliter debeat reddere gratiosum."

[2]See the identical report in Baluzius, *loc. cit.*, tom. i, cols. 1103–4 (ed. Mollat, vol. ii, p. 626).

of Todi saw that the *familiares* of some cardinals were busy collecting jewels and other valuables, and he concluded from this that the election was already finished. A short while afterwards the officials returned to the custodians, telling them with tears in their eyes that if no Roman were elected the people would blame them (the officials) and their lives would be in danger. They went to the window again, where Cardinal Orsini and the Cardinals of Florence and Geneva had now appeared. The Bishop of Marseilles saw how the *familiares* were packing even the sheets and bed linen of the cardinals, whereby he became convinced that the election was over. According to the testimony of the Bishop of Todi, Orsini said to the crowd : " Listen to me, Romans, if you should not have a pope who proves acceptable to you by this evening I will allow you to tear me to pieces,"[1] whilst according to the testimony of the Bishop of Marseilles this cardinal addressed the crowd in the following words : " You Roman pigs, get away from here with your impudent demands. When I get out I will chase you with my stick."

According to the evidence of the Bishop of Todi, the cardinals now closed the window, but in the meantime the Archbishop of Bari together with other prelates had arrived. The new arrivals had their midday meal in the palace. They, and the guardians, were puzzled as to why they were sent for, but a new outbreak of popular violence cut short all further discussions amongst them. The crowd shouted : " We have been betrayed, we have no Roman," and they were about to break into the conclave. Some shouted : " Let's kill them." When the cardinals had heard the excited crowds, they besought the Cardinal of St. Peter to save them and to allow them to pretend that it was he who had been made pope ; that is how the Bishop of Todi had been told of the events inside the conclave. The Bishop of Marseilles had a somewhat different version : he had, in a loud voice, asked the crowd to calm down, when one Roman attacked him with his sword and called him a traitor. The bishop feared for his life and ran away to his quarters in the palace. Then the people broke open the conclave and the Cardinal of St. Peter was enthroned. The bishop, still in fear of his life, left his chamber and wanted

[1] See also Baluzius, tom. i, col. 1437 (ed. Mollat, vol. ii, pp. 517–8).

to take refuge in the castle of St. Angelo, but he was captured on his way and led as a prisoner to St. Lorenzo, where he was later released through the intercession of an official. He then proceeded to the house of Cardinal Orsini, where he met the Cardinal of St. Eustace with whom he fled in the middle of the night to Vicovaro. Here the bishop's narrative ends, since he knew of the events in the palace only through reports from others.

But the Bishop of Todi was present at the palace and he relates that the old Cardinal of St. Peter remonstrated and told the crowd that it was not he who was the pope, but that another far worthier than himself had been elected. At this time, however, the witness did not know the nature of this fraud and wanted to pay homage to the " pope ". He had met the Archbishop of Bari who was ready to pay homage to the new pope. They had been stopped on their way, because so many people were there that it was impossible to advance. Whilst they were waiting, his brother Anthony approached them and said that the Cardinal of St. Peter was not pope, for he had himself denied that he had been elected. The witness, together with the Archbishop of Bari, returned to their quarters. A rumour had spread amongst the crowds that the Archbishop of Bari had been elected. This news had been received with the cry : " Non lo volemo ", and some Romans broke into the belfry of St. Peter's and began to ring the tocsin.

During these riots some officials approached the witness and suggested to him that the archbishop should renounce his election, supposing he had been elected. This request, the witness said, had been flatly refused, since it had not been by any means certain that the archbishop was pope. When, later, he heard of this, he remarked : " They do not know me —not under the threat of one thousand swords would I have renounced my election." This reply had greatly amused the Cardinal of Geneva, when he was told about it.[1]

The report of the Bishop of Todi about the flight of the cardinals is in essential agreement with the *Factum Urbani*.

[1] " Ipse dixit : ' Non cognoscunt me bene ; si tenerent mille spathas ad collum meum, non renuntiarem ' ; et quando ego recitavi postea ista verba domino Gebennensi, ridebat ita fortiter, quod est mirum, tantum gaudebat de responsione," Baluzius, tom. i, col. 1467.

He emphasized however the solicitude which the Cardinal of Geneva—the later anti-pope—had shown for the safety of the Archbishop of Bari. There had been signs, the witness says, that the Roman population was dissatisfied with the result of the election and he, the witness, requested several of his friends to guard the palace during the following night. In the morning of Friday, 9th April, the Cardinal of St. Peter sent for all the cardinals who were in the castle of St. Angelo and who at first showed little inclination to come to the palace; it was only upon repeated requests that they agreed. " There the cardinals assembled in the chapel and decided, as I afterwards learned, to perform the ceremony of the enthronement of the true pope." The Archbishop of Bari was sent for, the doors were locked, and he was enthroned upon the altar, whereupon the cardinals intoned the *Te Deum* and paid him homage. Through the now open doors the people entered and paid their reverence.[1]

The remaining statements of our witness are concerned with events which are identically described by the *Factum Urbani*; it is perhaps worth while noting that the Cardinal of Geneva busied himself conspicuously in collecting souvenirs for the pope; in fact, he presented the pope with a ring of the value of 400 ducats. As to the reports of the service on Palm Sunday, the distribution of palms and the administration of communion by the pope, the meals in common and the cardinals' treatment of Urban VI as true pope throughout their residence in Rome—all these are identical with those in the *Factum*. Lastly, some of the cardinals received benefices from the pope, as, for example, the Cardinals of Brittany and St. Eustace and Milan. The Cardinal of Glandève was created cardinal bishop of Ostia. All the cardinals had included prayers for the pope in their daily masses.

This statement, taken in conjunction with the previous statements, supports the curial memorandum in nearly all essential points, though we find differences and deviations in matters of detail. But, considering the unusual circumstances, these differences and deviations are easy to explain: the masses of armed people screaming and clamouring, the excitement of the witnesses, the quick sequence of the events,

[1]Baluzius, tom. i, col. 999.

the issues at stake—all these considerations afford a ready explanation of the inconsistencies. On one point, however, the curial memorandum remains unsupported, and that is with regard to the " complete silence " outside the conclave. Every witness stresses the disorderly nature of the Roman assembly outside the palace, and even Urban himself referred to the riots of the Romans and offered a plausible explanation ; he said that it was " vinolentia " rather than " violentia " which characterized these street scenes outside the palace. And this pun finds some support in the testimony of Thomas of Acerno, a lawyer and Bishop of Lucera,[1] who stated that the Romans spent most of the night between the 7th and 8th April in the taverns near St. Peter's and went into the streets in an uproarious and drunken mood.[2]

This testimony is also interesting from another point of view. The witness reports that whilst the cardinals hesitated to publish the result of the election, the " thirsty Romans broke open the papal cellars, drank Greek wine and Malmsey in great quantities, some crying : ' We want a pope,' others : ' We want a Roman.' " Now it will be recalled that the Bishop of Marseilles also spoke of damage inflicted by the Romans on the foodstuffs. The allegation of our witness that the Romans made merry in the cellars may, therefore, refer to one and the same event. Whilst the member of the household of Peter de Luna and the Bishop of Todi do not mention the words by the Bishop of Marseilles to the Roman mob, " Allez à St. Pierre ", Thomas, on the other hand, does report it, but puts it into the mouth of Cardinal Orsini. But this witness also states that it was this exhortation which misled the Romans into believing that the Cardinal of St. Peter had been elected. In agreement with the Factum, but in disagreement with the other witnesses, Thomas testifies to the misunderstanding created by this exhortation in the morning, and also to the fact that the cardinals, frightened by the approaching mob, made use of this misunderstanding and " created " the Cardinal of St. Peter pope. The deception in

[1]The statement of Eubel, Hierarchia Catholica, tom. i, pp. 67, 329, that Thomas was made a bishop by Urban VI in 1380 is not correct.

[2]Muratori, Rerum Italicarum Scriptores, vol. iii, 2, cols. 715 seq., especially col. 718.

the afternoon, according to the *Factum* and Thomas, was based
upon the misunderstanding in the morning, whilst according
to the other witnesses the deception was merely caused by the
threatening approach of the Romans. It would appear,
therefore, that the former statements deserve the greater
credit, since they explain far more satisfactorily than the other
testimonies, why the Cardinal of St. Peter, and he alone, had
to be the chief actor in the farce. It is significant, as we shall
see, that the *Declaratio* of the cardinals also leaves this point
open.

A short, but instructive account is also to be found in the
three volume work, *De Schismate*, of Dietrich of Niem, another
eyewitness of the election. This celebrated lawyer had come to
Rome with Gregory XI as " notarius sacri palatii ". It may,
therefore, be profitable to quote at length from his statement,
since what he has to say sheds a somewhat different light upon
the events, and is not always in keeping with the statements
of other witnesses.

" When the cardinals entered the conclave, the archbishop of Bari was in their company.[1] He waited until all
the prelates who had accompanied the cardinals had
dispersed and then spoke with some cardinals in their rooms
and requested them to be guided in all things by God and
the law. I was present and saw and heard all this myself.
After the cardinals had elected him pope unanimously, they
sent for him and other prelates on Friday, at the third hour.
He immediately moved his books and other valuables into
a safe place, so that they would not be stolen, if the rumour
were spread abroad that he had been elected. The prelates
had hardly entered the Vatican, when the rumour reached
the people that the election had been finished : the Romans
now waited to know its result. Somebody shouted from the
palace : ' Barensis est electus in papam ', whereupon a
vehement commotion arose amongst the people, and I think
the reason was that many Romans had repeatedly asked the

---

[1]*De Schismate*, lib. i, cap. 2. This fact is not reported by any
other witness, but this may be explained by his access to details
which were inaccessible to other individuals. Dietrich's statements
of detail are not always correct, though this defect may be due
to the terseness of his accounts.

cardinals before the entry into the conclave to elect a Roman
or at least an Italian. I myself heard how, when the cardinals
entered the conclave, all those who stood on the steps of
St. Peter's demanded a Roman. Many maintained that
Cardinal Orsini had instigated this, in order to be elected
himself. But there was also another reason for the commotion : the late pope had a chamberlain called Jean de
Barre, a Limousin, a proud and lascivious man who was
hated not only by the Romans, but also by most people in
the curia ; and since the Romans believed that it was he
who had been elected, they were duly incensed about it.
They never thought of the Archbishop of Bari, *for he was
entirely unknown to many of them, and others despised him because
of his poverty*. In order to quell the popular turmoil, the
cardinals allowed the rumour to spread that the Cardinal
of St. Peter had been elected, whereupon his friends rushed
upon him and put him upon the altar of St. Peter (it should
be : of the chapel in the conclave), although he declared :
' The Archbishop of Bari is pope, not I.' He was nearly
crushed. Some cardinals left the city, whilst others went
into the castle of St. Angelo. Next day the cardinals of
Marmoutier, Poitiers, Geneva, Aigrefeuille, Viviers, Glandève, de Vergne, St. Eustace, Brittany and de Luna came
to the elect who was in the Vatican.[1] When the Romans
heard that it was not the chamberlain Jean de Barre who
had been elected, they calmed down and refrained from
further interference, so that all the cardinals who were
assembled in the palace in the evening of this day, performed
the enthronement."

Dietrich further reports that at that time nobody had the
slightest doubt about the canonical character of the election :
no rumours were heard to the contrary, neither amongst the
cardinals nor amongst other dignitaries. Indeed, all the
cardinals publicly and privately, in the written and spoken
word, stated that Urban was *verus papa* and that he had
been elected canonically and unanimously *per ipsos*. Dietrich
concludes : " And this is the truth and it cannot be
denied."

We may conclude this chapter with a brief review of the

[1] These names are not correctly reproduced by Dietrich.

deposition of St. Catherine of Sweden before the tribunal set
up in Rome in the early spring of 1379 to investigate the events
leading up to the election of Urban VI. The Swedish saint
was present during the critical days : she was active in promoting the canonization of her mother, St. Bridget.[1] The
protocol concerning her deposition before the tribunal is still
preserved and partly reproduced by Raynaldus.[2] She stated
that she herself had heard from trustworthy prelates that the
cardinals before their entry into the conclave had talked about,
and agreed upon, the election of the Archbishop of Bari.
She expressly denied that there was any agitation on the part
of the Romans before the conclave.[3] Moreover, she knew from
the Cardinal of Poitiers and also from other cardinals that
Prignano was elected unanimously " concorditer et cum bona
voluntate atque perfecta." " I firmly believe and hold Urban
VI to be the rightful pope." The tribunal also asked her
whether there was any intimidation on the part of the Romans.
The saint's answer was not quite clear and does not tally with
the testimonies of other witnesses. During the election itself, she
maintained, there was no *impressio*, but afterwards there was
some agitation (aliqualis rumor), because the Romans wanted a
Roman pope. On the other hand, she herself draws attention
to the petitions of the Roman officials as regards the election
of a Roman.[4] The saint appears to have been correct in her
observation in that she ascribes the farce with the old Cardinal
of St. Peter to the fear of the cardinals who knew that they had
not met the wishes of the Roman population. As she says,
the cardinals had every reason to fear for the life of the pope
elected.[5] Asked her opinion as to what was the cause of the
Schism, the saint declared that the Schism was caused by the
rigor justitiae which Urban VI had exhibited towards the

[1]See *supra*, p. 27.

[2]*Op. cit.*, tom. vii, pp. 380, col. 2—381, col. 1.

[3]" Interrogata, si pro tunc aliquis rumor Romanorum erat, dixit,
quod non."

[4]*Loc. cit.*, p. 381, col. 1.

[5]" Cardinales dubitantes, cum fuissent requisiti a Romanis, quod
papam Romanum haberent et non annuissent eorum petitionibus,
timuerunt, cum alium elegissent praeter Romanum, quod dictum
electum aut interficerent aut interfici facerent : propter quod
finxerunt dicti cardinales dominum S. Petri fore papam "—*ibid.*

cardinals to whose petitions he was not kindly disposed ; the saint perceived another cause of the Schism in the desire of Urban to reform the cardinals. It is worth while to quote from the deposition of the saint : " Interrogata, quae fuit ergo causa istius schismatis : respondit et dixit, quod credit, quod rigor justitiae domini nostri, qui eis (scil. cardinalibus) non erat blandus in eorum petitionibus, et corrigere eos optabat."

III

THE STORM

THE RELATIONSHIP between pope and cardinals in the days that followed the coronation disclosed nothing abnormal ; above all, there was nothing to suggest that the cardinals felt themselves to be acting under compulsion. Their known attitude towards the pope during this time lends no support to their later plea that they were, in fact, in constant fear of their lives : on the contrary, everything goes to show that they regarded Urban as *verus papa*. The cardinals themselves could not deny that, as the *Factum Urbani* stressed, they made numerous petitions to the pope for grants and privileges, assisted him in public and private consistories, were active in the appointments to vacant sees, proposed the Cardinal of Glandève as cardinal bishop of Ostia (which office he accepted from the hands of the pope), participated in various proceedings which ended with excommunication and anathemas, etc., and assisted Urban as pope in every conceivable way. Gifts were made to him, and there was indeed nothing which would have suggested that the cardinals did not consider him as lawful pope. If any further proof were needed, it would be furnished by the quite spontaneous homage which the Cardinal of Amiens paid to the new pope : he was not present at the election, but, as soon as he had finished the particular task with which he was entrusted, he hurried to Rome and arrived there on 24th April, 1378. And even after the cardinals had left Rome for Anagni, they inundated Urban with petitions for benefices which, as a rule, were granted : and yet they afterwards described Anagni as a safe place in which they had sought refuge and to which they had escaped from the pope's tyrannical treatment.

Although to the outside observer there was nothing in the behaviour of the cardinals which would have indicated that they did not recognize Urban as true pope, the mutual relations between them soon deteriorated considerably. Urban appeared

as a pope who solemnly and repeatedly pronounced his
intention to eradicate the evils within the Church. And he
seemed desirous to begin his scheme of reform from the top
downwards, singling out the cardinals and other prelates of
the Church for primary attention. But his methods were, to
say the least, undignified, and defeated the whole object of
reform, however praiseworthy his intentions. Of a rather
sanguine, impulsive and pugnacious nature he was prone to
outbursts in which he used most abusive and vituperative
words about the cardinals and other high dignitaries assembled
around him. These rages, which made his face red and his
voice hoarse, as Dietrich of Niem reports, were bound to be
resented by cardinals and prelates, who were not accustomed
to this kind of treatment. Thus, on Easter Monday, the day
following his coronation, during a service in the great chapel
of the Vatican, he inveighed against some bishops and prelates
who had stayed in Rome, calling them traitors, because they
had deserted their sees and preferred to live at the curia. The
Bishop of Pampeluna, himself an official of Urban and a
famous doctor of canon law, immediately took the challenge
up, whilst others were merely stunned ; the bishop replied
in a bitter tone that he was not there for the sake of his private
enjoyment, but for the sake of the public good : he would be
ready to resign his office rather than to suffer these insults.[1]

A fortnight after this incident the pope held a consistory,
all the cardinals and many prelates being present. The text
of the pope's address was : " I am the good shepherd." As
a contemporary chronicler puts it, the sermon was delivered
" minus caute necnon etiam minus ornate." Urban denounced
the life which the cardinals and prelates were leading—a charge
which they took very much amiss.[2] There are many instances
of the new pope's great lack of self-control. A papal tax
collector, for example, when delivering his collected revenues,
was shouted at by the pope and cursed as a simonist for
the money he had brought with him. On another occasion
it was the Cardinal of Limoges who was singled out as the
target of a furious outburst. During a private consistory the
pope actually fell upon the cardinal with the intention of

[1] Raynaldus, *loc. cit.*, p. 314, col. 2.
[2] " Ipsi aegre tulerunt."

beating him,[1] but the Cardinal of Geneva (the later Clement VII) threw himself between the two and said to the pope : " Holy Father, what are you doing ? " meanwhile putting the raving man gently back into his seat. Nor were these unedifying scenes restricted to private consistories. During a public consistory the Cardinal of Limoges made a grimace of annoyance behind the pope's back. The pope noticed this and challenged the cardinal in threatening words to look him in the face and to say publicly what he disliked. Another cardinal, who stood next to the Cardinal of Limoges, seeing that the pope was " blazing like a lamp ", said to his colleague : " Turn round, turn round, to our master."[2]

As a practical reform measure Urban decreed that the cardinals must restrict themselves to one course at meals— an order which must have greatly exasperated the princes of the Church, accustomed as they were to the luxury of Avignon. Another measure of reform was the prohibition against accepting gifts (*pensiones*) from outside, especially from secular princes. This, Urban declared, was simony and induced them to lead a life of pomposity and splendour. No less a witness than St. Catherine of Siena testified that the continual invectives of the pope wounded the pride of the cardinals and prelates. It became a daily occurrence for the pope to fulminate against simoniacs and to attack the cardinals personally. On one occasion Cardinal Orsini was called a half-wit (*sotus*). Can we be surprised at the statement of a chronicler[3] that the cardinals, such as they were, regretted having made him pope ?

A special target for Urban's fits of rage was the Cardinal of Amiens. In fact, some chroniclers held him to be the author of the Schism, and considering the personality and craftiness of this cardinal, it may well have been that he was very active in promoting discontent and dissatisfaction, for which Urban gave ample justification. The cardinal, having been unsuccessfully censured for his lascivious and luxurious life, was seized by an implacable and violent hatred of the pope. Urban

---

[1] " In consistorio privato surrexit de sede cum furia ad percutiendum dominum cardinalem Lemovicensem," Baluzius, *loc. cit.*, tom. i, col. 1067 (ed. Mollat, vol. ii, p. 585).

[2] The whole scene is described in great detail by Baluzius, *loc. cit.*

[3] Raynaldus, p. 315, col. 2.

himself expressed the opinion that there would have been no Schism, had it not been for the Cardinal of Amiens. Soon after his arrival in Rome on 24th April, 1378, he attended a consistory in which the pope dwelt upon the moral duties of ecclesiastical dignitaries and immediately went on to thunder against the avarice of the cardinals. They were, he said, debauched by the yellow metal—" qui fulvo corrupti metallo " —and blinded by money ; more anxious to grab wealth and mundane power than to seek the peace of the nations. The Cardinal of Amiens more than any other cardinal had been guilty of this sin : he had been a traitor and accessible to brib- ery. For, when commissioned by the late pope to negotiate peace between England and France, the cardinal had accepted large sums of money from both sides and, instead of procuring peace, had done everything to prolong the quarrel by playing off the one side against the other. Each time his money bag was empty, he contrived ways and means to fill it up again. Pre- tending to be a sincere friend to each side, he accepted money from both and " filled his burse heinously ". But the cardinal did not seem unduly shaken by this tirade—though there was a good deal of truth in the pope's indictment—and rose to his feet *in furore mentis* and in " unspeakable haughti- ness " he pointed his finger at the pope saying that his speech was a lying statement delivered by the Archbishop of Bari, not by the pope.[1] On another occasion the pope charged this cardinal with treachery, this time in his dealings with Milan and Florence. The cardinal replied : " I cannot answer you back now that you are pope ; but if you were still the little Archbishop of Bari—*Archiepiscopellus Barensis*—as you were only a few days ago, I would say that this *Archiepiscopellus* lies in his throat."[2] On yet another occasion, when this cardinal intervened in a somewhat heated altercation between the pope and his future rival, he was called " a wicked man ", because he had sown discord between the Kings of Aragon, Navarre and Castile ; this cardinal had, the pope continued, many lives on his conscience. A witness reported that the pope was alleged to have said to the Cardinal of Amiens : " This

[1]See Raynaldus, p. 332, col. 2 ; Baluzius, tom. i, col. 1159 (ed. Mollat, vol. ii, pp. 677–8).

[2]Baluzius, *loc. cit.*, col. 1158 (ed. Mollat, vol. ii, p. 678).

black robe has committed every evil deed in the world."[1] Soon afterwards the cardinal found himself deprived of his hat. It was on the occasion of one of these brawls between Urban and the Cardinal of Amiens that the Cardinal of Geneva, Robert (the later Clement VII), obviously taking exception to the language employed by the pope, made the following significant remark : " Unlike your predecessors, Holy Father, you do not treat the cardinals with that honour which you owe to them. You are diminishing our authority, but verily I tell you that we will do our best to diminish yours."[2]

To make the picture complete, we cannot omit the pope's en-counter with the quiet and learned Cardinal of Milan, Simon de Bursano, a former professor of canon law at the University of Naples. When, in May 1378, an English friar preached in the papal palace, taking as his subject the vice of simony, the pope, who was in the audience, suddenly jumped to his feet and cor-rected the friar in these words : " You may also say that excom-munication can be used against simoniacs, of whatever standing or rank they may be, even cardinals." In a quiet, dignified manner the Cardinal of Milan said : " Holy Father, there can be no lawful excommunication unless you have warned the guilty person three times beforehand," which statement brought the pope again to his feet and in one of his fits of rage he shouted at the cardinal : " I can do everything—and so I will and decree it."[3]

It is certainly not difficult to see that a friendly atmosphere cannot be maintained when pope and cardinals are wont to employ language of this kind to each other. It is unquestion-able that the pope had hit upon one of the sorest maladies afflicting the higher clergy, but, on the other hand, it was precisely the delicate nature of this malady which should have prompted the pope to be more cautious, dignified and prudent. The cardinals, in their turn, cannot but have strongly resented this dictatorial manner on the part of a man who had always

[1] Baluzius, *loc. cit.*, col. 1159 : " Iste habitus niger perpetravit omnia mala mundi " (ed. Mollat, *loc. cit.*).

[2] Deposition of Bishop Alphonso of Jaën : " In effectu, Pater beatissime, vos non tractastis dominos cardinales cum illo honore, quo debetis, sicut antecessores vestri faciebant, et diminuitis honorem nostrum. Dico vobis in veritate, quod cardinales conabuntur etiam diminuere honorem vestrum," see Raynaldus, p. 379, col. 1.

[3] Baluzius, *loc. cit.*, col. 1139 (ed. Mollat, vol. ii, pp. 659–60).

been regarded by them as socially inferior and who, after all, owed his position entirely to them : the *Archiepiscopellus* had become supreme pontiff through their election.

The deterioration in the relations between pope and cardinals was accompanied by a like deterioration in his relations with the secular princes. Duke Otto of Brunswick, Queen Joanna's husband, who had come to Rome to congratulate the new pope, received treatment that was humiliating when the pope kept him kneeling whilst the duke, in his office as cup bearer, vainly tried to offer him wine. The queen herself, hitherto a devout daughter of the Church, was also to suffer from the pope's tactlessness : her request for a delay of twelve months in the payment of her dues for the Neapolitan fief was bluntly refused by the pope, who, in addition, threatened to use his power over her and to place her in a nunnery and confiscate all her goods.[1] The legates of the queen were no better treated. Urban told the embassy, headed by the Duke of Brunswick, that he was going to improve the government of her kingdom, which, he said, was ruled inefficiently and badly. The cause of all this bad government was to be found, the pope was convinced, in the fact that the ruler was a woman.[2] Since all this must change, he would depose the queen and put in her place a man, namely, the son of the French king, Charles de la Paix. To lessen the effect of this startling news upon the legation which had come to congratulate him, the pope suggested that the queen should voluntarily enter a nunnery. But a more personal element caused considerable estrangement. At a dinner party in the papal palace on 23rd May, 1378, Nicholas Spinellus, the seneschal of the queen and a famous lawyer in Naples,[3] was made the target

---

[1] Baluzius, col. 1124 (ed. Mollat, vol. ii, p. 646).

[2] *Ibid.*, col. 1125, see also *Chronicon Siculum*, p. 33, *Giornali Napoletani*, in Muratori, *Rerum Italicarum Scriptores*, tom. xxi, col. 1038, and tom. xvii, col. 262.

[3] He was one of the shining examples of the Neapolitan seat of learning, see Panzirolus, *De Claris Legum Interpretibus*, pp. 161–2. At one time he was also in the service of Galeazzo Visconti II. Baldus de Ubaldis, who will engage our attention later, maintained that Nicholas was the instigator of the Schism, see Panzirolus, *loc. cit.*, and Baldus, *Consilia*, tom. ii, consilium 147, col. 4. Nicholas died in 1380, in Padua, where he had taught civil law since 1379.

of one of Urban's dreaded outbursts. The seneschal was placed by the master of ceremonies next to some ecclesiastical dignitaries. The pope objected to the precedence given and sent word to the seneschal asking him to leave his seat. In a dignified manner the seneschal left his seat, approached the pope and said that he had been sitting there by the arrangement of the master of ceremonies, and added that he had always occupied the same seat in the reign of Urban V and Gregory XI, who had known how to treat the seneschal and chancellor of the queen. Thereupon the Neapolitan embassy left the hall and returned to Naples. Cardinal Orsini had thus no trouble in producing, a few months later, an open breach, the ground having been prepared so well by the pope himself. In fact, Urban was compelled to ask the queen for armed support against the rebels and their forces, but not more than a token force was dispatched, obviously only to keep up appearances.

Of greater practical consequences was the pope's unnecessary affront to the Duke of Fondi. This prince had lent Gregory XI the sum of twenty thousand ducats, but Urban would not hear of repayment. The duke's formal request was bluntly refused, on the ground that the money had not been used for ecclesiastical purposes and that no obligation to repay it lay, therefore, upon Gregory's successor. The Duke of Fondi never forgot this : he was to become Urban's most determined enemy and a welcome friend to the cardinals. Though deposed by the pope as *comes campaniae*—for no other reason except that he demanded the repayment of a validly contracted debt—the duke was still strong enough to assist the cardinals effectively.

Even with the Emperor Charles IV, the pope only narrowly escaped a quarrel. In this case, too, the pope refused to pay the tithe of forty thousand ducats which Gregory XI had borrowed from the Emperor, on the ground that he had not received the money. But Charles IV's death prevented any breach with the imperial authorities.

So far no open rupture had occurred between pope and cardinals; to the outside observer relations still appeared harmonious, though internally, as we have seen, a good deal of tension and unrest prevailed. Obviously it was the cardinals who took the decisive step when they submitted to the pope

St. Catherine of Siena—an eighteenth-century engraving

*Effigy of William Courtenay,
Archbishop of Canterbury
(1382-1396) in Canterbury
Cathedral*

Anagni Cathedral

their proposal to take the curia back to Avignon. This proposal necessitated a clear-cut answer, affirmative or negative, and, as could only be expected, it precipitated the course of events. This step was nothing but the outward manifestation of the cardinals' dislike of the pope's policy. Urban flatly refused even to consider the proposal. To the cardinals this refusal meant, first, that the pope was bent upon asserting his superiority over them, and, secondly, that steps must be taken to ensure that Urban should have no further opportunity to appear as their taskmaster. The discontent, which had hitherto only smouldered beneath the surface, now became apparent —and to no one more than to Urban himself. The cardinals experienced one more disappointment : Urban, not being a Roman, and only partly Italian, and being quite unknown to the Roman populace, might have been expected to meet with antagonism, if not open hostility, from the Romans. But, from all accounts, it does not appear that Urban was received by the Romans in an unfriendly way. On the contrary, the Roman populace seemed not dissatisfied with the result of the election. And whatever antagonism there might have been, Urban took great care to forestall any manifestation of opposition towards him by trying to placate the Romans as much as possible. But no opposition was in fact forthcoming from this quarter. The cardinals, who had only themselves to blame for this state of affairs, saw themselves deprived of an influential ally ; the Roman populace was completely pacified by the pope's decision to stay in Rome, if for no other reason. On the other hand, at a later date, Urban correctly perceived that his refusal to return to Avignon alienated the cardinals to the degree of rebellion against him. Canon Thomas Petra reported the pope as replying to the cardinals that " it is neither possible nor admissible for us to go there, because Urban V and Gregory XI returned to Rome in order to restore this city and its ecclesiastical and spiritual life, which were near collapse ; and this intention is not yet fulfilled and for this reason we cannot go."[1] The mundane, not to say materialistic, outlook of the cardinals is very significantly illustrated in their reply to Urban : never, they declared, would Italy be guided by the apostolic see, and Italy's bad

[1]Raynaldus, p. 315, col. 2.

financial position could easily be remedied by selling the possessions of the order of St. John of Jerusalem—then all wants would be satisfied.[1] In his usual fashion the pope was infuriated by this argument of the cardinals and declared that he would suffer a thousand deaths rather than " destroy the right arm of the Christian Faith ".

We need little imagination to see that the cardinals, such as they were, could never be reconciled to the somewhat austere and severe life in Rome, nor could they easily have submitted to the tactless, dictatorial manners of a pontiff who owed them everything. So it was that to remove the pope from his Roman surroundings appeared to them imperative, if they were not to become mere tools in his uncivilized hands. They blamed the environment as much as the nature of the pope himself. Once back at Avignon, they thought it would be easy for them, realizing as they did the great influence environment is apt to play upon a man's decisions, to handle the pope and to shape his policy according to their own designs.

The cardinals had every intention of resuming their former mode of life. Having failed to persuade the pope, however, they were compelled to resort to subterfuges, and accordingly, by the end of May, 1378, under the pretext of escaping from the unbearable heat of Rome, some of the cardinals obtained permission to leave Rome for Anagni. More and more of them followed, so that by 21st June all, except the four Italians, had taken up residence there.

Two ways were open to the cardinals to effect a release from their obligation of loyalty and obedience to the pope : they could proceed either by his physical removal, or by his legal deposition. After unsuccessfully tempting the pope to join them at Anagni and to settle outstanding matters there in the interests of the universal Church, they realized that only the latter alternative promised any success. The pope was seriously considering joining them at Anagni when he heard, as the Bishop of Todi tells us, that if he went he would find himself the prisoner of the cardinals, who had secured the assistance of the Duke of Fondi—alienated now by the pope's own

[1]Raynaldus, *loc. cit.* It should be borne in mind that the possessions of the Templars, after their dissolution, were handed over to the Order of St. John.

behaviour. Another witness, Bishop Thomas, knew of still worse things which would have been in store for Urban : if he had gone to Anagni he would there have met his death. Accordingly, the pope abandoned the idea.

The cardinals, though growing bolder, did not even yet break with the pope. It is true that they spoke of him as a *delirus*,[1] or considered him a *furiosus* and *melancholicus*,[2] but they still, outwardly at least, treated him as pope, sending him numerous requests for benefices and grants, so that when the pope heard that they would no longer recognize him, he laughed and said : " First they say I am not the pope, and then they send me petitions all day long."[3] Nor did their letters show any sign of what they had in mind : they began *Sanctissime Pater* or *Beatissime Pater* and ended with phrases like these : " humilis et devotus Sanctitatis Vestrae . . ." or " humilis creatura vestra . . ." or " devotus servus vester. . . ."[4]

While thus they pretended that they recognized Urban as pope, they took steps to communicate with the French king.[5] Here emerged for the first time the theme of an election caused by fear. They asked the king, Charles V, for help in their efforts to declare the election null and void. But the French king did not appear too enthusiastic about the role he was to play. A united papacy under his influence was possibly of inestimable value to him, but a curia with a serious cleavage in its ranks was of little avail ; moreover, the wars with England, the uncertainty of imperial policy and of the possible consequences of Edward III's death in the summer of the previous year (1377), preoccupied him at the moment and he

[1]Dietrich of Niem, *De Schismate*, lib. i, c. 7 : " Eum delirum communiter ipsi cardinales habebant."

[2]Baluzius, tom. i, col. 1143.

[3]Raynaldus, p. 317, col. 2.

[4]A number of examples are given by Raynaldus, p. 317, col. 1 ; see also Gayet, *Le Grand Schisme d'Occident*, vol. ii, pp. 261 seq.

[5]On this correspondence, see N. Valois, *La France et Le Grand Schisme*, vol. i, p. 89. About the envoys sent to Charles V, see Hefele-Leclercq, *Histoire des Conciles*, vol. vi, part 2, p. 1071 note, and Valois, vol. i, p. 92. In August, 1378, the cardinals had dispatched an envoy (Jean de Guidnicourt) to Charles V, see Valois, p. 96, and A. Coville, *L'Europe Occidentale* (1270-1380) p.639.

delayed giving a forthright answer. Nor was Charles V a king who conspicuously pursued a policy of expansion or aggrandisement. That he was disposed to be friendly to the cardinals, some of whom—Robert of Geneva, for instance— were relatives, cannot seriously be doubted, but this fact alone did not seem to weigh unduly with him.[1] He commissioned a number of outstanding jurists to draft a report on the question. But the jurists, guided by purely juristic arguments, replied that the whole dispute was one to be settled by a general council. Even if it were assumed, they declared in their memorandum, that fear had caused the election, it would still be an open question as to whether the candidate elected was instrumental in causing the fear which eventually led to his election. The cardinals, these royal jurists continued, had no legal power to initiate proceedings against the man elected pope, nor to anathematize him. Moreover, they could not possibly be plaintiffs, witnesses and judges in one. The only way left for a just solution was the convocation of a general council. The lawyers were, however, instructed to say that so far as immediate help and counsel were concerned, the king would lend the cardinals any aid they might desire to ensure their personal safety.[2]

Now, according to canon law, the convocation of a general council was a prerogative of the pope. The cardinals were quick to turn the situation to their own advantage. On 20th July, 1378, they dispatched a letter to the Italian cardinals, peremptorily summoning them to appear at Anagni within five days of receipt of the letter : the Holy See was declared vacant. On 9th August they issued their famous *Declaratio* from Anagni, in which they announced to the whole of Christendom that the election of Urban VI was null and void and that the Holy See was declared vacant. Urban himself was cited to come to Anagni, since he was a criminal who wrongfully usurped the throne of St. Peter. As to the General

[1] The questionable part played by Charles V is the subject of a very penetrating analysis by Valois, *loc. cit.*, vol. i, pp. 85–9, 112–5, 141–4. The charge sometimes brought against this king, that is to say that he was the instigator of the Schism, is very properly dismissed by Valois, *loc. cit.*, p. 141. See also Salembier, *Le Grand Schisme*, pp. 69–70.

[2] Raynaldus, p. 330.

Council suggested by the French jurisconsults, the cardinals had now a ready answer : there was no pope who could lawfully summon the council. It appears, furthermore, that they took literally Charles V's promise of help and counsel. Seeing that the king was not ill-disposed towards them, they proceeded to distort events and to represent themselves to him as the victims of oppression. In a further communication, if the report of the papal legate to the King of Castile is trustworthy, the king was alleged to have gone even so far as to leave the French-English war aside and to extend all his help *in schismatis causa*.[1] With this promise, and the assistance readily offered by the Duke of Fondi, the scene was set for the final stages which culminated in the election of Cardinal Robert of Geneva as Pope Clement VII on 20th September, 1378. The cardinals' political acumen is indicated by their addressing a letter to the Chancellor of the University of Paris on 7th September and another letter to the members of the university on 12th September, in which they described Urban as an intruding archbishop possessed by the spirit of anger (*truculenta rabies*) and malice against them.[2] But no less political foresight was displayed by Urban, who, as early as 3rd July, foreseeing the difficulties and attempting to forestall mischievous machinations, had sent his own description of the events during the election to the University of Paris.[3]

One more occurrence quickened the course of events. Urban had several times tried to induce the cardinals to return to Rome or at least to Tivoli, where he had betaken himself in July. Whether upon instigation of the cardinals, or only through the intervention of the Duke of Fondi, a considerable force of Breton and Gascon mercenaries now advanced against Rome, a city without defences. The Romans were heavily beaten near the Ponte Salario on 16th July, 1378, losing several hundred of their poorly equipped soldiers. It was now that the pope made his humiliating request for succour to Queen Joanna. The token force which she sent arrived and may have prevented worse disaster. But the victory over the Romans gave fresh incentive to Urban's enemies, the Duke of Fondi

[1] "Etiamsi Anglicorum bellum ea de causa intermissurus foret."
[2] See Bulaeus, *Historia Universitatis Parisiensis*, tom. iv, p. 479.
[3] Bulaeus, *loc. cit.*, p. 464.

and the cardinals. The Roman population, however, had accumulated sufficient hatred of the mercenaries to withstand successfully a much more serious onslaught a few months later.

The cardinals had now secured themselves against any immediate danger from Urban ; they felt confident of success and it was immediately after this battle that they prepared for the final steps : hence the quick succession of events; 20th July the summoning of the Italian cardinals, 9th August the promulgation of the *Declaratio*, and 20th September the election of the new pope.

IV

ATTEMPTS AT PREVENTION
AND RECONCILIATION

D U R I N G those momentous days in mid-July, 1378, the pope stayed with the three Italian cardinals in Tivoli—the Cardinal of St. Peter was too ill to make even the short journey from Rome to Tivoli. The " invitation " of the cardinals at Anagni to the Italian cardinals was favourably received by them and by the pope ; all appeared ready to take steps towards a reconciliation. After having, without success, requested the cardinals to come to Tivoli, Urban VI now believed that this opportunity should not be lost : the deterioration of the political situation and the growing tension within the curia cannot have failed to bring home to him the serious impasse for which, he had no doubt any more, it was he who was chiefly responsible. Hence his readiness to negotiate.

On 26th July the three Italian cardinals left Tivoli ; they were met by the Cardinals of Geneva and St. Eustace in the chapel of Palestrina. Obviously carrying out the instructions of Urban the three pressed for a general council before it was too late to save Christendom from a terrible disaster. We cannot decide whether the anti-Urbanist cardinals already knew of the proposals of the French jurisconsults : in true diplomatic fashion they referred Urban's proposal back to their colleagues, since they themselves had no powers to make agreements. The reply from Anagni was in the negative. On 6th August the Italian cardinals informed the pope of the breakdown of the negotiations.

The unfavourable reply from Anagni was drafted by the Cardinal of St. Eustace. After examining the legality and admissibility of a general council he arrived at the conclusion that the convocation of a council would, in this case, mean a departure from old established traditions and would, in effect, amount to an innovation in the history of the Church. It had happened several times before that popes had been " intrusi in apostolica sede," but no case could be quoted in which a council had been convoked to declare " whether such a one was really pope or not ". According to canon law, every council must be summoned by the properly constituted authority, that is to say, by that authority which has jurisdictional powers over those who are to be summoned. But now, since the pope had no longer authority over them—the Holy See having been declared vacant—nobody was in a legal position to summon a council. Nor could lay princes be legally entrusted with the convocation of a council. " Ergo non est haec via modo superstitione invenienda."[1]

This answer, as it stands, is perfectly correct : there can be no general council without the pope's authority. The purely legalistic attitude, to which the cardinals were always prone, will not withstand serious criticism, for they were themselves arrogating powers which canon law did not confer upon them. According to canon law, the Sacred College had no right whatsoever to declare the Holy See vacant. And it was precisely this illegal arrogation of legal powers which enabled them to reject the proposal for a general council for purely legalistic reasons. The legality of their views rested upon the illegality of their powers. They would have been right if the Holy See had been vacant : they were not right, because there was legally no vacancy. The basis of their rejection was thus untenable.

How far Urban and his three cardinals were sincere in their proposal for a general council, it is difficult to assess ; they were certainly not more than lukewarm. Nevertheless, Urban did at least suggest a council, whilst this suggestion was firmly resisted by the anti-Urbanists throughout the period of the Schism. St. Vincent Ferrer, a fiery zealot in the fold of the later anti-pope, reasoned in the typical manner—like all others on the side of the anti-Urbanists he begged the question when he declared that it would be improper to justify a council on this count alone,[2] since Pope Clement VII and his followers would thereby implicitly admit the existence

[1]Raynaldus, p. 331, col. 2.
[2]Baluzius, tom. i, col. 1108 (ed. Mollat, vol. ii, p. 631).

of a doubt as to their legal position : and their legal position was unassailable, according to St. Vincent Ferrer.[1] One cannot but detect a certain uneasiness on the part of all the Clementine followers at the prospect of a general council : it appeared to them a safer device to generate emotional heat by referring to imponderables, such as decency, prestige and propriety. There was certainly a readier response to their appeals addressed to the crowds when the suggestion of a general council was turned down as *damnosa et praejudicialis*, as the Cardinal of St. Eustace put it,[2] than when it was proposed to submit the matter to arbitration.

On 9th August, only a few days after the meeting with their Italian colleagues, the cardinals issued another proclamation to the Christian people of Europe. They declared, once again, that the Holy See was vacant and that Urban was anathematized, because he was an *intrusor* and an " invasor, qui per ostium non intravit."[3] The faithful were instructed to renounce all allegiance to this " wicked man " (*scelestus vir*) ; in no wise must his orders be obeyed. Urban, they maintained, had been bidden to abdicate and to abstain from the exercise of all spiritual and temporal functions. Lastly, they solemnly requested Urban to return to private life in order to spare Christendom any further scandal.

The well-meaning efforts that were made to prevent irrevocable disaster were doomed to failure in view of the uncompromising attitude of the cardinals. No greater and no more heroic efforts were made than by St. Catherine of Siena. We fortunately possess her opinions, which were preserved by her confessor, the later Dominican Master General, Raymund delle Vigne, of Capua. From the outset the saint appeared as one of the staunchest defenders of Urbanist rights ; and with Catherine we feel a genuine revolt against the conditions prevailing within the Church and a sincere dismay at the luxury and splendour of the cardinals. She prophesied

---

[1]See Baluzius, *loc. cit.* On St. Vincent Ferrer see especially H. Finke, " Drei Spanische Publizisten aus den Anfängen des Grossen Schismas " in *Spanische Forschungen der Goerresgesellschaft*, vol. iv (1934), pp. 174–95.

[2]Baluzius, *loc. cit.*

[3]Baluzius, *loc. cit.*, and *Chronicon Siculum*, p. 32.

the Schism three years before its actual outbreak. Her bio-grapher met the saint in 1375, at a time when a great number of cities had risen against papal domination. It is interesting to see how much the temporal dominion of the Church was, in the minds of men, intrinsically linked up with its spiritual authority, as is clearly shown in the lamentations of the saint and her biographer, who both came to consider the prevailing conditions with horror. The increasing antagonism of the cities against the temporal sovereignty came to be clearly associated in the minds of the people with a corresponding lack of faith in the truths of Christianity. When the biographer met St. Catherine, he spoke of the gloomy outlook for the Church now that whole cities rose up against her : on the same occasion he complained of the small effect that excommuni-cation and interdict produced upon the faithful, and of the selfishness which dominated private and social life ; the rights of Holy Church had not been respected, since her government had been seditiously rejected. When Perugia followed the example of other cities in raising the battle cry of liberty and independence, the biographer, bursting into tears, bewailed this " new scandal for the Church."[1] St. Catherine tried to console him and said : " Do not weep now, you will have still more to weep for in the future ; what you see now is just milk and honey compared to what will follow."[2] " How," asked the biographer, " how can we witness greater evils than a sedition of Christians against the Church ? Her commands are no longer obeyed, her punishments not feared and the faithful have lost all respect for her. There is just one more thing lacking, and that is the complete denial of the Christian faith."[3]

To which the saint replied—correctly as the event proved: " At the moment it is only laymen who act thus ; soon you will see how much more heart-wringing the actions of clerics will be." Would the clerics rise against the Church ? the biographer asked. " Yes, I maintain that as soon as the pope tries to improve the moral standard of the clerics, they will

[1]Raynaldus, p. 323, cols. 1 and 2.
[2]" Istud enim, quod nunc videtis, est lac et mel respectu eorum, quae subsequantur."
[3]" Nihil restat amodo nisi, ut Christi fidem totaliter negent."

cause immense dissension within the Church, which will be divided, as it were, by a heretical pestilence."

When in Rome, soon after the outbreak of the Schism, St. Catherine remarked to Raymund : " What we witness at the moment is child's play (*ludus puerorum*) by comparison with what is in store for the Church." She was perfectly aware of Urban's abusive tongue and courageously wrote many letters to him urging greater tolerance and understanding of the difficulties of the cardinals : as the true vicar of Christ he, above all others, should use moderate language in his dealings with the cardinals and should treat them gently. " Do what you do with moderation," she counselled Urban, " with good will and a peaceful heart ; for excess destroys rather than builds up. For the sake of your crucified Lord, keep your natural hastiness somewhat in check."

Realizing that the creation of a common enemy was always the safest means of uniting contending factions, St. Catherine strongly urged a crusade against the infidels. She tried to persuade the Cardinal of Florence to use his influence with the pope to kindle in him the old crusading spirit. But both cardinal and pope were concerned with more personal and realistic issues. The saint also wrote a number of letters to Queen Joanna of Naples begging her not to withdraw her allegiance from the " one, rightful pope ". Nor did the saint omit to approach the Duke of Fondi—but all these efforts were made with inadequate means and were purely personal appeals. Little response could be expected from an adversary who went to work in a calculating, shrewd and political manner. That the saint cannot have fully grasped the situation is shown by her approach to the French king himself, even after the outbreak of the Schism.[1] On the other hand, this fact alone indicates that St. Catherine was far from considering the break as a conflict between purely nationalistic aims. The personages to whom she had addressed all her letters did not even deem it worth their while to reply or to take any of her appeals into consideration. Nevertheless, the strength of her conviction of the rightfulness of Urban's cause emerges clearly from her letters. But the spirit of the time moved in a direction averse to her fervent, mystic appeals. The outbreak

[1]See Raynaldus, pp. 398–9.

of the Schism was but one symptom of a crisis besetting men
who had come to question the institution of the papacy itself
—all attempts to shift the scene from the purely rational to
the purely emotional plane were doomed to failure. The unity
of Christendom cannot be saved by emotional appeals.

This emphatically emotional approach to the question
found no favour with the Emperor Charles IV. He too was
most anxious to preserve Christendom, or rather to retain the
papacy as a political ally. A divided papacy, with divided
allegiances and loyalties, was useless to an emperor. In contrast to the saint, the emperor's endeavours to prevent a
rupture were purely political moves dictated by self-interest :
the rickety and tattered Empire (itself soon to be the scene
of an imperial schism) was compelled to seek alliance with
conservative forces to make good its resistance against the
pretentious assertions of the component national states.
Consequently, the emperor too tried to reconcile the rival
factions and appealed to the cardinals, urging them to a more
conciliatory policy and reminding them of the great responsibility of their office. After the cardinals had betaken themselves
to the territory of the Queen of Naples, Charles appealed to
her also to use her influence to heal the wounds.[1] But constructive proposals were lacking on all sides—once men are
resolved to pursue a certain course, mere appeals will tend to
confirm them in it rather than to effect a change of mind.

The election of Cardinal Robert of Geneva as pope took
place in the palace of the Count Honorato at Fondi. The
composition of the Sacred College had remained unchanged,
and even the three Italian cardinals were present. The fourth
of the Italians, the old Cardinal of St. Peter, had died on
7th September. The wavering behaviour of the three Italian
cardinals merits some attention. Their letter of 6th August
informing the pope of their failure to achieve any agreement
with the other cardinals does not convey the impression that
they had any doubt about the validity of Urban's election.
More than that : they corresponded with the pope as late as
4th September and in none of their letters can one detect any

[1]On the Emperor's correspondence see Hefele-Leclercq, *Histoire
des Conciles*, vol. vi, part 2, p. 1083 note 2, and Valois, *La France et
Le Grand Schisme*, vol. i, p. 265 note 6.

shade of doubt as to the validity of the election. Nevertheless, they did not accede to the pope's request that they should return to Rome, and their letters to him were evasive on this point. Whilst they were thus vacillating, the French cardinals, who cannot have failed to perceive this indecision on the part of their Italian colleagues, resorted to a device which was bound to prove successful. Each of the three Italians was secretly informed that a new pope was to be elected and that he alone had been selected as a suitable candidate.[1] The three were thus played off against each other. Thus cajoled they joined the other cardinals and went with them into the conclave. Each of the Italians, believing that he was the future pope, refrained from voting. Robert was elected unanimously. The three Italian cardinals could not but recognize his election as valid.[2] The new pope, who called himself Clement VII, was enthroned and crowned on the day of his election—a remarkably speedy affair. Little more than two months later Pope Clement VII found himself excommunicated by Pope Urban VI (29th November, 1378).

It is true that the election of Robert may appear " as the triumph of the French idea ",[3] if purely external appearances had decided this issue. Yet, one may detect very little triumph, when one calls to mind that, up to this election, Urban was the undisputed pope, recognized as such by all nations, including the French. The recognition of Clement VII by France was by no means a foregone conclusion : on the contrary, matters took a turn for him which seemed, in the following months, to question the wisdom of his somewhat hasty election. In retrospect, Clement's elevation to the pontificate may appear a triumph of the French idea ; at the time, however, this opinion would certainly not have been shared by him or by his followers.

[1]These intrigues are reported at great length by Baluzius, tom. i, col. 1049 (ed. Mollat, vol. ii, p. 565).

[2]The Italians were in a constant state of vacillation. Cardinal Orsini was typical : two days before his death (13th August, 1379) he made a declaration in which he said that he personally would favour a General Council to settle the dispute, though Urban was *verissime papa*, see Raynaldus, p. 371, col. 1.

[3]Workman, *John Wyclif*, vol. ii, p. 58.

For quite understandable reasons, attempts at a reconciliation after the break were few, as the attitudes of men stiffened the deeper the chasm went. This made a reconciliation all the more difficult. Nevertheless, some nations and their clerics had not yet declared their loyalty to the one or the other of the two claimants, and it is amongst these that we may find some pleas for reconciliation. Perhaps the ablest attempts in this direction came from the pen of the Archbishop of Toledo, Petrus Tenorius, who, as late as August, 1380, tried a reconciliation in a memorandum submitted to the Cardinal of St. Eustace.[1] This memorandum is a strong and direct appeal to the cardinals for unity, and it is notable not only because of the impartiality and unbiased attitude of this ecclesiastical dignitary, but also because of the frank and dignified language : the arguments of the Castilian betray a genuine sense of justice ; he endeavours to convince the cardinals by emphatically and bluntly stating the wrong character of their actions. This memorandum is a truly rational appeal and attempt at a reconciliation. In it the archbishop says that on the one hand the cardinals maintain that they had been under the impression of fear throughout their stay in Rome, that they had never been at liberty whilst in the city, and that all their actions had been dictated by fear ; Urban, on the other hand, denied all this. Consequently, this is a dispute which must be decided in some juridical way : " Locus est juridicae determinationi ". For it appears most absurd, the archbishop reminds the Cardinal of St. Eustace, that the man who had been held pope throughout the world for four months should be expelled without giving him any hearing or any possibility of a defence against the most serious charge of the cardinals, e.g., that he was an *intrusus, apostaticus et antichristus*.[2] And the cardinal is

---

[1] The greater part of this memorandum is printed by Raynaldus, *loc. cit.*, pp. 43ᴏ, col. 2—431, col. 2, whilst Martène and Durand, *Thesaurus Novus Anecdotorum*, tom. ii, cols. 1099–1120, print the whole memorandum under the title : *Acta Domini Toletani super facto schismatis ad Dominum S. Eustachii Cardinalem.*

[2] " Satis enim videretur absurdum, si vobis et dominis meis cardinalibus accusantibus ipsum apostaticum et antichristum, qui receptus, habitus et reputatus fuit per totum mundum ut verus papa, qui per quatuor menses fuit in possessione pacifica, absque aliqua audientia expellatur et eidem defensionis copia denegetur."

referred to the canon law itself which lays down that nobody is allowed to renounce allegiance to a pope before the charge against him is proved.[1]

To whom, then, does the right to make this juridical decision belong ? asks the Archbishop of Toledo. The Cardinal of St. Eustace, in a former communication to him, had maintained that it lay with the cardinals. Bowing before the wide learning of the cardinal and before his expert knowledge of canon law, the archbishop, with all the respect due to a legal expert, requests the cardinal to enlighten him on this legal point, since his own blindness and feebleness of mind allow him to interpret canon law in a different manner.[2] He believes— and we can readily agree with him—that *Clem.*I. iii. 2 quite plainly rejects the interpretation of the cardinals : " Revera, imbecillitas mea credit totum contrarium, videlicet, quod juridica determinatio et finalis seu sententialis definitio cum causae cognitione in hoc casu non pertineat ad dominos cardinales." In short, the cardinals were acting as if there had already been a juridical decision—and, surely, cardinals ought to know that this method is quite illegal.[3] Even if the Holy See had been vacant, the archbishop goes on to say, the cardinals, according to the plain sense of the above-cited passage in the *Clementines*, have no powers or jurisdictional authority.[4] " I flatly deny," writes the Castilian to the cardinal, " that the cardinals after having elected and enthroned the pope who occupied St. Peter's chair for four months peacefully, have the right to sit in judgment over the pope, without summoning him and without proper legal safeguards, when they themselves had previously consented to, or at least, not contradicted, his

[1] Causa viii, quaestio 4, canon 1 : "Lex ecclesiastica pontificem ab aliis accusatum, priusquam sub luce objecta constiterint, exigit non relinqui."

[2] " Sane, reverendissime pater et domine mi, ut saepius dixi, rudis sum et de apicibus juris non tantum didici, ut aperire possim os coram tanto patre, qui est arca juris canonici ; tamen, cum pace loquar cum domino meo, ut me caecum et vacillantem in isto passu velitis et dignemini illuminare, quia revera . . ."—*Thesaurus Novus Anecdotorum, loc. cit.,* col. 1114.

[3] The archbishop properly refers to *Decretales,* I. iv. 10 ; 29 ; 53.

[4] " Praesuppono etiam, quod sede apostolica vacante cardinales nihil potestatis aut jurisdictionis habent nec exercere possunt."

actions."[1] Since, then, this juridical decision is not the business
of the cardinals, to whom else does it belong ? The archbishop
replies that the dispute must be submitted to a council, because
this matter affects the whole universal Church. He seems to
sense the difficulty inherent in his proposal: for, according to
canon law, as he himself points out, only the pope or his legate
can summon a council. Here is the weak point of the memorandum: he asserts that the council can be convoked by the cardinals themselves—he omits to say whether he thinks of both
" Sacred Colleges "—because in this case they succeed to the
papal authority: *Hoc casu succedunt in jurisdictione papali.* Only a
very liberal interpretation of two passages in canon law[2] enables
the archbishop to maintain a point of view which finds but
remote support in the passages referred to. If this should not be
correct, the archbishop argues, the council can be summoned by
either pope. In spite of the defect from which this memorandum
suffers in legal respects, it certainly was an attempt to reconcile
the two parties in that it honestly and bluntly demonstrated the
wrong basis of the cardinals' actions towards Urban. The Castilian concludes his memorandum with a fervent appeal to all
cardinals to put an end to this tragedy and exclaims: "My lords
and glittering and radiating lights, lend relief and succour to the
blind, vague, wavering, timid, unintelligent and uncritical
through your splendours, enlighten them and bring solace to
them with your combined strength . . . I beg and pray through
the inexhaustible mercy of Jesus Christ that the unity of the
Catholic Faith may be restored and that you may join together
in a general council."[3]

[1] " Sed quod cardinales possint juridice definire, et quod stetur
eorum determinationi et definitioni in praejudicium electi, jam per
ipsos cardinales inthronizati et per quatuor menses possidentis paci-
fice et quiete, ipsis cardinalibus praesentibus, videntibus et consen-
tientibus, vel saltem non contradicentibus, ipso non vocato, non
convicto, hoc omnino nego ; quia decretum ' Ne Romani' ipsos
cardinales privat omni potestate et jure et jurisdictione, sede
vacante," Raynaldus, p. 411, col. 2.

[2] *Distinctio* lxxviii. 8 ; *causa* vi, *quaestio* 4, *canon* 1.

[3] " Succurrite ergo et subvenite, patres conscripti et luminaria
super candelabrum radiantia, et caecos, vagos, fluctuantes et trepi-
dos, ac insipientes in populo, vestris illustrate splendoribus, vestris
injunctis viribus comfortate . . . oro et obsecro per illam, inexhaustam
misericordiam Jesu Christi, ut unitatem catholicae fidei, quatenus a

We may profitably conclude this chapter with extracts from two letters written by St. Catherine of Siena, the one to the pope, and the other to the three Italian cardinals after they had deserted Urban. In the first she said : " I have heard that these devils in human form have made an election. They have not chosen a vicar of Christ, but an anti-Christ. Never will I cease to acknowledge you, my dear Father, as the representative of Christ upon earth. Now go forward, Holy Father, without fear into battle, for that is your sure defence."[1]

The second letter, though addressed to the three Italian cardinals, is actually applicable to all the cardinals. The sincerity of tone, the depth of grief and emotion are strikingly illustrated in it.

" To what have you come, since you did not act up to your high dignity ! You were called to nourish yourselves at the breast of the Church ; to be as flowers in her garden, to shed forth sweet perfume ; to be as pillars to support the vicar of Christ and his bark ; as lamps to serve for the enlightenment of the world and the diffusion of the faith. You yourselves know if you have accomplished that to which you were called, and which it was your bounden duty to do. Where is your gratitude to the bride who has nourished you ? Instead of being her shield, you have persecuted her. You are convinced of the fact that Urban is the true pope, the sovereign pontiff, elected lawfully, not through fear but by divine inspiration, far more than through your human co-operation. So you informed us, and your words were true. Now you have turned your backs on him, as craven and miserable knights, afraid of your own shadow. What is the cause ? The poison of selfishness which destroys the world. You, who were angels upon earth, have turned to the work of devils. You would lead us away to the evil which is in you, and seduce us into obedience to anti-Christ. Unhappy men ! you made truth known to us, and now you offer us lies. You would have us

[1]Pastor, *History of the Popes*, vol. i, p. 130.

vestrae splendidae puritatis lucibus tantae obscuratis maculam abradentes et in hoc instantibus malis et periculis occurrentes ad propositum dicto generalis concilii remedium concurratis ", Raynaldus, p. 413, col. 2.

believe that you elected pope Urban VI through fear. He who says this, tells a lie. You may say, why do you not believe us ? We, the electors, know the truth better than you do. But I answer that you yourselves have shown me how to deal with truth. If I look at your lives, I look in vain for the virtue and holiness which might deter you, for conscience' sake, from falsehood. What is it that proves to me the validity of the election of Messer Bartolomeo, the Archbishop of Bari, and now in truth Pope Urban VI ? The evidence was furnished by the solemn function of his coronation, by the homage which you have rendered him, and by the favours which you have asked and received from him. You have nothing but lies to oppose to these truths. O ye fools ! a thousand times worthy of death. In your blindness you perceive not your own shame. If what you say were true as it is false, must you not have lied, when you announced that Urban VI was the lawful pope ? Must you not have been guilty of simony in asking and receiving favours from one whose position you now deny ? "[1]

[1]Pastor, *loc. cit.*, Raynaldus, p. 340-1.

V

THE CASE OF THE CARDINALS

W H A T reasons did the cardinals themselves put forward to justify their extraordinary procedure ? How far can they be said to have acted in the interests of the universal Church ? Why did they adopt so uncompromising an attitude towards the pope ? By what methods did they choose to lend a semblance of legality to their own proceedings and a semblance of illegality to those of Urban ? To answer these questions we must examine still more closely the documents drafted and signed by the cardinals and the other available evidence also. Their case is best stated in the lengthy document entitled *Declaratio* issued at Anagni on 9th August, 1378 ; it runs as follows :

" Be it known to all the faithful that, after Gregory XI's death on 27th March last, officials of the city of Rome conferred with the Cardinals, both in secret and in public, as it is the custom when important business has to be decided upon. These conferences dealt with the procedure and attitude to be adopted by the cardinals. As it was reported by some witnesses, the officials compelled the cardinals to elect a Roman or at least an Italian[1] to ensure that the curia remained at Rome. The then Archbishop of Bari was present at one of these conferences, as he himself has publicly confessed, although he advised that the cardinals should be treated gently. Some creditable witnesses testify that this same archbishop had frequently recommended himself to the officials, in the church of S. Maria Nova, before the

[1] " Ut omnino cogerent (scil. officiales) dominos cardinales ad eligendum Romanum vel saltem Italicum," Baluzius, tom. ii, col. 822 (ed. Mollat, vol. iv, p. 174).

It should be noted here that in the official declaration of the cardinals one of their most important claims is confirmed by " some witnesses ".

entry into the conclave.[1] Immediately after Gregory's death
the city officials were desirous to guard all gates and bridges,
including those which had traditionally been guarded by
the officials of the Vatican. Indeed, they guarded these
localities safely night and day. It was everywhere thought
at the time that they did so to prevent the cardinals leaving
for any place to perform the election. During the ten days
that elapsed between Gregory's death and the beginning
of the conclave, the city officials approached the cardinals
several times in the company of a great number of citizens,
in order to beg them to elect a Roman or at least an Italian
pope ; they added that the cardinals should declare publicly before the whole people that they would comply with
the wishes of the population : in order to avoid grave perils
and dangers, the cardinals should comply with the wishes
of the people. At the same time individual citizens were
sent to the private quarters of the cardinals to submit this
request personally. All members of the nobility were to
leave the city within three days. The request of the cardinals
that at least the Counts of Nola and Fondi should be permitted to stay in Rome, since they were officials of the
curia, was flatly rejected. The cardinals sent for the officials
and made it clear to them that they had erroneous conceptions of the cardinals ; moreover, the requests of the
officials were simply threats and intimidations, and an
election thus influenced would be null and void. If they
tried to keep the curia in Rome by such measures, they
themselves would be the cause of losing it for ever. The
cardinals put two requests to the officials. Firstly, they
should send back the great numbers of country folk who had
streamed into the city recently ; they should give orders
to the people to abstain from public meetings which inflamed the passions of the people. Secondly, they should
detail a suitable captain and an adequate number of
citizens, to guard the Borgho of St. Peter ; the expenses
would be met by the cardinals ; care should be taken

[1]Here again, the cardinals vaguely refer to " some creditable
witnesses " on a point which is surely of greatest importance and
which would have merited a somewhat more detailed elaboration,
especially as regards the personalities of those witnesses.

that the people could not advance up to the palace.

"The officials complied with this request and appointed one *banderensis* (district governor) as captain, who selected four citizens as constables. They all swore solemnly to protect the cardinals effectively and efficiently and to preserve them from all violence. But actually these officials kept none of their promises.

"Thus, when the cardinals were about to go into the conclave they had difficulty in entering the palace, because the square in front of it was thronged with people, many of whom were armed. Moreover, a huge crowd entered the palace together with the cardinals, and the doors had to be kept open throughout the night, because the crowd would not allow them to be shut. The whole palace was surrounded by armed men, so that nobody could go in or out without the mob's permission. All left the palace, except the senator and a few individuals, and the cardinals requested him to lock the doors so as to prevent anyone getting in. The district governors and officials, however, pressed to be admitted into the conclave. They repeated their request, when it was made clear to them that their entry into the conclave would be quite unusual, especially at such a late hour. Fearing that the doors might be broken open and that they themselves would be in grave danger, the cardinals permitted the entry of the governors. As soon as they had entered, they repeated the request that a Roman or at least an Italian be elected, otherwise the cardinals would be in great peril. The cardinals had heard from trustworthy persons that there were some prelates in the city, partly Romans, partly Italians, who incited the population and promised them money in case of their election. At the time of Gregory's death there were sixteen cardinals at Rome,[1] of whom twelve were ultramontane, and only four Italian. The ultramontane cardinals had a two-thirds majority and, as soon as the vacancy had occurred, had decided to elect one of the College and a non-Italian, until they had been subjected to the pressure to be described later. The Italians, though desirous to elect one of the College, suggested one of their own nationality. After the entry into the conclave

[1] Their names and titles follow here.

there was no change of mind until the next morning, when they all said mass according to tradition—all this regardless of the fact that the Romans, in contradiction to the old custom, refused to allow the bricking up of the door of the conclave. Only after the cardinals had gone to bed was it possible for the guards to put a beam across the door of the conclave. The crowd, however, occupied the palace, particularly that part which lay under the conclave, and caused great noise throughout the night, clashing their arms and shouting all the time : ' Romano lo volemo o Italiano '. Some are reported to have heard the cry, ' Moriantur '. All this commotion continued until next morning, so that the cardinals could find little sleep. Tired out by their continued shouting, the crowds abstained for a little while, but the clamouring started again while the cardinals were saying their masses, so that one could hardly hear or understand the words of the mass. Just when the cardinals were about to begin the election, the bells of the capitol and of St. Peter's began to ring, as if to summon the people, and immediately afterwards the cries, ' Romano lo volemo o al manco Italiano ', became more furious than ever before. The cardinals were advised by some of the guards (some of whom were ultramontane, and some Romans) immediately to elect a Roman or an Italian, if they wanted to safeguard their own lives. For this reason the ultramontane cardinals condescended to the election of an Italian, only in order to escape the danger of death, as they then declared—in no other circumstances would they have agreed to it. Moreover, some of the Italian cardinals declared that, if they happened to be elected, they would not accept the election, because of the obvious pressure. Since they all were anxious to escape danger, they hastily nominated the Archbishop of Bari without any discussion of his merits. They immediately elected him pope, as he was well known to them and, they trusted, greatly experienced in the business and customs of the curia, though later experience plainly proved the belief erroneous. Some cardinals added that they elected him as true pope,[1] but they did so only out of fear for their lives.

[1]*Quod ipse esset papa*, Baluzius, tom. ii, col. 827 (ed. Mollat, vol. iv, p. 178), but Bulaeus, *Historia Universitatis Parisiensis*, tom. iv,

An exception to this was an Italian cardinal who said that, because of the notorious intimidation, he would not give his vote for anyone, unless he were in a position to do so freely. An ultramontane cardinal declared that he had first voted for an Italian cardinal, but later *timore mortis* had cast his vote for the Archbishop of Bari. Another ultramontane cardinal though voting for the archbishop, did so protesting that the election was null and void, whilst a third ultramontane cardinal had declared before a notary and prior to the conclave that if he were to elect an Italian, he would do so only under pressure. Moreover, some cardinals said amongst themselves that they had the firm intention to go to a safe place as soon as possible, and to re-elect him (sic !) there anew.[1] In the meanwhile the crowd made unmistakable signs that they were preparing to break open the conclave, and the cardinals did not dare to announce the result of the election to the masses, which had become seriously enraged. Instead, they sent out three cardinals, who told and promised the people that they would be comforted on the next day at the third hour with news of a Roman or an Italian pope. The cardinals asked the mob to withdraw. Only a few did so, whilst the great majority remained and even prevented food being brought to the cardinals for their lunch. They did not allow anyone to go in or out of the palace. In the meantime the cardinals had sent for some prelates, amongst whom was the Archbishop of Bari, the newly elected pope. When he arrived, he saw the disorderly state of the crowd and heard cries ; as it was thought at the time, he had forebodings of his election, to which he tacitly agreed, and he quietened the crowd, so that the cardinals could receive their food. The crowd was

[1] " Quod quam primum commode possunt, secederent ad locum tutum et securum, et tunc ipsi reeligerent de novo," Baluzius, tom. ii, col. 828 (ed. Mollat, vol. iv, p. 179).

---

p. 471, reads : quod ipse non erat verus papa. On this point see Gayet, *Le Grand Schisme d'Occident*, vol. ii, pp. 14, 79, 82–3. One may be inclined to agree with the opinion of the late Dr. Rashdall that Bulaeus " was perhaps the stupidest man that ever wrote a valuable book ", *Universities of Europe in the Middle Ages* (ed. F. M. Powicke, vol. i, p. 269).

somewhat calmer, though it still remained in the palace
armed. Then the cardinals had their meal, after which all,
except three cardinals, went to the palace chapel. After
they had gathered there, an Italian cardinal said that the
fury of the people had now abated and that they could now
proceed to a re-election. But one of the ultramontane
cardinals maintained the opposite view and said that the
danger was now greater than before. Nevertheless, without
informing the three absent cardinals, they proceeded to a
re-election, but whilst still engaged in it, the crowd, incited
by some officials, broke into the conclave ' cum maximo
furore ' clamouring : ' Per lo clavellato de Dio Romano lo
volemo,' and smashed the whole conclave in pieces. The
cardinals, hardly knowing if they were dead or alive, withdrew into a secret chapel of the palace, but its door was
forced and smashed. In surged the armed crowd and
surrounded the cardinals. They believed that all, or at
least the ultramontane cardinals, would have been slain,
if one of them had not had the idea of announcing to the
people that they had elected the Cardinal of St. Peter,
who was alleged to have resisted election : they begged the
people to induce him to accept. As soon as the crowd heard
this, they rushed to the reluctant Cardinal of St. Peter and
elevated him twice upon a throne. The cardinals took
advantage of this scene : they slipped away as well as
they could and hastened on foot to their private dwellings,
some of them without hats or coats. Towards the evening
some cardinals fled disguised into the castle of St. Angelo,
others betook themselves outside the city, and others again
remained in their own homes. Next morning, when the
crowd had become quiet, the Archbishop of Bari, who had
stayed behind in the Vatican, in spite of three demands
made by the cardinals that he should leave the palace,
sent for those staying in the castle or in their private quarters
in order to avoid placing their lives in greater danger.
First they all failed to comply with this request, but later
they became tired of refusing, and the cardinals who were
in the castle sent a note (*cedulla*) to the Archbishop of Bari,
in which they agreed to his enthronement. Those who spent
the night in their dwellings came to the palace. But he was

displeased with the absence of the cardinals in the castle and again sent word to them that they should come to avoid still greater danger and trouble. Although still doubting the gravity of the threatened trouble, they went to the palace, because all their possessions and the members of their households were dispersed throughout the city; furthermore, the food situation in the castle was precarious, and the castle itself was not a particularly safe place. He was enthroned in the usual manner. Shortly after this ceremony those who had fled outside the city also returned, with a bad grace, but fearing that if they did not come, the Romans might suspect them of impugning the election, and might take reprisals against them. Then he was crowned by all cardinals.

" From this time onwards the cardinals treated him as pope and paid homage to him, but never in the intention that he should be true pope. In consistories and in all ecclesiastical functions he acted as pope. Yet all this was within the city of Rome where the cardinals, especially the ultramontanes, never felt themselves secure. They believed that if they had cast any doubt on the election, they would all have been killed, since they were still under duress. For this very reason they did not even dare to confer with each other and to discuss this matter whilst in Rome. Since he did not want to leave the city in their company, nor to permit them to remove their residences from Rome, they were forced to withdraw one by one to Anagni, whilst he *quasi solus* went to Tivoli without a single cardinal."

This *Declaratio* is signed by all the non-Italian cardinals who took part in the election.[1]

The weak points in this official declaration can easily be discerned. The main idea was to represent the whole election as a rushed and precipitated affair, caused by the violent threats of the mob outside the palace. In order to please the

---

[1]The document is printed in Baluzius, tom. ii, cols. 826 seq ; see also *Chronographia Regum Francorum* (ed. H. Moranville, tom. ii, p. 366). There are still two MS. copies in the archives of Vaucluse, see Leclercq in Hefele-Leclercq, *Histoire des Conciles*, vol. vi, part 2, p. 1060 note.

population, they elected an Italian. If this was correct, one may legitimately ask why they were so frightened of announcing the result of the election. On the one hand, they elected an Italian in order to appease the stormy demands of the crowds ; on the other hand, they were so terrified of this result that they dared not publish the name of the man elected. This is a contradiction which cannot be explained. Moreover, the refusal of those cardinals who were in the castle to go to the palace was based upon the cardinals' fear of the furious crowd : a statement which is in agreement with the *Factum Urbani*. According to their contention it was their fear of the Romans which kept them in the castle, and in rejecting Urban's summons they do not say one word about the invalidity of his election as the reason for their refusal. Surely, these statements are incompatible with their chief assertion that the election of Urban was caused by popular pressure. Furthermore, the document speaks in two places of a possible re-election of the archbishop. If he was elected by the threat of force, why should they think of re-electing him, once they were in a free and secure place ? The fear of the cardinals, therefore, appears wholly inexplicable, unreasonable and unfounded. One explanation of their conduct is possible : they may have expected that the man elected would fail to find favour with the Romans ; in other words, they may have assumed that they had acted against the wishes of the populace. This explanation of their fear, reasonable as it seems, excludes the possibility of the election being carried out under pressure and destroys, furthermore, the main argument of the *Declaratio*.

The declaration does not lack contradictions and omissions. In one place it says that the city officials posted sentries on all roads and bridges leading to the palace, whilst a few lines later the cardinals ask the officials to see that roads and bridges are guarded. Had the officials already done so, why should the cardinals submit this request ?[1] It should be pointed out that the declaration omitted to state that the Sacred College itself appointed guardians for the conclave and the Vatican. This fact was not only maintained by Urban's declaration, but also by the *Vita Secunda Gregorii XI*, which is

[1] On this point see also Noel Valois, *La France et Le Grand Schisme*, vol. i, p. 13.

most unfriendly to the cause of Urban, as well as by the statements of the guardian of the conclave.

But, apart from the obvious deficiencies of the *Declaratio*, it also suffers from defects of a more subtle character. Whilst not attempting to conceal facts which were reported by nearly every witness, the document tries to shift the emphasis so as to create a distorted picture of the many and doubtlessly confusing events. Only a few of these distortions can be noted here. The cardinals state that, at the beginning of the conclave, the crowd surged into the palace when they themselves were entering it. This is true ; but the entry of the crowd may have been a customary rather than a hostile or threatening act : the people may simply have accompanied the cardinals in a more or less tumultuous (Roman) fashion. The cardinals themselves had to admit that the crowd soon withdrew from the palace : if they had had any hostile intention, they would surely have remained within the palace. Furthermore, the mere fact of the presence of a huge crowd on the occasion of a papal election cannot be regarded as extraordinary, especially considering that this was the first papal election at Rome within living memory. That there was a certain agitation and excitement is undeniable, as might be expected amongst a mob of Romans, but that the crowd maintained a hostile attitude for three whole days and that they stayed put before the palace all this time—as the cardinals try to make out—is highly improbable. A similar attempt to create a misleading impression of the facts occurs in their emphasis on the fact that the crowd was armed. It is undeniable that the people in the Middle Ages were armed to a far greater extent than we care to imagine nowadays. Certainly this fact by itself carries no perturbing implications. Their carrying of arms necessarily entailed rattling and noise, especially when there were such huge crowds as the cardinals claimed to have seen. And when they speak of the clash of arms in the room underneath the conclave and deduce therefrom a menacing attitude of the arm-bearers, we are driven to the conclusion that the cardinals resorted to a falsification of this particular point. For it was the guards who had their quarters beneath the conclave, and a clashing of arms issuing from the guardroom can hardly be considered a legitimate source of alarm. It is true that there were about 6,000 peasants from the hills in the city at the time of the election, but the cardinals fail to prove that this gathering had any connexion with the election itself. That these illiterate and rough mountaineers did not behave in a befitting manner cannot be held surprising. It is more than probable that—as Urban himself said—these unruly masses showed *vinolentia* rather than *violentia* : as we saw in the second chapter, wine was consumed in tremendous quantities.

The cardinals' description of the actual electoral proceedings lacks all precision, and the vagueness appears to be deliberate. The cardinals are made to appear like frightened sheep crowding together under the threat of a mortal danger ; electing a pope, in order to please the population, but still fearing the publication of the result of the election. The brief statement in the declaration cannot invalidate the statements previously given by some of the cardinals who now signed this declaration : Cardinals Peter de Luna and de Vergne, and the Cardinals of Poitiers, Geneva and St. Eustace, who all appear to have taken a great part in the discussions concerning the candidature of the Archbishop of Bari.

The *Declaratio* refers to a protestation made by the Cardinal of Glandève before a notary prior to the entry into the conclave. This protestation is, in fact, the only objective proof the cardinals are able to offer, and one which might lend some support to their plea. Let us look into this. The protestation is printed by Baluzius, in his second volume.[1] After referring to the negotiations between the cardinals and the city officials the Cardinal of Glandève goes on to say that the officials bluntly declared that, if they did not elect a Roman or at least an Italian, they would all be *in periculo mortis*. He therefore declared before the public notary Stephen Bertrand that it would be entirely against his will and intention that an Italian should become pope. But, unfortunately for the Cardinal of Glandève, this public notary died in November, 1378, and his papers, documents and protocols were lost—thus the original protestation disappeared also. Therefore, on 10th December, 1378, the same cardinal made a new document in which he referred to the original. Whether the alleged protestation was really genuine cannot now be decided : the fact remains

[1]Tom. ii, cols. 816–21 (ed. Mollat, vol. iv, pp. 169–73).

that only the original declaration would have afforded full proof—and not the one devised eight months later.

Nevertheless, there was no lack of attempts to prop up the *Declaratio*. Two biographies of Gregory XI in particular strongly support its main argument. Both biographies emphasize the fear of the cardinals and the element of compulsion. The *Prima Vita* says that the mountaineers who had arrived in the city were an unruly gang, behaving themselves like beasts and *ratione carentes*. They had been standing around the palace in armed bands and had abused the cardinals and the members of their households. Throughout the procedure of the election they all had been clamouring *una voce tumultuosa et horribili*. While this description errs on the side of exaggeration, the statement which follows about the actual election not only suffers from gross inaccuracies, but also introduces an entirely new element.[1] After saying that the archbishop was elected hastily, the anonymous biographer goes on to reveal that the cardinals firmly believed that the archbishop would soon renounce his election. They contended that, being versed in canon law and in the business of the curia, he necessarily knew that the election was invalid. But why the cardinals elected this particular archbishop, who was no member of the Sacred College and inferior to them in status and wealth, remains—so far as this account goes—a mystery. The biography simply says : " Aspectum habuerunt ad Bartholomeum de Prinhano tunc archiepiscopum Barensem." If the populace had to be deceived and pacified, would it not have been a far more plausible deception for the cardinals to pretend that a Roman cardinal had been elected, as they actually did pretend during the course of the election ? This statement of the biography is therefore quite unsatisfactory and inadequate. Precisely the same inconsistency can be observed in the statements of St. Vincent Ferrer, the fiery follower of Clement VII, in his *De Moderno Ecclesiae Scismate*. He studiously avoids speaking of an election, but declares that the cardinals had " nominated " the Archbishop of Bari. They had known him as an intelligent and worthy individual well acquainted with curial matters: as such he must have recognized the invalid character of his " election ", and the cardinals therefore assumed that he

[1] Baluzius, tom. i, col. 450.

would not accept his election at all, or that he would pretend to accept it " only for the time being to free them from danger."[1] Here again, the questions remain unanswered, viz., why just this archbishop was chosen to pretend something, and why the cardinals feared to publish the result of the election when the man elected was supposed to be *persona grata* with the Romans.

The second (anonymous) biography of Gregory XI, though highly coloured and unfriendly to Urban VI, is more cautious and seems to try to convey a picture more consonant with the facts. Though it also maintains that Urban's election was a compulsory affair, this biography omits all reference to the actual election, such as we find in the *Declaratio* and in the other biography. Its descriptions of the popular commotion and of the discussions between the cardinals before the conclave are far more in agreement with the description of the *Factum Urbani*. In particular, the statement as to the fraud committed in the name of the Cardinal of St. Peter is hardly distinguishable from the evidence listed so far. This document[2] deserves more credit than the other biography of Gregory XI. An especially interesting feature is the long verbal report of the speech made by one of the city officials to the cardinals after they had entered the conclave. The biography says that the official *Deum non habens prae oculis* addressed the cardinals in a speech in which he referred to the grave consequences which the election must inevitably entail for the whole of Christianity. " The Roman people," the official continued, " have been deprived of the supreme pontiff for over seventy years and they are like orphans. This city is the centre of Christianity as was ordained by the apostles Peter and Paul, to whom Christ had given the keys of heaven and to whom He said : ' Thou art Peter and on this rock I will build the Church ', and this was the reason why the two apostles made this city the *funda-*

---

[1] " Domini cardinales . . . nominarunt dictum Bartholomaeum in papam, quem reputabant hominem intelligentem et devotum et in factis curiae satis expertum, quatenus ipsemet per suam scientiam et experientiam cognoscens nullitatem notorissimam illius modi electionis, eam propter timorem Dei retractus nullatenus acceptaret, vel solum ad tempus eam acceptasse simularet ad liberandos dominos cardinales," *De Moderno Ecclesiae Scismate*, fol. cclxiii, sexta objectio.

[2] In Baluzius, tom. i, cols. 451–78 (ed. Mollat, vol. i, pp. 439–59).

mentum totius fidei Christianae. We beseech you, therefore, to elect a Roman pope, and you will find a great number of famous clerics, who are wise and capable of governing the Church. It would be strange if you could not find a suitable man in this land. But if you do not want to do this, you may know, most reverend Fathers, that first we, the officials of the city, would be killed, and most certainly you also, as you can hear from the clamourings of the population : Romano lo volemo lo papa."

Although this second biography of Gregory XI continually strives to impress the reader with the fear and anxiety felt by the cardinals, the love of truth had not entirely forsaken the biographer. His detailed report of this interview—quite in agreement with the *Factum Urbani* and other witnesses— therefore deserves all the more attention. For the manly behaviour of the cardinals towards the city officials is clearly to be inferred from this record of the episode. After the official had ended his address, the cardinals said to him and to his colleagues that they should withdraw from the door so that the cardinals could converse with each other. This the officials did. Thereupon the Cardinal of Florence, as the senior of the cardinals, spoke and expressed his astonishment that they as *antiqui, sapientes clerici* and being perfectly aware of the requirements of a valid election, should have listened to these supplications. " An election like this," said the cardinal, " should be free from the influence of supplications, favouritism or fear, and should be solely inspired by the divine will and by the grace of the Holy Ghost." The city official to whom this reply was given somewhat threateningly re-iterated his request, whereupon one cardinal—the biographer does not say which—said : " We are in your power and you can kill us, if you like ; but even if we knew that it entailed our death, we would do nothing but what God's will bids and commands us to do."[1]

This report, the truthfulness of which we need not impugn, since it is amply corroborated by many other witnesses, leaves no room for doubt that there was not only no fear on the part of the cardinals, but that they manfully withstood the tactless requests of the officials. If there had really been

[1] *Ibid.,* i, 459.

that degree of anxiety which the biographer wants the reader
to believe and of which the *Declaratio* itself speaks, it is difficult
to explain the cardinal's dignified and correct response to the
officials. The steadfastness of the cardinals in the presence of
the officials and in face of the clamourings of the people tends
to confirm the correctness of our interpretation of their fear,
the interpretation, namely, that *their fear was based upon the
assumption that their elected candidate would be unacceptable to the
Romans.*

There were naturally many more attempts to " describe "
the critical events from the standpoint of the cardinals. From
these attempts we may single out an allegedly objective description which is contained in a manuscript at Liège and which
was brought to light by Martène and Durand in their *Amplissima Collectio.*[1] The document is anonymous and undated,
but most certainly written before the Council of Pisa (1409).
The author or authors were obviously desirous to portray a
picture of the events which would not admit of any other
conclusion than that of the election of Urban VI being due
to the pressure exercised by the Romans. This document, in
some places, goes even farther than the original declaration
of the cardinals and paints the pressure of the mob as irresistible.
Without attempting to prove any of its statements by reference
to depositions of witnesses, the document, which is entitled
De Initio Schismatis quod multum perturbavit Christianum populum,
begins with the somewhat startling statement that the Roman
officials held in the Capitol several meetings which were directed
against the cardinals : " *Diversa consilia tenuerunt in capitolio
Urbis contra collegium cardinalium.*"[2] In these meetings the decision was reached that the cardinals should be compelled to
elect a Roman or an Italian, so that the pope would henceforth
have to reside in Italy.[3]   In order to enforce their decision,
the officials sent for 6,000 armed men from the mountains
who, soon after their entry into the city, molested the cardinals

---

[1]See Martène and Durand, *Veterum Scriptorum . . . Amplissima
Collectio,* tom. vii, cols. 426–33.

[2]Col. 426, sect. I.

[3]" Conclusum fuit, ut cardinales compellerentur eligere Romanum
vel Italicum, ut sic sedes apostolica de caetero in Italia remaneret,"
—*Ibid.*

frequently.[1] This is a novel statement, as none of the cardinals interpreted the presence of these men in this manner : nor can we find a single witness who confirms the personal molestation by these mountain peasants. Other uncorroborated statements follow. Thus, the document says that in the evening of the day of the election, and after locking the doors of the conclave, thirteen Roman officials, the district governors, broke the doors open, entered the conclave *violenter* and demanded from the cardinals the immediate election of a Roman or an Italian, otherwise the inflamed passions of the populace would bring them into deadly danger. Thereupon, the document goes on to say, the mob threw stones, stormed the buildings, broke the walls down with their heavy weapons and rushed furiously into the interior of the conclave with swords drawn and shouting in their vulgar manner : "*Par la bodella de dyo vo morere o ferrate papa Romano.*"[2] This statement, as it stands, is not supported by any witness : most probably the author had heard of the events from individuals in the Clementine camp and compressed several events into one statement, thereby distorting the sequence of events. Moreover, the document makes Urban say to the officials on the morning after the election : " You have made me pope, and unless the cardinals come and obey me, your efforts will have been in vain." But the document fails to adduce any evidence of an understanding between Urban and the Roman officials before the election. It is, furthermore, alleged that the officials immediately after this utterance of Urban, sent for the cardinals who, in the tumult, had fled to various places : the inconsistency of these two statements does not dawn upon the author of the document, for why should the cardinals flee when they had met the wish of the officials by " nominating " an Italian ? Although the Duke of Fondi had received the cardinals " with delight and great pleasure ", and although they enjoyed all liberty in Anagni, as the document itself emphasizes, it con-

[1]" Romani statim miserunt pro VI millibus rusticorum, quae sunt de obedientia et comitatu Romano, qui Romam intrantes armati, cardinales Gallicos saepe irritaverunt," col. 426, sect. I.

[2]" Instrumentis ferreis, effractis januis et parietibus irruerunt super cardinales ensibus evaginatis clamantes in suo vulgari : ' Par la bodella . . .'," col. 427, sect. II.

veniently omits all reference to the numerous petitions which they sent to the pope in Rome. On the contrary, the document tries to convey the impression that the cardinals, as soon as they saw themselves freed from the shackles of Rome, wrote to the pope and " persuaded " him to renounce his claim to the papacy, as his election was null and void. Quite in contrast to the actual facts, the document declares that Urban (who, even at this late stage, is unwittingly referred to as " papa ") opposed their plea with the proposal of a General Council, where the whole matter could be thrashed out.[1] This document is one of the many attempts to portray a picture partly vague, partly accurate and partly wrong.[2]

Other attempts to support the case of the cardinals consisted merely of tirades and diatribes against Urban VI. Amongst these the sermon of the Patriarch of Constantinople, Cardinal Itro, is an especially good example of the unrestrained language employed by its author.[3] He took the invalidity of Urban's election for granted and argued on this basis throughout the sermon : Urban was the anti-Christ, the man who had caused the Schism and had disrupted Christianity. The patriarch made lavish use of a legal apparatus and legalistic arguments to prove that the position of Urban was untenable. The facts upon which he based his legal deductions, however, were those as supplied by the Clementines and they were accepted by him unchallenged.

The cardinals could not possibly deny that they treated Urban as Pope whilst in Rome and even for a considerable time after, during their stay in Anagni. We have already mentioned that they received communion from his hands, begged favours from him and assisted him on all occasions. How could the cardinals reconcile this attitude with their plea that his election was invalid ? Their highly untenable justification shows a really remarkable degree of hypocrisy.

[1] " Papa obtulit eis concilium generale, ubi posset res decidi," col. 428, sect. V.

[2] Thus, for instance, it states that the Cardinal of Geneva had asked for and received the cardinalate of Ostia ; in fact, it was the Cardinal of Glandève who was made Cardinal Bishop of Ostia, sect. III.

[3] See Martène and Durand, *Thesaurus Novus Anecdotorum*, tom. ii, cols. 1075–81.

As to their general behaviour in Rome, they pretended that they were compelled to assume their role by Urban and the officials : they dared not even converse with each other ; the slightest questioning of the validity of the election would have endangered their lives. At the same time witnesses for the cardinals' party want us to believe that, as early as the evening before the coronation, the Cardinals de Vergne and Glandève were " making fun about this business throughout the night ", which they spent in the quarters of Bishop John de Castro, who reported this.[1] Moreover, the Cardinal of Glandève declared that " to-morrow we will have to perform this farce ". There are several more reports by which it is purported to prove that, even during their stay in Rome, the cardinals knew that Urban's election was invalid. These, however, are hardly consonant with the statement that they dared not communicate with each other.

As to the particular powers of the pope, the cardinals said that, owing to the invalidity of his election, he had no power to absolve them from sins by his own authority, but only by the authority of the Church : therefore, he acted not as Pope but as representative of the Church.[2] They received communion from him not as Pope but as the Archbishop of Bari. Their motives whilst in Anagni were of a different character. Here, they maintained, they asked for favours in order to prevent anyone else from receiving them. In the words of the Cardinal of Aigrefeuille, they would have given their eyes to prevent anyone else obtaining benefices or other favours.[3]

The letters written by the cardinals to inform ecclesiastical and secular princes of their election deserve particular attention. They wrote not only to their colleagues in Avignon but also to a number of secular dignitaries, expressing their satisfaction at the result of the election. Later they maintained that they were compelled to do this by Urban, and, as one cardinal declared (Cardinal of Aigrefeuille), their letters began with the formula " De mandato domini nostri scribo vobis ". Upon the objection that no letter could be found which

[1]Baluzius, tom. i, col. 1078 (ed. Mollat, vol. ii, p. 599).

[2]Testimony of Cardinal de Vergne, Baluzius, tom. i, col. 1120 (ed. Mollat, vol. ii, p. 642).

[3]Ibid., tom. i, col. 1005 (ed. Mollat, vol. ii, p. 523).

actually contained these words, the same cardinal gave no reply.[1] Cardinal Orsini, in his deposition, wants posterity to believe that the pope dictated those letters and that he inspected them before they were dispatched. The statements of all the other cardinals, especially of Peter de Luna and of Robert of Geneva, are to the same effect. The latter even declared that it was the city officials who compelled them to write these letters of notification. He wrote them " timore potius quam amore ".[2] Here again, the pretext of compulsion could no longer be upheld after they had left Rome. Nevertheless, during this period they wrote letters to various ecclesiastical and secular princes and signed these letters " pontificatus sanctissimi in Christo patris et domini nostri domini Urbani, divina providentia papae VI anno primo." Their argument about this was that although knowing that Urban was not truly pope, they signed the letters in this way because as individuals they were not entitled to declare Urban's election invalid : this declaration being a matter for the whole Sacred College, which had not yet issued it. They are never at a loss for a reply.

The conduct of some of the cardinals deserves a more detailed examination. The Cardinal of Glandève, who was most active in his intrigues against Urban, did not deem it expedient to renounce the high honour which Urban had bestowed upon him by creating him Cardinal Bishop of Ostia. If, as he afterwards maintained, he knew all the time that Urban was not truly pope, why did he accept this office and, having accepted, why did he not renounce it ? Indeed, the incongruity of his actions must have dawned upon him. He declared that the late pope, Gregory XI, had promised him this office, but was prevented from formally conferring it, owing to his premature death. What Urban did was simply the formal realization of Gregory's promise.[3] The point made by the Declaratio as to the re-election of Urban was also mentioned

---

[1] *Ibid.*, tom. i, col. 1004. Valois, *op. cit.*, vol. i, p. 65, proves convincingly that only one letter written by Peter de Luna to the King of Castile, was *seen* by Urban, who did not finish reading it ; see also Gayet, *op. cit.*, vol. ii, Pièces justif., pp. 121, 156.

[2] Baluzius, tom. i. col. 1106 (ed. Mollat, vol. ii, p. 629).

[3] *Ibid.*, col. 1079 (ed. Mollat, vol. ii, p. 600).

by the Cardinal of Glandève : in order to avoid scandal they would have elected him in Anagni if he had been suitable.[1] Thomas of Acerno reported that this cardinal had quite openly boasted of the support he had given to Urban, but complained that as pope he had failed to keep his promises and " would not give even a single benefice to my nephew ".[2] And the pretext of compulsion is plainly exposed as such by a statement of the Cardinal of Glandève the day after the coronation. Asked how he was feeling after so much strain and labour on the previous day, the cardinal answered : " If there had not been so much food, refreshments and good wine provided for us by our lord the pope, things would have taken a bad turn."[3] Referring to this feast on another occasion, the same cardinal declared that the pope had been with them and had drunk a considerable amount : everyone was in good spirits.[4] This statement was enlarged on by the Cardinal of Brittany to the effect that the pope had drunk eight times as much as any of them.[5] These statements and reports by no means bear out the plea of the cardinals and go to show that the atmosphere was free from tension and that there was no trace of compulsion exercised by the pope.

Let us now turn to Cardinal Orsini, the remaining Italian and Roman Cardinal in the Sacred College. Already during the election he left no doubt as to his real intentions, i.e., of becoming pope himself. His proposal to clothe a Franciscan friar with the papal vestments and to make the Romans believe that he was the newly-elected pope clearly indicates his ulterior motives. This proposal is an established fact, but whether Orsini openly opposed Urban's election in the conclave, as some witnesses said, or whether, as other witnesses stated, he declared he would give his vote to whatever candidate had the majority of votes, cannot now be decided. The fact

[1]*Ibid.*, col. 1080 (ed. Mollat, vol. ii, p. 601).
[2]*Ibid.*, col. 1076 (ed. Mollat, vol. ii, p. 599).
[3]*Ibid.*, col. 1078 (ed. Mollat, vol. ii, p. 599).
[4]*Ibid.*, col. 1270 (ed. Mollat, vol. ii, p. 790).
[5]In this context a bishop, who was at the same time a doctor, testified that Urban never ate, but always drank : " Of two things he could not leave one, and that was the wine," Baluzius, tom. i, col. 1270.

remains, however, that Cardinal Orsini joined the rebel cardinals, if for no other reason than to be elected pope by them in Anagni. How little he himself was convinced of the case he promoted can be gathered from the report of the cardinal's own chamberlain, who declared that the cardinal, so long as he was with Urban, had never doubted that he was the true pope : he had come to this conclusion only after having been acquainted with the frame of mind of the other cardinals.[1] It was Cardinal Orsini who put the tiara on the pope's head at the coronation and who later declared that his letters were dictated by his master.[2] Is one to believe these incompatible statements ? The truth must be that Cardinal Orsini's aspirations to the papacy revived as soon as he saw that the other cardinals contemplated the deposition of Urban.

Orsini's dealings with Queen Joanna of Naples demonstrate his ulterior motives quite unmistakably. A brief review of his relations with the Queen will throw further light upon his character. The fact that the cardinals doubted the validity of Urban's election was not unknown to the Queen of Naples. Now, during their stay at Anagni, the cardinals not only tried to procure the French king's help but also the assistance of other secular princes. Owing to the political ties binding the kingdom of Naples to the French monarchy, and owing to the tactless behaviour of Urban towards the Queen's envoys, the cardinals were bent upon winning her support as well. As we know from the deposition of Cardinal de Vergne, the Cardinal of Cosenza and other witnesses, the cardinals, attempting to win over the Queen, dispatched Cardinal Orsini and the Cardinal of Cosenza (Nicholas de Brancaciis) to Naples, in order to inform her of the true situation. The Queen still proved herself a staunch adherent of Urban—for understandable reasons—but when she heard the rumours that his election was alleged to be invalid she naturally wavered in her devotion to her fellow countryman, all the more so as the opposition to Urban came from the French cardinals towards whom undoubtedly she was not unbiased. When the deputation from Anagni arrived at her court, they were

[2] *Ibid.*, col. 1100 (ed. Mollat, vol. ii, p. 623).
[1] *Ibid.*, cols. 1095, 1096 (ed. Mollat, vol. ii, p. 616).

received with due honour by the Queen. She told Cardinal Orsini of the rumours she had heard and asked him to inform her of the truth.[1] And Cardinal Orsini, laying his hand on his breast, swore that Urban was not truly Pope. Grasping the Queen's hands with a theatrical gesture he affirmed that he was speaking the pure truth, not omitting, however, at the same time to recommend himself to her. The suggestion was made to the Queen that she should lend her weighty support to the cardinal so that he could be elected pope in Urban's place " pro evitatione istius scismatis ". Yet the Queen showed herself less yielding than the cardinal expected her to be : she declared that she would support the Cardinal of Florence. As soon as the latter heard of this, his brother made strong overtures to the Queen, promising many things to her and her people.[2]

Reviewing the statements of the cardinals one cannot but arrive at the conclusion that their case was weak. It is their actual conduct as recorded by witnesses and their own friends which deprives their statements of credibility. The real reason for their leaving Rome and the pope was very human, simple, understandable : it was their disappointment at the result of their own choice which first of all united them against the pope they themselves had elected and then, later, led them to choose a road from which there was no return. In other words, they had been deceived by the character and personality of Urban, and now wanted to undo what, only a few months before, they had deliberately done.

Urban, deserted by all his cardinals, was indeed like a " sparrow on the housetop " and saw, at long last, that he had gone too far. Dietrich of Niem reports that in those dark summer days of 1378 the pope wept in his presence and admitted to him that he had acted *minus caute*. But the die was cast. A week after Clement's election Urban created twenty-eight new cardinals on one day. To the incalculable loss of Christendom, the gulf now opened was not to be bridged for the next forty years.

[1] " Rogabat eum, quod ipse diceret sibi veritatem," *Ibid.*, col. 1098 (ed. Mollat, vol. ii, p. 620).

[2] *Ibid.*, col. 1098 (ed. Mollat, vol. ii, p. 620).

VI

EFFECTS AND CONSEQUENCES

THE CALAMITY of two popes necessarily entailed for
Catholic Europe a divided allegiance. Excommunication and
counter-excommunication of and by the rival popes, the tirades
delivered by the one against the other, and the inevitable
political intrigues made it almost impossible to entertain
much hope of any reconciliation or rapprochement between
the two contending factions. And it is highly significant that,
in the early days of the Schism, we can search in vain for
any serious, constructive proposals to settle this dispute
amicably and with as little detriment as possible to the authority
and prestige of the Church. Attempts to bring about a reconciliation were doomed to failure from the very beginning,
either because impracticable or because put forward so half-
heartedly that their originators could themselves have had
but little hope that their proposals would be realized. Instead,
within a remarkably short time and as if they had been waiting
for this excuse, we see the nations of Europe ranged behind
the two claimants and aligning themselves in battle array :
the unwillingness or, shall we say, the incapacity of responsible
secular potentates to bring this state of affairs to a speedy end
is as significant of the mentality of princes and nations as is
the Schism itself of the mentality of the ecclesiastical hierarchy.
No document can be produced showing any effort on the part
of a secular prince to end the Schism by making constructive
proposals. What efforts there were, were mainly characterized
by feeble lamentations which at best merely proved the grief
felt by princes and others at this disaster, and which, at the
same time, palpably demonstrated their complete lack of
strength and influence. The Schism was but one symptom of
the depths to which fourteenth-century society had sunk, in
the temporal as well as the spiritual sphere. The blame for
the outbreak of the Schism and for its continuation must be

shared equally between ecclesiastical and secular rulers ; but no less blame should be attached to a legal system which cut off, *ab initio*, any argument of dispute concerning the government of the Church and left this entirely in the hands of one man who was not controllable by, or responsible to, any human power, however questionable or harmful his policy might have been. The relevant passages of canon law had emerged from widely different conditions, and were unadaptable to the complicated machinery of fourteenth-century Church government, inextricably interwoven as this was with day-to-day politics. As usual, the law lagged behind the circumstances to which it was to be applicable. But we will return to this point later, and may now review the political and religious consequences produced by this twofold headship.

One of the first papal actions of Clement VII was the creation of a number of cardinals, so that by December 1378 he had a fully established Sacred College. From this same month onwards his legates were dispatched to nearly all the influential princes. The Cardinal of Limoges was entrusted with the official mission to France and with the representation of Clement VII at the French court. This mission was more a formality than anything else, and it proved successful. Charles V of France, after revealing a certain reticence in the summer and early autumn months, had declared his adherence to Clement on 16th November, 1378, and was henceforth resolved to support him. Very great powers were conferred on Clement's legate by a number of bulls, all signed at Fondi on 18th December, 1378.[1] On 6th April, 1379, the cardinal was solemnly received at Notre-Dame.[2] The French king even induced the majority of the masters of the University of Paris to join the ranks of Clement, though Urban, foreseeing this development, had already sent a memorandum to the rector and masters urging them not to listen to the falsehoods and distortions of the cardinals, but to remain faithful

[1] The gist of these bulls is to be found in Noel Valois, *La France et Le Grand Schisme*, vol. i, p. 129, note 1.

[2] A contemporary chronicler reported : " Cardinalis Lemovicensis venit in ecclesiam, et per ordinationem dominorum fuit chorum paratum, et de omnibus campanis pulsatum et de organis lusum ", quoted after Valois, *op. cit.*, p. 129, note 2.

to him, the true pope.[1] But whatever opposition there was in University circles, the monarch's influence proved stronger than the written message of the pope.[2] The support of Clement by the University does not seem to have been enthusiastic. An influential party within it pleaded for a general council, but this body met with the resistance of Charles V.[3] With all the fervour characteristic of French policy towards papal questions, the king issued a proclamation throughout his realm forbidding obedience and allegiance to Urban and threatening with confiscation of goods all who disregarded this royal order,[4] the laymen no less than the clerics.

[1]Baluzius, *Vitae Paparum Avenionensium*, tom. i, col. 549, and Bulaeus, *Historia Universitatis Parisiensis*, tom. iv, p. 524.

[2]Bulaeus, *loc. cit.*, tom. iv, p. 480.

[3]Raynaldus, *loc. cit.*, p. 343, col. 2. In fact it was not until May, 1379, that a majority of the masters declared themselves for Clement VII, see Baluzius, *loc. cit.*, tom. i, cols. 490–2, Bulaeus, *loc. cit.*, pp. 481, 585, seq., Hefele-Leclercq, *Histoire des Conciles*, vol. i, part 2, p. 1092, and Valois, *op. cit.*, vol. i, pp. 120, 326–9, 334–59. For a review of the University's attitude towards the Schism, especially as regards the stimulating effect of the Schism on University circles, see Rashdall, *Universities of Europe in the Middle Ages* (ed. F. M. Powicke, vol. i, pp. 558–74). It is perhaps worth recalling Rashdall's dictum that "the difficult position in which the Schism placed the Germans at Paris (as followers of Urban) contributed to the growth of universities in Germany," first edition, vol. i, p. 557 note. Thus, famous theologians, such as Henry of Langenstein, Conrad of Gelnhausen and Marsilius of Inghen, were in open opposition to Charles V. They preferred to leave the university. The first became one of the lights of the newly-founded university of Vienna, see Scheuffgen, *Beiträge zur Geschichte des Grossen Schismas*, p. 41; it was he who completely reformed that university and established the theological faculty there, after Urban VI had granted what Urban V had refused, see Aschbach, *Geschichte der Wiener Universität*, vol. i, pp. 366, 402. Henry was later chancellor of the university and took a prominent part in the theological dispute on the Immaculate Conception, in which dispute he stood against the Dominicans who had followed St. Bernard. The two other Parisian scholars went to Heidelberg, where Conrad became rector, see Rashdall-Powicke, vol. ii, pp. 240, 251. Gerard of Calcar, another of the Parisian theologians, settled, after a brief stay at the university of Vienna (see Aschbach, *op. cit.*, p. 431, and Scheuffgen, *op. cit.*, pp. 40–1), at the university of Cologne, see Valois, *op. cit.*, vol. i, p. 368.

[4]Thomas of Walsingham, *Historia Anglicana*. vol. i, p. 391, *Chronicon Angliae* (1328–1388), pp. 222–3.

Cardinal Peter de Luna had the task of winning over the kings of Castile, Aragon, Navarre and Portugal, but his efforts were not crowned with success until two years later, the kings not wholly trusting the fiery cardinal's message. The neutral attitude which was decided upon in the national synod of Complutum (Castile) and convoked by the already-mentioned Archbishop of Toledo, Petrus Tenorius, was maintained for the next two years,[1] though it is difficult to see how, in a conflict of this kind, neutrality can be maintained.

The ambassador to Germany and Bohemia was the Cardinal of Aigrefeuille, whose mission ended in complete failure. The new Emperor, Wenzel, remained adamant in his determination to support Urban VI,[2] and he was successful in bringing the Diet of Frankfort, in February 1379, to issue a proclamation of loyalty to Urban, whilst Clement's ambassador was not even admitted to the assembly. Wenzel, also, in his capacity as king of the Romans, declared himself, as early as 18th October, 1378, at Nuremberg, wholeheartedly for Urban: " Declaravimus et denuntiavimus fidelibus universis ipsum dominum Urbanum esse Jesu Christi vicarium et beati Petri apostolorum principis successorem."[3] Wenzel gave instructions that emissaries of " Robert, the anti-pope " should

[1]See Baluzius, loc. cit., vol. i, cols. 492, 502, 517 ; Valois, op. cit., vol. i, pp. 198–239, especially as regards Portugal, pp. 225–39. The declaration of the King of Castile to Clement VII is printed in Martène-Durand, Thesaurus Novus Anecdotorum, tom. ii, cols. 1098–9. On the attitude of the King of Aragon, see also the paper by J. Vincke, " Der König und die Curia Apostolica in den Anfängen des Grossen Schismas " in Spanische Forschungen der Goerresgesellschaft, vol. viii (1939), pp. 84–126. According to Mansi, Sacrorum Conciliorum . . . Collectio, tom. xxvi, cols. 655–6, the " Concilium Complutense Nationale " disputed " cuinam parendum esset tamquam vero pontifici, an Urbano VI, an Clementi VII. Videtur ea gravissima quaestio tunc in medio relicta, suspensis inter utrumque animis."

[2]The old emperor, Charles IV, died on 29th November, 1378. Though there were some who maintained that Charles IV was inclined to support Clement VII (see, e.g., Gayet, Le Grand Schisme d'Occident, vol. ii, Pièces justif., pp. 184–5) it is more likely that the opinion of Henry of Langenstein came nearer to the truth, that is, that the emperor on his death-bed enjoined his son Wenzel to adhere to Urban VI and to remain faithful to him, see Valois, op. cit., vol. i, pp. 267–8.

[3]Baluzius, loc. cit., col. 558 ; Deutsche Reichstagsakte, i. 232 ff.

not be admitted, whether appearing privately or publicly, nor should any documents or letters be accepted : all his agents should be mercilessly expelled. These measures, Wenzel declared, were dictated by *imperialis justitia*. The devotion of Wenzel to Urban is, perhaps, best illustrated in a letter addressed to Richard II of England, soon to be his brother-in-law. This letter was written at Prague on 20th May, 1379.[1] Whatever his defects as a ruler, Wenzel appears sincerely grieved at the disaster besetting Western Christendom. Briefly recalling in the letter the events during the conclave and afterwards, Wenzel expresses his amazement that the cardinals could honestly entertain any hope of being taken seriously : they had become *destructores Christianae unionis* and he would keep in the archives *ad aeternam memoriam* their letters expressing satisfaction at the choice of Urban. Robert was the anti-Christian, anti-pope and a schismatic and, together with his followers, would be in danger of hell fire, unless they saw fit to cease their mischievous activities. " We intend," Wenzel continued, " to lend all our secular power to the pope to help him defend himself against the schismatics : with our temporal sword and our own blood let us defend Holy Church against all perils and storms, so that the spiritual and secular world may become united into one body." This letter concludes with an admonition to Richard II to pursue the same aim since, like Wenzel himself, he was young and therefore more apt to work effectively for the unification of Christendom.[2]

Urban's rude and tactless treatment of Queen Joanna of Naples, taken together with the allurements of Cardinal Orsini, were bound to create an estrangement between her and Urban and they led eventually to a fateful antagonism between the kingdom of Naples and the papacy. By April, 1379, Clement had gathered a considerable force consisting mainly of Breton mercenaries under the leadership of a captain of the family de la Salle. This captain led his force against Rome, but the Romans inflicted a crushing defeat upon him and his band at Marino : he himself was killed and, according

[1]Raynaldus, *loc. cit.*, pp. 292–3.

[2]Raynaldus, *loc. cit.*, p. 292, col. 2—p. 293, col. 2. On the Clementine mission to Germany and Bohemia, see also Valois, *op. cit.*, vol. ii, pp. 286–97.

to a contemporary report, 50,000 of his men slain. What was, perhaps, of greater importance was the surrender to Urban of the garrison of St. Angelo. This castle, as we have seen, was in the hands of the Breton soldiers, who, upon hearing that John Hawkwood, the dreaded English warrior, was in command of a Roman unit,[1] were so intimidated that they immediately entered into negotiations with the pope.[2] They were granted a secret exodus to prevent an attack by the infuriated Roman mob, whilst all treasures, gold, silver and jewelleries—stored in the castle since the riots in April—were transferred to the palace by night. In view of this military situation, which had taken such a grave turn for Clement, he no longer deemed his abode at Fondi secure and resolved to move his court to Naples. Here he was solemnly received by the Queen, who put at his disposal the magnificent Castel Nuovo. But, in spite of the royal favour, the Neapolitan populace received the new pope with mixed feelings. After all, Urban was their fellow-countryman and Clement a Frenchman. In no ambiguous language he was made to understand that he, together with his entourage, were " undesirable aliens ". Once again they were on the move, in a ship lent by the Queen, which carried him and his cardinals to Marseilles ; they arrived there on 10th June, 1379.[3] Under French protection the party reached Avignon, the city of delight, splendour, luxury and magnificence which, for the next few years, was to become an effective rival to historic yet poverty-stricken Rome.

Urban replied by excommunicating Queen Joanna and deposing her, thus strengthening the bonds between her family, the house of Anjou, and the French monarchy. When, next, he conferred the Neapolitan throne on Charles of Durazzo, Urban drew upon himself the active enmity of Louis of Anjou : Louis consequently became a special protégé of

[1] John Hawkwood was held in great esteem by Gregory XI, see his letter full of praise for the English warrior which is printed by E. Seckendorff, *Die Kirchenpolitische Taetigkeit der Heiligen Katharina von Siena*, Leipzig, 1917, p. 159 ; cf. also F. Gaupp, " The condottiere John Hawkwood " in *History*, xxiii (n.s.), 305–21.

[2] *Chronicon Angliae*, p. 227.

[3] See Baluzius, *loc. cit.*, col. 494, *Chronographia Regum Francorum*, vol. ii, p. 375.

Clement and, fortified by this spiritual and political support, thundered against the nepotism of Urban, who made his own protégé Charles promise to hand over considerable territories in the Neapolitan realm to his nephew Francis Prignano (Butillo)—"a thoroughly worthless and immoral man."[1]

The various satellites of the great powers naturally sided with their protectors. Hungary immediately recognized Urban, whilst Scotland, as the ally of France and enemy of England, staunchly defended the cause of Clement. Nothing better illustrates the practical implications of the dual papacy than the divergence in the number of bulls issued by the two popes to Scotland and England : of 86 bulls issued by Clement before July, 1381, no more than three were addressed to England and English individuals, whilst all others were written to Scotland or referring to Scottish matters. The case is exactly reversed as regards the number of bulls issued by Urban to Scotland and England.[2]

In retrospect one cannot but come to the conclusion that this division of allegiance to the " heads " of Christianity greatly accelerated the break-up of Western Christendom in the sixteenth century. But, in at least one way, the division in the fourteenth century went deeper than those of two hundred years later : the division went even so far as to affect the internal administration of the ecclesiastical government. For it was not only secular rulers who dragged their subjects into this cataclysm. There can be little doubt but that the secular rulers were almost wholly prompted by political motives and national sentiments in their religious allegiance. But worse than this was the occurrence of divisions amongst the heads of dioceses. Many a diocese had at its " head " two bishops, the one passionately defending Urban, the other no less passionately contending for Clement : all this, of course, accompanied by mutual sentences of excommunication and interdict. Breslau, Constance, Dorpat, Liège, Mainz,

---

[1]Pastor, *History of the Popes*, vol. i, p. 136. See also Valois, *op. cit.*, vol. ii, pp. 9, 65.

[2]Although Ireland adhered to Urban VI, there was a determined attempt to set up a Clementine party in the island, see Valois, *op. cit.*, vol. ii, pp. 316–7.

Basle, are but a few instances of dioceses ruled by two bishops. The mass said by the Urbanist bishop or his adherents was proclaimed a blasphemy, and the mass celebrated by the Clementine rival was equally loudly condemned as sacrilege. In many dioceses public worship was an impossibility,[1] and the populace was left in a confused state of bewilderment and cynicism. The influence of the Schism was not confined to the secular clerics. It affected monasteries and orders, too : Carthusians, Dominicans, and the other Mendicant Orders[2] in particular were drawn into the conflict. Many houses in these, and others too, had two abbots or priors. One needs very little imagination to picture for oneself the practical implications of this division within one and the same order or monastery. Thus the chapter of Bayonne was divided into two parts, the one upholding the rights of Urban, the other those of Clement.[3] Nor was a change of opinion infrequent. The Bishop of Marseilles who, as we saw, was a guardian of the conclave, was first a follower of Urban, and then became a zealot in the fold of Clement.[4] Nor were saints immune from a change of mind. St. Colette may serve as a typical example for the vacillating attitude which had befallen mortals. She first had joined the Urbanist Poor Clares, and later turned to Benedict XIII, the anti-pope and former Cardinal Peter de Luna, by whom she was empowered to found new convents.[5] With some exaggeration one might speak of a Schism within human personalities. Abbot Ludolph of Sagan described this catastrophic situation thus : " Surrexit regnum contra regnum, provincia contra provinciam, clerus contra clerum,

[1]Dietrich of Niem, *De Schismate*, lib. i, c. 19.

[2]On the Franciscans see Eubel, " Die Avignonesische Obedienz im Franziskanerorden zur Zeit des Grossen Schismas " in *Franziskanische Studien*, vol. i, pp. 165–92, 312–27, 479–500.

[3]On contemporary conditions in Strassburg, see the interesting paper by J. Rott, " Le Grand Schisme d'Occident et le Diocèse de Strasbourg " in *Mélanges d'Archéologie et d'Histoire*, vol. lii (1935), pp. 366–95.

[4]Further examples in Salembier, *op. cit.*, pp. 77–8 ; cf. also Rose Graham, " The Great Schism and the English Monasteries of the Cistercian Order " in *E.H.R.*, vol. xliv, pp. 373 ff.

[5]See also Valois, *op. cit.*, vol. iii, p. 442, note 3, vol. iv, p. 509, and *Gesta Benedicti*, in Muratori, *Rerum Italicarum Scriptores*, vol. iii, pars 2, col. 792.

doctores contra doctores, parentes contra filios et filii in parentes."[1] To strengthen their position in the secular field the two popes vied with each other for the favours of secular princes and were consequently compelled to make ever-growing concessions to them, thereby lowering still further their own authority and the prestige of the Church.

And what was the ordinary citizen to think of all this? It is evident that—as in modern elections—the programmes of the two popes were of less importance than the personalities involved. This element certainly carried much weight with rulers and princes, together with the political advantages they thought they could reap from a recognition of the one or the other pope. These two elements—personality and political profit—were the criteria decisive for the rulers' choice and we shall try in vain to detect any religious motive for their declarations of loyalty. Their access to the facts was limited, if ever they were really interested in forming an impartial judgment. Now if the rulers' knowledge was so limited, how much more so was that of the ordinary people? The people were only informed of those events of which higher authorities deemed it expedient for them to know. Thus, even if the individual citizen was eager to form his own opinion, he could necessarily only arrive at one identical with that of his rulers and superiors. Moreover, the facts which were set before the people were not presented in a detached manner : the emotional argument against the " other " pope, mainly consisting of a tirade delivered from the pulpit, or originating in some other officially inspired source, so clouded the real issue that it was far beyond the grasp of ordinary people. The spiritual salvation of the common people was simply determined by the attitude of their rulers and superiors, guided as these were by motives far enough removed from the spiritual, religious or moral. As usual, the people were drawn by appeals to the emotions and swayed by the likes and dislikes formed by their rulers, spiritual or temporal. Nevertheless, it would be rash to pretend that the whole population of Europe inevitably saw in either Clement or Urban merely the anti-Christ and the scoundrel. The few cases cited by chroniclers,

[1]*Tractatus de longaevo schismate*, cap. 2, quoted by Loserth in *Archiv für oesterreichische Geschichtsforschung*, vol. lx, p. 404.

and registered in the collections of State documents, as well as the rigorous legislation of rulers, especially France and England, go to prove that open doubt as to the respective positions of the claimants was by no means unknown.

The picture thus presented to us is one of indescribable mental confusion. The Church, the reality of whose power and the actuality of whose existence remained an unshakable axiom with all, constituting a determinative factor in the moral and political life of nation and individual, now provided a repulsive spectacle of unworthiness and dishonour. Although strenuously upheld throughout the tempests of centuries, the very foundations of the Church now seemed shaken : not indeed through the action of an external foe, but through that of the Church's own internal working mechanism. The tide which was to rise against the Church two centuries later was moving. Doubt concerning the divine foundation and claims, hitherto confined to a few intellectuals, thrust itself vigorously upon the indiscriminating, yet devout, individual—thus also intellectually paving the way for the cataclysm of the sixteenth century. The fundamental basis of the ecclesiastical hierarchy, and of the whole edifice of the Church, now became matters of dispute and uncertainty. " Abstruse questions that ordinarily were discussed by scholars in the closet were now noised abroad on the housetop."[1] Or, as another modern writer says : " An important effect of the Great Schism had been to make men think more seriously about the institution which they had accepted as part of their daily lives."[2]

But there were not only intellectual doubts about the very foundations of the papal supremacy—a greater disruptive force than one is perhaps inclined to think—but also loss of respect for the institution of the papacy as such, and of the clergy. The moral disintegration of the clergy had already set in during the Avignonese adventure, but now that personal passions came into full play and, in many cases, individual existence depended on joining " the right side ", the moral disintegration gained momentum. The corrosion of the morals of the clergy changed into rapid decay. Corruption and bribery, neglect of spiritual duties, lascivity and luxury,

[1]Creighton, *History of Papacy*, vol. i, p. 212.
[2]Jacob, *Essays in the Conciliar Epoch*, p. 7.

characterized a considerable part of the clergy : and the popes themselves—especially when later in 1409 a third pope was added, and the contesting duumvirate expanded into a quarrelling triumvirate—set a poor example of morality ; as the popes were so dependent upon princely favour to keep themselves in power, however shadowy this power may actually have been, papal policy naturally consisted in the main of granting concessions.[1] We may select as an important contemporary witness one who was present at the Council of Constance, the monk Dietrich Vrie, who, in a Latin poem written at Constance, set forth the wailings of the dishonoured Church :

" The pope, once the wonder of the world, has fallen, and with him fell the heavenly temples, my members. Now is the reign of Simon Magus, and the riches of this world prevent just judgment. The papal court nourishes every kind of scandal and turns God's houses into a market. The sacraments are basely sold ; the rich man is honoured, the poor despised ; he who gives most is best received. Golden was the first age of the papal court ; then came the baser age of silver. Next came the age of clay. Could aught be worse ? Aye, dung, and in dung sits the papal court. All things are degenerate, the papal court is rotten. The pope himself, head of all wickedness, plots every kind of disgraceful scheme and, while absolving others, is himself hurrying to death."[2]

Another witness is Nicholas de Clémanges, the Parisian doctor, papal secretary, scholar and ecclesiastical statesman. In his *De Corrupto Ecclesiae Statu* he writes that priests were concerned solely with revenue :

" Salvation or edification of those entrusted to their care, the divine services, are hardly mentioned. Papal collectors devastate the land and excommunicate or suspend those who do not justify their demands. Judgment is given in favour of those who pay most. The loss of ten thousand souls is easier borne than the loss of ten thousand shillings. The study of Holy Writ and theological professors are openly turned into ridicule. Bishops do not hesitate to sell

[1]See Pastor, *loc. cit.*, p. 146, and in many other places.
[2]Quoted by Creighton, *op. cit.*, p. 261.

licences to priests to keep concubines. Priests blaspheme the name of God and the Saints, and from the embraces of prostitutes hurry to the altar."[1]

Such was the verdict of men qualified to judge—the disaster which had befallen the Church was on such a scale that her recovery was bound to be slow and painful. But let us now turn to review the English attitude to the dual papacy.

[1]This tract is in Van der Hardt, *Concilium Constantiense*, tom. i, pars 3. On the disputed authorship of this tract see Hefele-Leclercq, *Histoire des Conciles*, vol. vi, part 2, p. 1118, note 1. See also Pastor, *loc. cit.*, p. 146, and Creighton, *op. cit.*, p. 263.

VII

THE ENGLISH REACTION

THE REACTIONS of England towards the drama un-
folding itself on the Continent are of particular interest to the
student of English history. There is no information available as
to when England received the news of Gregory's death, of Urban's
election, and of the subsequent events. But when we keep in
mind that news from Italy took about four to six weeks to
reach this country, it is plain that the news of the pope's death
must probably have been received here at a time when his
successor was already in full exercise of the papal functions.
It is possible that unofficial news of Urban's election was
received through a messenger of the already-mentioned John
Hawkwood, who was at that time battling in Lombardy and
other Italian parts ; he had sent a friar minor, Walter
Thorpe, to England with a request for financial aid. On 1st
June, 1378, a hundred shillings were advanced to him.[1]
Richard II was officially informed through the Archbishop of
Canterbury, Simon of Sudbury, who had received a papal
Bull announcing the election of the Archbishop of Bari to the
throne of St. Peter. This Bull, dated 19th April, one day after
the coronation, speaks of a unanimous and canonical election.[2]
In order to be able to fulfil the heavy tasks of his pontificate
and to carry the *jugum apostolicae servitutis* successfully, the pope
asks the English for their prayers to help him in the discharge
of his duties " which we alone cannot do ". On 26th June the
king sent a deputation, headed by Walter Skirlaw, to Rome to
convey the royal felicitations to the new pope.[3]

Generally speaking, the election of Urban cannot have

[1]*Issue Roll*, 468 m. 5.

[2]Wilkins, *Concilia*, tom. iii, pp. 127–8 : " De ipsorum fratrum
concordi voto parique concordia, eodem afflante spiritu, processit de
nobis . . . ad Petri cathedram canonica, communis et concors electio."

[3]*Issue Roll, ibid.*, m. 8.

caused anything but joy and satisfaction in English lands. Not only did he not belong to the loathed French nation, but he also appeared to be resolved to stay in Rome and thus to be determined to shake off the shackles of an unholy alliance with France.[1] Moreover, his personal integrity and his desire to introduce long overdue reform measures must surely have appealed to the English. The unmistakable sincerity of tone revealed in his first Bull, and the frank recognition of the difficulties ahead, no doubt made a deep impression upon the nation. Always prone to interpret actions in a sense favourable to themselves, the English, somewhat groundlessly, considered all the new pope's official activity as manifesting friendliness towards them and unfriendliness towards the French. They were especially confirmed in this belief by a Bull of 9th May, 1378, addressed to the Archbishop of Canterbury and the Bishop of Lincoln,[2] in which the pope granted Richard II considerable privileges with regard to the appointments to vacant benefices in churches in England, Wales, Ireland and in the English possessions on the Continent.[3] Power was granted the king to nominate two suitable individuals for the first canonry, prebend or other dignity, in all cathedral and collegiate churches.[4]

The papal envoy himself enjoyed the highest honours during his stay in this country. A great number of gifts were

[1]Though it is certainly true to say with Noel Valois, *La France et Le Grand Schisme*, vol. i, p. 241, that " l'attachement au pape de Rome ne marche pas toujours de pair avec l'hostilité à l'égard de la France."

[2]Th. Rymer, *Foedera*, tom. iii, p. 85, Wilkins, *op. cit.*, tom. iii, pp. 130–1 (Reference is made to the third edition of Rymer's *Foedera*, Hague, 1740).

[3]Precisely the same privileges were granted to other princes, notably Charles V of France and the Duke of Normandy, but this fact remained unknown to the English.

[4]For practical application, see *Calendar of Patent Rolls* (hereafter quoted *C.P.R.*), tom. i, pp. 328, 333, etc. The privilege granted to the prior and chapter of the Benedictines at Canterbury whereby they were dispensed from attending a general chapter (Bull of 24th April, Wilkins, pp. 126–7) was another act of the new pope, which was interpreted as showing favour to the English. The Bull of 4th May, addressed to the same (Wilkins, 130), concerning the dispensation of clerics from certain irregularities, should also be mentioned in this context.

offered him as a mark of the special devotion towards the new pope. On 25th September a friar minor was sent to Rome to negotiate a number of outstanding points between Richard and Urban.[1]

Meanwhile, however, Clement VII had been elected and a complete break in the government of the Church effected. Passions ran high on the Continent, but the somewhat cooler temper of the English made them view these events with less emotionalism and with, perhaps, a more calculated political rationalism. The alleged invalidity of Urban's election appeared to have had no effect upon the English : no chronicler gives any description of the first reaction of people and ruler towards this extraordinary new situation. But in October, 1378, a decision had to be made concerning England's position. By sheer coincidence the envoys of the rival claimants arrived simultaneously, both legations asking for help against the anti-Christ and intruder. Neither king nor Parliament was in London. Gloucester had been chosen as the meeting place of Parliament and there the sessions began on 18th October. It was at this time that the two legations arrived. The choice of the meeting place was determined by the main issue of this session, that is, the supposed violation of sanctuary rights at St. Paul's in London.[2] The gloomy financial position of the country was another matter that considerably preoccupied the minds of the boy king's Government and his Parliament at the time. Chroniclers were, consequently, far more interested in the financial situation than in the question of recognizing the one or the other of the two rivals. This session lasted until 16th December, 1378.[3] Although the chronicler of St. Peter's, Gloucester, records many interesting details at great length—he deals fully with the domestic arrangements designed by abbot and monks for the personal comfort of the king and his household—there is no mention of the arrival of the envoys, nor of any proceedings initiated by reason of their appearance. Indeed, it appears that the legates were kept waiting for some time before they were allowed to submit their respective

[1] *Issue Roll*, 468 m. 12.

[2] About the decisions of the synod of Gloucester, see Mansi, *Sacrorum Conciliorum . . . Collectio*, tom. xxvi, cols. 617–20.

[3] *Historia et Cartularium Monasterii S. Petri Gloucestriae*, p. 52.

cases. Archbishop Sudbury was commissioned by the king to examine the statements of both legates and to decide *cum quo tenendum esset*.[1] He was to hear the counsel of clerics before he arrived at a final decision. After a rapid review of the credentials and statements of the two deputations, the archbishop and clerics reached their conclusion, which was announced to Parliament in public session : " You may receive Urban VI as the true pope."[2] Clement's emissaries were not even admitted to Parliament to plead their case before the assembly. After this announcement Sudbury preached a sermon on the text : " I will set up one shepherd over them " (*Ez.* 34: 23), in which all the arguments propounded by the cardinals were refuted. He attacked them vehemently, declaring that their actions were dictated by malice and that their detestable falsehoods should have all the publicity they deserved.[3] Thereupon Parliament resolved unanimously and without discussion that Urban should be recognized as the only true pope.[4]

This theoretical, political and religious recognition of Urban was followed by two acts of Parliament, which had far-reaching consequences. In the first the king obtained the right to oppose all activity within the realm made by or on behalf of Clement VII.[5] The second act proclaimed all those who favoured Clement's cause traitors and rendered their goods liable to confiscation by the Treasury.

It is an eloquent testimony of the efficiency of the royal administration in the fourteenth century that, as early as 8th November, an order was served upon the coastal guards in Sussex, Cornwall and various southern ports, to make search " in accordance with the ordinance of the Council that no person pass beyond the seas with gold or silver in money or bullion or with jewels or letters of exchange, under pain

---

[1] *Eulogium*, tom. iii, p. 347.

[2] *Ibid.*

[3] Walsingham, *Historia Anglicana*, vol. i, p. 381.

[4] Selden declared in a characteristic epigram : " Urban was made pope by act of parliament against pope Clement ", *Table Talk* (ed. Arber, p. 87, quoted by Workman, *John Wyclif*, vol. ii, p. 60).

[5] *Statutes of the Realm*, tom. ii, ch. vii, p. 11.

of being arrested and brought before the Council."[1] Now it is interesting to note that, on the very same day, Urban— who cannot have possibly known of the decision of the Parliament of Gloucester—issued a Bull to Richard II in which he reveals that he has disposed of the goods, estates and revenues belonging to the seditious cardinals : he had decided that two-thirds of the income derived from their benefices should go to the apostolic see and that the remainder should be reserved for repairs or other expenses charged upon the goods and estates.[2] This proposal of the pope was of great importance, as we shall see later.

The Act of Parliament was implemented with all speed. The arrest of Clement's emissaries was immediately ordered. Roger Foucault, the head of the delegation, together with his companions was taken into custody by the town authorities and delivered to the king on 5th November. Taken to the castle of Gloucester on 20th November, Roger was later transferred to Windsor and not released until August, 1380. His release was conditioned by his abjuration of loyalty to Clement VII and his promise to go to Rome to ask Urban for pardon. The very fact that twelve years later Roger was still in correspondence with the rebellious cardinals, and with Clement himself, does not indicate any great sincerity on his part. His companions were deprived of their freedom for only a few months. The shrewdness and political skill of the cardinals and of Clement shows itself in their choice of legates : they were all, technically speaking, subjects of the king, and Roger, moreover, had been in the service of the Black Prince, the king's father. The nationality of the envoys was to shield them against any encroachments upon their rights.

The confiscation of all benefices and revenues proceeded with great speed. This legislative measure[3] met with all the more approval on the part of the nation in that the holders

[1] *C.P.R.*, i. 309.

[2] The following passage in the Bull is of particular interest : " De fructibus beneficiorum, quae cardinales rebelles olim in regno tuo obtinebant, sic disposuimus, quod duae partes eorundem fructuum pro camera nostra apostolica, tertia vero pars pro reparationibus necessariis et aliis eis incumbentibus oneribus, reserventur ", *Foedera*, tom. iv, col. 177.

[3] See *Rotuli Parliamentorum*, vol. iii, p. 46.

of the benefices were almost exclusively Frenchmen. The rich benefices which the cardinals held in England were a source of serious discontent amongst the people, as the enormous revenues were thought to go to the French king, thus possibly aiding the national enemy. It had become more and more a feature of the Avignonese papacy to confer almost exclusively benefices situated in England.[1] The temporary character of this confiscation indicates clearly that, so far, no general animosity against foreign holders of benefices was entertained by the English ; their hostility was restricted to the French holders.[2] For, within three years, most of the benefices were again given away to the cardinals newly created by Urban and not possessing French nationality. Let us briefly show the extent of these benefices.

The Cardinal of Aigrefeuille possessed the Archdeaconry of Berkshire and a prebend at Worth (diocese of Salisbury), another in Lincoln and another Archdeaconry at Taunton. The Cardinal of Poitiers held a prebend at York, whilst Cardinal de Vergne received revenues from a prebend in Lincoln and the Archdeaconry of Exeter. The Cardinal of Glandève was Chancellor of Hereford, Robert of Geneva (Clement VII) Archdeacon of Dorset, and the Cardinal of St. Angelo Archdeacon of Suffolk. Italian cardinals, too, were in possession of large English benefices : Simon de Bursano (the Cardinal of Milan) held the Archdeaconry of Wells and received revenues from a prebend in Salisbury ; Cardinal Orsini was Archdeacon of Leicester and also of Durham. Nepotism in the French curia had caused the late Pope Gregory XI to confer the Archdeaconry of Canterbury upon his nephew, Adhémar de la Roche. Altogether there were seven major benefices in the diocese of Lincoln, nine in that of Salisbury, four at York, three at Wells, and one benefice each in Canterbury, Norwich, Hereford and Meath in Ireland, which fell under the statute of confiscation passed at Gloucester upon the recommendation of Archbishop Sudbury.

[1]Perroy, *L'Angleterre et Le Grand Schisme d'Occident*, p. 59, gives the sums as they were yearly delivered ; he was fortunate enough to be able to make use of the records of the Avignonese clerk, who, as the procurator of the Cardinal of Aigrefeuille, kept strict accounts.

[2]A different view-point in Trevelyan, *England in the Age of Wycliffe*, pp. 118–20.

The king and his officials acted swiftly. On 28th November, barely four weeks after ordering the confiscation of these long-coveted revenues, all procurators and tenants of the benefices concerned were ordered to Westminster to give all necessary information to the Exchequer. At the same time the transfer of money and any other goods out of the country was forbidden. It is surprising that none of the French cardinals raised the slightest protest against this procedure. Their Italian colleagues, however, probably relying upon the lack of proper information in the country, were bold enough to demonstrate against the confiscation. The king appeared satisfied with the truth of their protestations and revoked the confiscation by an order of 20th February, 1379, " the king being assured of their obedience to that pope and friendship towards himself."[1] These Italians could certainly claim that they had wavered between Urban and Clement for a considerable period, although by the time that they issued this protest they had already joined the ranks of the rebels. Their protestation was fraudulent in the highest degree. But the case of the Cardinal of Albano, Angelicus (or Anglicus) Grimoard, whom his brother Urban V had raised to the cardinalate (1366),[2] was still worse and shows a disregard for the most fundamental moral principles that indicates a complete loss of self-respect. Having as early as 9th August, 1378, publicly proclaimed his allegiance to the rebellious cardinals, he yet had no scruple in remonstrating against the confiscation of his revenues. The king entertained no doubt that the protest was genuine and that the cardinal was loyal and faithful to Urban : in his letter to the treasurer on 20th February, 1379, Richard II revoked this order of confiscation in an almost apologetic tone.[3] It was not until the following year that this decision was reversed when the true facts became known.[4]

[1]*C.P.R.*, 342, membr. 15, *Foedera*, iii, col. 82, and *Cal. Close Rolls*, p. 175, membr. 17.

[2]Raynaldus, *Annales*, tom. vii, p. 147.

[3]See *Foedera*, iii. 82.

[4]See *Cal. Pat. R.*, p. 491, membr. 15, of 23rd May, 1380 : mandate to the president and chapter of St. Peter's, York, to proceed to the election of a dean, in the room of Anglicus, cf. also *Cal. Close Rolls*, p. 449, membr. 10.

As already mentioned, Urban deprived all the seditious cardinals of their dignities, but the case of the Cardinal of Albano had some repercussions in this country. He too was, of course, deprived of his hat by the pope who, as a sign of special favour to the English, suggested William of Courtenay as the Cardinal of England. But the Londoners made three applications to the pope, on 4th December, 1378, 25th April and 16th May, 1379, to beg him to abstain from raising the Bishop of London to the cardinalate, since this appointment would have deprived Londoners of a very popular ecclesiastical figure.[1] Whereupon, complying with the Londoners' request, Urban gave the hat to the Benedictine, Adam Easton of Norwich, later known as the Cardinal of England.

Urban's Bull of 29th November, 1378, excommunicating Clement VII received the widest publicity in England : by an order of Archbishop Sudbury, issued on 30th March, 1379, at Canterbury[2] to all his suffragans, this Bull was read in all the English churches. But it is interesting to note that, four days before the Bull of excommunication was promulgated, the pope addressed a Bull to the Archbishop of Canterbury, which sheds very significant light upon conditions then prevailing. This Bull is noteworthy, not only because it was written at a time when the pope could not have known the decision of Gloucester, but also because it strikingly illustrates the typical medieval mixture of religion, ecclesiastical policy and national politics. It would be erroneous to assume that the pope wanted to reward England for its adherence to him, since the Gloucester decision could not yet have reached him. This Bull (*Dignum arbitramur*) of 25th November[3] was incorporated in a letter which Sudbury sent, in the first place, to the prior and chapter of Canterbury and also to " all whom it may concern ". In the Bull the pope declares that upon that very day he had been informed of the case of the

[1] It is certainly an exaggeration to say with Workman, *op. cit.*, vol. ii, p. 57 note 1, that the Londoners " wrote in protest to Urban " ; the supplications themselves show nothing of this kind ; they were simply petitions to the pope not to make Courtenay a cardinal. It was still the rule that diocesan bishops if raised to the cardinalate resigned their sees and went to reside in the curia.

[2] Wilkins, *Concilia*, tom. iii, col. 138–41.

[3] Wilkins, *loc. cit.*, 148–9.

Archdeacon of Canterbury, Adhémar de la Roche. Although the cure of souls had been entrusted to him, the archdeacon had never taken up his residence in Canterbury and had allowed his manors, houses and other buildings to fall into decay. Moreover, by birth an Aquitanian, he had now joined the enemies of " our most beloved son in Christ, Richard, the illustrious King of England ". The pope, therefore, instructed the archbishop to summon Adhémar de la Roche by a public edict, firstly, to proceed in person to his archdeaconry and, secondly, to take up his residence in Canterbury forthwith. If he should disregard this summons, the archbishop must deprive him of his office *sententialiter*. These instructions are followed by the statement that John Fordham, canon of Lincoln, had submitted a humble supplication to the pope on this very same matter. John Fordham, the pope declares, had been much commended to him on account of the purity and blamelessness of his life and because of many other virtues, and was the special counsellor of the king and the keeper of his privy seal : in view of all this, and out of consideration for the king's interest in this favourite cleric, the pope instructs the archbishop to confer the archdeaconry, if its present holder should be deprived of it, upon John Fordham after careful examination as to whether the said John was able to read and write in Latin with facility, as well as to sing and adequately to converse in that tongue. In the opinion of the pope it would be no obstacle to conferment of this office upon John, if he, whilst passing all other tests, failed to reach a satisfactory standard in singing, provided that he swore by the gospels that he would studiously apply himself to the practice of singing during the year following the examination. The conferment should be carried out without regard to any existing laws and customs in the country and without waiting any subsequent apostolic confirmation. Apart from the revenues and incomes of the said archdeaconry (which, it was estimated, did not exceed 600 marks sterling), John was understood to have obtained canonries and prebends in the dioceses of Lincoln, Chichester, St. David's and Lichfield not exceeding 500 marks sterling. This Bull was dated at Tivoli.

In his letter the archbishop says that he had examined

John Fordham and had found him a fit and proper person for this office.[1] On 3rd June, 1379, the king publicly proclaimed that, upon advice of his council, he had seized all goods of Adhémar de la Roche and transferred them to the Archbishop of Canterbury.[2] John Fordham later became Bishop of Durham, on the very same day on which Courtenay succeeded to the Archbishopric of Canterbury.[3]

As soon as the news of England's adherence to Urban had reached Rome, missionaries and preachers arrived in this country in growing numbers, thunderously denouncing Clement VII and "the devils in human form" supporting him—though not all of those preachers lived up to the high ideal which, professedly, was the reason for their missionary activity. It is reported, for example, that a Dominican, Martin Halscombe, became so infamous for his sale of indulgences that the Bishop of Exeter had to take steps to put an end to this practice.[4] Such missionaries, and more thoroughgoing impostors also, swarmed into the land under the pretext of being envoys of Urban. The pope was himself informed of this mischievous use of his name, as he says in a letter addressed to the Archbishop of Canterbury, dated 18th March, 1380, from Rome.[5] In this letter the pope refers to lay as well as to clerical personnel who had produced forged bulls and letters granting indulgences, dispensing applicants from matrimonial impediments, legitimating illegitimate children and bestowing many other privileges. These forged bulls were fabricated, as the pope puts it, " by the son of iniquity, Stephen de Cusa, who falsely pretended to be the pope's secretary." The archbishop was therefore instructed to do everything in his power to stop this practice : the pope suggested that the archbishop should act as ecclesiastical censor and demand the production of the bulls and letters by those claiming to act on behalf of the pope : if necessary, the archbishop should invoke the assistance of the royal authority. If these bulls seemed to him suspicious, he should register and forward them for further

[1] Wilkins, *loc. cit.*, 149.
[2] *Foedera, loc. cit.*, col. 85.
[3] 23rd December, 1381, *C.P.R.*, ii. 44, 48.
[4] See *Exeter Registers*, vol. i, pp. 410, 418, 428.
[5] See Wilkins, *op. cit.*, 145, and *Calendar Papal Registers*, vol. iv, p. 257.

inspection to the curia in Rome. How far the archbishop was successful in his drive against the forgers, and whether he ever made any use of the powers granted by the pope in this respect, is difficult to say in view of the silence of the chronicles on this point.

Amongst many notable preachers, who arrived in England in the spring of 1379, was the Archbishop of Cashel, Philip of Torrington, O.Min., Magister Theologiae. Coming straight from Rome he had all the zeal and fervour of a missionary and preached several times in London, fiercely denouncing Clement and his adherents, and telling the people that the pope had bestowed upon him " great powers to bind and to loose."[1] A preaching crusade against the arch enemy France went hand in hand with his missionary zeal. In the cause of God as well as in the cause of the king of England the time had come, he declared, when the kingdom of France should be invaded, all the more so as the anathematized French king would not have the strength to resist. Other chroniclers report that the archbishop maintained Charles V had given orders to kill all partisans of Urban VI.[2]

The crusading and missionary spirit also inspired lesser dignitaries, who had not visited Rome, to accumulate hatred against the Avignonese pope. And it is interesting to note that, as time went on, the campaign against Clement VII took more and more the form of a purely political campaign against France or other political adversaries. The sermons of a Carmelite friar furnish a good example of this curious mixture of religious zeal and political motives. In the Fragment preserved in the *Fasciculi Zizaniorum* (pp. 506-11), the friar maintained that Clement was, properly speaking, an alien, that is, a false pastor, who pretended to belong to the flock of the true pope ; after electing him and consenting to his coronation and to his exercise of the papal functions this false pastor deemed it advantageous to turn from his true master and to take upon himself the office of pope. In fact, he was nothing else but a thief and a wolf bent upon drawing others of the flock into the dreadful abyss into which he himself had fallen. According to this good friar, there was one striking instance of the spread-

[1]Walsingham, *Historia*, vol. i, p. 391.
[2]See Perroy, p. 63 and notes.

ing of this pernicious example. The "false king" of Spain, John I, adhered first to Urban, asked him for favours and did not appear to have had any doubt upon the legitimacy of his position. When, however, Clement VII arrogated to himself the papal office, the king, after an initial period of hesitation, joined the side of the rebels. What was the reaction of our pope to the rebels in Avignon? asked the zealous friar. After admonishing them suavely and softly, he was bound to excommunicate the false pope and all his followers, branding them as apostates and depriving them of all ecclesiastical dignities. Therefore the pope appealed for a crusade against the impostor in Avignon and—this is most revealing—against the false king of Spain, who had usurped the throne of the rightful ruler, who was no other than John of Gaunt, the Duke of Lancaster, uncle to Richard II. "The pope has now raised his banner, that is the cross, on behalf of the Duke. . . . And in order to ensure the success of this crusade, the pope has granted certain indulgences and privileges to all who take part in it."

But opponents—theological as well as political—were quick to point out that the grant of indulgences and other privileges was illegal because not given *gratis*, and therefore ineffective. The friar himself points out this objection: "Dicunt isti, quod indulgentiae, quas papa concedit pro expeditione huius cruciatae, nullius sunt vigoris, quia non dantur gratis, ut jubet Christus in evangeliis, dicens ' gratis accepistis, gratis date ' " (Matt. x. 8). These arguments he brushes aside, referring to William of Auvergne's treatise on the sacraments: these indulgences are not granted *for* money, although they are obtained *through* money, but are given for the sake of two spiritual goods, of which the one is the return of Spain into the flock of the true pastor, and the other the desire of all faithful Christians to bring about an effective union of Christendom. Thus an indulgence is not granted *propter pecuniam*, but *pro reformanda unitate ecclesiae* —an aim which cannot be achieved without money—" quae non reformari potest sine pecunia ". How far the friar was successful in his appeal, it is difficult to judge, since the chroniclers contain no reference to the response of the people.

The amalgamation of religious with purely political considerations manifests itself still more glaringly in the mandate given by Pope Urban VI to the Bishop of Norwich, Henry Despenser, in 1382. This mandate cannot easily be reconciled with the aims of reformation, so earnestly desired and repeatedly professed as necessary by the pope himself. The importance of the pope's mandate and the significance of the episcopal appeal warrant a closer examination.

In the Bull of 23rd March, 1381 (*Dudum cum vinea Dei*), Henry Despenser was empowered by Urban to take drastic action against Clement VII and his adherents : the bishop was to appeal to the country for a crusade against the schismatics in order to destroy the Clementine pretensions for ever ; everyone taking part in this crusade against France's pope was to be granted an indulgence for his sins. In another Bull (*Dudum cum filii*), dated 25th March, 1381, general permission was granted, through the Bishop of Norwich, to every cleric to take up the cross without the consent of his superior ; the duty of residence in his benefice was cancelled. For various political reasons, amongst which the Peasant Revolt was conspicuous, the bishop deemed it advisable to delay the publication of the bulls. It was, in fact, not until 1382 that the publication of these bulls, together with a mandate to the clergy, was considered expedient.[1]

In the first-mentioned Bull the pope recalls the atrocious behaviour of the troops owing allegiance to Clement and to France, especially that of the Breton mercenaries. Robberies, murders, rapes, sacrileges, expulsions of the population—these, according to the pope, were some of the deeds of the troops owing allegiance to Clement. The pope justifies his sentence of excommunication against Clement and his close collaborators by referring to the great excesses and heresies of the cardinals : he could tolerate this state of affairs no longer and was forced to employ drastic measures. They had, so to speak, asked for excommunication and deprivation of all their official functions. Now, the Bishop of Norwich was empowered to use equally drastic measures against anyone who tried to help the rebels : by giving shelter to their emis-

[1]These Bulls are contained in Wykeham's *Register*, Hampshire Record Society, vol. ii, pp. 198–211, Brit. Mus. King's MS, 7 E x, fol. 71 *verso*—74, and summarized in Walsingham, vol. ii, pp. 71 seq.

saries, by defending their heretical conduct ; in short all activity which was designed to help the cause of the rebels automatically entails excommunication, from which only the pope had power to absolve them. Even the bodies of those who had been guilty of this condemned conduct, had to be exhumed, before they could be absolved. Whoever referred to Robert as true pope was automatically excommunicated, or, in the case of a whole community, came under the interdict and was thus cut off from all intercourse with the rest of mankind. In conclusion the Bull lays down that indulgences are to be granted—analogous to those given for the rescue of the Holy Land—to all who, according to their means and faculties, contributed sufficient subsidies—*qui ministrabunt sufficientia stipendia*—for the maintenance of the soldiers entrusted with the campaign.

The specific powers granted to the Bishop of Norwich were of a far-reaching nature. In particular, he was charged to arrest all who had favoured the cause of the schismatics : after a summary examination he was entitled to imprison them and to confiscate their goods. This mandate referred to layfolk as well as to clerics. In the latter case, the vacancies caused by their removal could be filled with suitable personnel at the discretion of the bishop. On the other hand, indulgences were to be granted to all who effectively contributed to the maintenance of suitable warriors. The pronouncement of excommunication was put into the hands of the bishop.

Despenser was not slow in putting these vast powers into operation. He issued a mandate to all clerics and rectors enjoining them to publish the Bulls, and the publication was thoroughgoing, as these Bulls appeared on all church-doors and the porches of monasteries. Furthermore, he ordered the clerics to record the name of every individual parishioner, and to register the exact amount of money or other valuables given for the cause.[1] To those who would not pay—whether rich or poor—the example of the poor widow's mite (Mark xii 41-3; Luke xxi 1-3) should be quoted ; they should be treated prudently in the confessional and induced to assist

---

[1] " Nomina autem singulorum parochianorum vestrorum scribi faciatis, summas et donationes solventium super ipsorum nomina signando ", *loc. cit.*, p. 79.

in the " holy voyage ", i.e., the crusade.[1] Those who obstructed
the crusade and opposed the bishop's orders, or who favoured
the cause of the rebels, should peremptorily be summoned
to appear upon a fixed day before the bishop or his commissioners in St. Paul's Cathedral in London : there they would have
to give concrete proof of their innocence. Moreover, the
clergy should discreetly inform the bishop himself of the names
of the donors and the amount given. This mandate to the
English clergy was signed and issued by the Bishop of Norwich
on 9th February, 1382, from Charing. Not, however, until
6th December, 1382, did the king give permission to all his
subjects to join the crusade.[2]

Before effective action was taken, the whole affair came to
be discussed in the parliament whose session began on 23rd
February, 1383, in London. It busied itself with the papal
Bull, the bishop's mandate to the English clergy and, above all,
with the proposed expedition to Flanders. There was by no
means enthusiastic, or unanimous, support for this campaign :[3]
there were clashes between two opposing factions, the one
supporting the bishop's plea for swift action against France,
or as they said, against the enemies of Christ (Walsingham,
ii. 84), although these religious motives did not seem to be the
only decisive considerations : the French victory at Ghent,
the ensuing expulsion of Englishmen and of Urban's adherents,
and the recognition of Clement by Flanders were events
which greatly imperilled the flourishing wool trade and, as
M. Perroy very succinctly points out (pp.179,183), we find
" the London capitalists " aligning themselves with Bishop
Despenser of Norwich. The rival faction, less moved by this

[1] " . . . signando, et non solventes de diebus in dies, quotiens et
quando plus expedit, non solum divites, sed pauperes, ad similitu-
dinem pauperculae viduae, sanos et valetudinarios maxime, in
confessionibus prudenter tractetis et inducatis, ut huiusmodi sancto
viagio . . . manus apponant adjutrices ", loc. cit.

[2] Foedera, iii, 145. Workman, loc. cit., p. 66, gives the date for the
promulgation of the bishop's mandate as 1383, whilst Walsingham
has 1382 ; nor is it correct to say that " Richard authorized
Spenser to proclaim the crusade " ; Richard merely gave his subjects
permission to join the crusade—assuredly a royal prerogative.

[3] On this parliament see also H. G. Richardson, " The Commons
and Medieval Politics " in Transactions of the R. Histor. Society, 4th
ser., xxviii (1946), p. 30 n. 3 ; A. Steel, Richard II, p. 101.

mixture of religious and economic considerations, urged caution, maintaining that it would be inadvisable to entrust the military leadership of the king's people to an inexperienced priest ; the crown itself was unenthusiastic about the episcopal leadership of an expeditionary force. This party, therefore, proposed a royal army under royal command. The session did not lack liveliness ; there were outbursts on both sides, but finally the bishop succeeded. Parliament made various grants in respect of the campaign—the bishop now had a more or less free hand to go ahead with his plans.

Immediately afterwards he sent letters to all the clergy throughout the land and empowered rectors, vicars and curates of all English parishes when hearing the confessions of their parishioners to grant, by apostolic authority, absolution to those who would make donations. According to the chronicler, the response was overwhelming (Walsingham, ii. 85) : the people were inflamed by a " heat of devotion and faith " and made hasty preparations for the expedition. Those who were unfit gave goods and money with liberality, according to the advice of their confessors, in order to merit absolution. Thus there was hardly anyone " in this spatious kingdom " who did not either offer his personal services or give according to his means. Walsingham reports that large sums of money were accumulated and delivered to the bishop. Another chronicler, Henry Knighton, reports that the amount of money, gold and silver collected by the bishop was " incredible ".[1] The bishop was not less fortunate in his harvest of jewellery, rings, plate and other valuables; and " ladies and women " showed especial zeal in this respect, one lady, it was said, giving 100 pounds.[2] Those gifts were made so that the donors and their friends might obtain the indulgence.[3] Thus "a secret treasure of the kingdom constituted by the possessions of women " was greatly imperilled. Rich and poor, men and women,

[1]Knighton, *Chronicon*, vol. ii, p. 198. Here also the mandate is printed in French, pp. 201–3.

[2]" Collegerat namque dictus episcopus innumerabilem et incredibilem summam pecuniae, auri, et argenti, atque jocalium, monilium, annulorum, discorum, peciarum, cocliarum, et aliorum ornamentorum . . ."

[3]" Ut beneficium absolutionis consequerentur pro se et suis benevolis amicis ", Knighton, *loc. cit.*

each gave according to abilities and wealth. " For otherwise they were not granted the indulgence, unless they contributed in proportion to their wealth."[1] This astounding success was, as Knighton has it, due to the papal authorization—a procedure which is somewhat difficult to reconcile with the professed aims of Urban VI.[2] Archbishop Courtenay on 10th April gave the enterprise his special blessing, and ordered public prayers for its success, whereby an indulgence of forty days was promised.[3] Three days before this, Despenser had taken the cross to the abbey of Westminster in solemn procession.

The archbishop's part in this crusade merits a closer examination. From his manor of Otford, on 10th April, 1383, he issued a mandate to the Bishop of London and two letters to the suffragans and subjects of the diocese of Canterbury. In the first communication the archbishop, by way of introduction, recalls the utter wickedness of the seditious cardinals and their pope, and the disgrace which they had brought upon the Church : they provoked wars and dissensions amongst the Christian peoples, and their chief, the former Cardinal of Geneva, behaved like the *antiquus hostis*, i.e. the devil, and was busy sowing distrust and disturbing the peace of Christian nations. The deceased amongst the rebellious cardinals are referred to as *damnatae memoriae* : they had created Robert anti-Christ, not pope. The archbishop then goes on to recall the many well-meaning efforts which Urban had made to restrain the rebels from their last step, but they had behaved like venomous serpents and so incurred the wrath of the pope. He had been compelled " to rouse the might of the martial sword, so that this pest of discord may be extinguished."[4] And since wars are waged to achieve peace, the pope had commissioned the Bishop of Norwich to launch

[1] " Nam aliter non absolvebantur, nisi tribuerent secundum posse suum et facultatem suam ", Knighton, *loc. cit.*

[2] " Habuit namque praedictus episcopus indulgentias mirabiles cum absolutione a poena et a culpa pro dicta cruciata a papa Urbano VIo ei concessas, cuius auctoritate tam mortuos quam vivos, ex quorum parte contributio sufficiens fiebat, per se et per suos commissarios a poena et culpa absolvebat ", Knighton, *loc. cit.*

[3] Wilkins, iii, 176–8.

[4] Wilkins, *loc. cit.*, 177.

a crusade against the schismatics and their supporters. The pope himself had instructed the bishop to don his habergeon and to rise *vehementer* against the schismatics and all other foes of the Church. At the same time, the pope had " graciously conceded " indulgences for all partakers in the campaign. As a loyal son of the Church the bishop had taken this burden upon his shoulders—the following is an ingenious combination of varied motives—to ensure the peace of the Church, no less than the salvation and defence of this kingdom : the chief consideration of the bishop being that the interests of Church and State are inseparable.[1] " In order to ensure that the minds of the faithful are more inclined to works of this charitable character, we grant all penitents in our diocese of Canterbury an indulgence of forty days, and we ask you (i.e., the Bishop of London) and others of our brethren to do the same."

The letter to the suffragans and subjects of the Canterbury diocese is much shorter and says that Henry, Bishop of Norwich, " inflamed with zeal for the law of God and the Church, and with fervour for the kingdom of England ", has exposed himself to the dangers and rigours of war as an obedient son of the Church and his country. But since an army could not be maintained without food, and since some collectors of subsidies had either embezzled or hidden money, jewels, etc., given to them for the crusade, and had, therefore, brought the army into great peril " and, as one must fear, the Catholic Church and the kingdom of England ", the clergy were admonished to see that collectors in their dioceses should *cum omni celeritate* deliver the money and other subsidies to Master Walter Donnell and Philip Mascal, the collectors authorized by Henry.[2] The frauds must have reached a fairly high sum, for on 15th March, 1383, the king issued a writ to Thomas Savyll and others charging them with the investigation of all questionable cases and empowering them to examine minutely,

[1] This argument is highly interesting and it shows that Marsiglio's doctrines had unexpected adherents. Moreover, this argument is the basic contention of a forerunner of Marsiglio, the anonymous tract *Rex Pacificus*, about which see my paper in *E.H.R.*, vol. lxi, pp. 180 ff. It is equally interesting to note that these very same words are used by the archbishop as his exordium.

[2] Wilkins, *loc. cit.*, iii. 178.

wherever they could, all particulars as to the donations of money and valuables. The king referred to forged episcopal letters and instructed all public officials, such as bailiffs, mayors, ministers, etc., to give all possible assistance to the royal officers.[1]

Finally, the third letter, dated the same day, 10th April, and addressed to all clerics of the diocese of Canterbury, requested a favourable reception for the trustworthy agents : Thomas Ranf, the prior ; John Pecham, the archdeacon ; and Canon Simon Hetham, on their accession to office.[2]

Two days before, however, the king himself instructed all collectors to gather the money which still remained in the hands of sub-collectors and deputy collectors, and to deliver it to the appropriate episcopal authorities. The names of those who refused to hand in the money, should be taken, and severe measures were threatened by the king against the refractory.[3]

Headed by the bishop himself, the expeditionary force crossed the channel on 17th May, 1383, and fought between Dunkirk and Ypres with varying success.[4] The campaign produced no tangible results ; in fact a truce was signed between the French and the English, and, seen in retrospect, the whole campaign was a lamentable and costly failure : Despenser was blamed for bad leadership and, on his return to England, he was deprived of his temporalities, whilst his clerks were made to answer for the sums they had embezzled.

These crusading appeals were accompanied by literary productions, two of which deserve our particular attention, although both are anonymous. Even the title of the one document, purporting to be the reply of the bishops to the cardinals' letter, is controversial. Walsingham heads it " Responsio Episcoporum Catholicorum ad Literam Pseudo-Cardinalium " (pp. 385-7), whilst the version of *Chronicon Angliae* is " Responsio Episcoporum ad Literam Pseudo-Cardinalium " (pp. 216-9).

---

[1]*Foedera*, 149 ; a similar writ was issued on 17th March, 1383, to the *vicecomites* of London, see *Foedera*, 149.

[2]Wilkins, iii. 178.

[3]*Foedera*, 152.

[4]On this campaign see also Valois, *loc. cit.*, ii, pp. 225-32. According to Eubel, *Hierarchia Catholica*, tom. i, p. 389 note 4, Clementine prisoners were killed by Despenser's troops.

Baluzius (i. 553-7) again prints this document as the king's answer to the letter of the cardinals; in Baluzius' version the document itself starts off: " Eduardus Rex Angliae et Dominus Hiberniae . . .", whilst in reality Edward III had been dead for more than a year. Moreover, Baluzius does not mention that the royal statement was a reply to the cardinals' letter, but says that this document was simply a letter sent to the cardinals loyal to Clement.[1] The historian of the University of Paris, Bulaeus, transcribes the letter " Anglorum ad Cardinales schismaticos seu Clementinos " (iv. 518) which, he says, he copied from Walsingham.[2] Lastly, M. Perroy refers to a MS. in the Vatican library which begins: " Richardus Dei gratia Rex Angliae " (p. 64), though the text seems to be identical with that of Baluzius. Whoever the actual writer of the document may have been, English authorship cannot be denied.

This document shows none of the refinement of style and language evident in the controversial writings of both parties. Its author took obvious pains to employ a style as blunt and uncouth as possible. The very initial words themselves betray the character of the document : the Clementine cardinals should not claim to have been appointed to their high offices by *divina misericordia* ; *divina maledictio* had been thundered against these rapacious wolves. Having obviously been instigated by the devil, their letter afforded sorrow and anguish instead of joy and edification ; it had wounded the heart of each and every Christian, since a most pernicious and scandalous schism had been wrought within Holy Church. " Woe to you," cries the author, " by whom scandal has come." " You have committed sacrilege when you believed yourselves the upholders of law and order ; burning grief has been inflicted upon the whole of Christianity." " O vestra detestabilis et infelix ambitio." The cardinals said that they had been compelled to elect a Roman or an Italian, but no person was

[1]One need not go so far as to declare this document " an extraordinary forgery " (Workman, ii. 60 n. 2). Only the initial words differ, the rest of the document is identical to that as recorded by Walsingham and *Chronicon Angliae*. I am more inclined to attribute this " forged " initium to a scribe's interpolation in the interests of Clement.

[2]Bulaeus refers to this letter, as if it had been composed by the Masters of *Oxoniensis academiae*.

specifically named by the multitude. Thus—this conclusion is certainly somewhat rash and unconvincing—they had elected Urban freely. It was Urban, the lawfully elected pope, " to whom we owe and shall always owe allegiance." " We detest your base senselessness." They should be called a generation of vipers and callous snakes. The blindness of stupidity makes them maintain that they had acted in the interests of Holy Church and in the service of God : these were words of Pharisees. How could they expect to be recognized as protectors of the Church when they themselves had deserted the Eternal City and left the Church ? This was rebellion and they had acted like Judas, the traitor. After associating with the Duke of Fondi they were worthy of the proverb : " To be praised by wicked men is to be praised for wickedness." The last part of the letter addresses the Duke directly, but here, too, emotion takes the place of reason, and we shall look in vain for any reasoned refutation of Clement's claims. It may be that lack of factual knowledge caused the author to employ language far inferior to that of the cardinals themselves, who, however fiery their manner of writing, were rarely negligent of dignity of style and touches of diplomatic skill. The English letter is nothing but a vehement and verbose invective. The violence of its language and the heat of the argument are strangely reminiscent of Wyclif's writings.

These defects are less obvious in the second document, entitled *Rationes Anglicorum*. It appears a justifiable assumption to identify the author as the writer of the letter just reviewed. Raynaldus prints the text (p. 337, col. 1—p. 338, col. 2), which sets forth sixteen reasons why the English did not accept the cardinals' plea for the recognition of Clement VII. Firstly, it is pointed out, the Romans did not compel the cardinals to elect any certain person, but merely asked (*petebant*) that the choice should be consonant to reason, which, in practical terms, meant that a Roman or an Italian should be elected. Therefore, the cardinals were free to choose the actual person to be elected and thus Prignano's election was free and canonical, all the more so as the crowd did not ask for him especially to be elected. " It is true that the Romans had confined the cardinals' selection to a certain nation, but not to a certain individual, and, therefore, Urban's election is

valid." Secondly, Prignano refused to accept the pontificate
" cum magna et maxima instantia ": he accepted it only at the
urgent request of the cardinals. Since they had asked him, they
could not have elected him against their will. Thirdly, the
English gathered from reports of archbishops, bishops and
masters and doctors of theology—all of whom had been eye-
witnesses—that before they entered the conclave the cardinals
had nominated Prignano as Pope, *ex unanimi consensu*, since they
were unable to agree upon a candidate from the Sacred
College. The cardinals had even elected him three times,
whilst they were in the conclave, and had crowned him pope.
The succeeding *rationes* refer to the lengthy stay of the cardinals
in Rome and to their applications for benefices, etc. The
eighth reason is rather interesting : if the cardinals knew that
Urban was not truly pope, they had deceived the whole of
Christianity. How could one give credence to a cardinal who
thus misled the world ? " Igitur de caetero non est credendum
eis." According to the author (or authors) there were three
reasons why the cardinals seceded from Rome. Urban justly
desired to show more favour to the King of England and less
favour to the King of France; he also wanted the cardinals to
change their ways of life, and, lastly, he compelled them to live
in accordance with the Christian faith and not against it, as had
been their custom. The reference to the vision of an Augustinian friar should also be mentioned. This monk, whose name
is not given, had written to England—to whom is not said—
three letters, which, he claimed, were dictated by the Holy
Ghost : the first concerned the government of the country,
the second related to the reformation of his order in England,
and the third showed how during mass Prignano was shown
in the Eucharist to be the true pope. The monk had accordingly admonished all the faithful to adhere to Urban and, in
conclusion, he stated that Clement was unworthy of being
pope, since he was a " man of blood ", because he had ordered
the killing of several people and was the leader of warriors.
   Whilst the cardinals did not deem the first document worthy
of a reply, the second was taken so seriously that they issued
the *Responsiones ad Rationes Anglicorum*.[1] These answers all
betray the characteristic style and touch of the Avignonese
   [1]Edit. by Baluzius, ii, 895–915, together with the main texts.

cardinals. Each of the *rationes* was singled out for a special reply, though these *responsiones* contain nothing that was new.

Despite the grave dangers to which the Clementine propaganda was exposed in England, Clement and his cardinals never ceased to give up hope of gaining some support there by skilful management of their missions. Clement was probably unaware of the decision of Gloucester when he entrusted the Cardinal of Poitiers with the mission to England and, in a Bull addressed " to all the faithful in Christ " of 18th December, 1378, announced that he was sending " to the realms of England, Ireland and Scotland, Guy, cardinal priest of S. Croce in Jerusalem " (the Cardinal of Poitiers). Clement recounted in the same Bull " the circumstances whereby, on the death of Gregory XI at Rome, last March, the cardinals, the present pope being one of them, entered the conclave and —owing to the violence of officers of the city and the terrible uproar of the people—were compelled to intrude into the holy apostolic see a certain Bartolomeo, then Archbishop of Bari, who, being blinded by ambition, presumes to call himself Pope Urban VI " ; Clement commends the Cardinal of Poitiers " to all the faithful and warns, exhorts and commands them to show him due obedience and reverence. Otherwise the pope will ratify the sentences of the cardinal against those who oppose him or rebel against him."[1] In another Bull, issued on the same day, addressed to the prelates and clergy, secular and regular, " throughout the realms of England, Scotland and Wales ", Clement VII orders them to provide Guy with 50 gold florins a day, and grants the cardinal himself the right to exact the sum of 50 gold florins from prelates and other clergy as his daily procuration.[2] Another 58 Bulls were issued simultaneously to the Cardinal of Poitiers, in which truly vast powers were conferred upon him.[3] The cardinal was, to all intents and purposes, pope in England.[4] Ironically

[1] *Calendar Papal Registers, Letters*, iv. 228.

[2] *Ibid.*, 229, 230.   [3] *Ibid.*, 228–36.

[4] He had the power to convoke general councils (231), to negotiate peace between England and France, to grant indulgences, to make provision of any benefices, secular or regular, to absolve offenders from excommunication (234), to deprive adherents of Urban of their benefices (235), to hear and terminate all civil and criminal causes brought before him.

enough, with all these powers bestowed upon him, the cardinal was not even able to procure an assurance of safe conduct from the English King—with the result that he never set foot on this island. But Clement VII was undaunted by this miscarriage : his optimism did not allow him to admit this palpable defeat, and, in succeeding months and years, emissaries carrying the Clementine banner tried their luck in this country, always meeting with the same fate, i.e., imprisonment. Two of these embassies are especially interesting, the one in the summer of 1379, and the other as late as 1384.

The Gascon knight, Jean Chamberlhac, in the company of Bernard de Aula Viridi (de Couvert), a citizen of Aquitaine, set out to obtain the conversion of England to the Avignonese party. Their activities came to an end when they were thrown into the Tower of London and charged with committing high treason and rebelling against Urban VI by adhering to " Robert the anti-Pope, misguided by heretical wickedness ".[1] Upon the intervention of the Bishop of Dax (Aquensis), investigations were made, as a result of which the king issued a writ to the constable of the Tower on 10th April, 1380 : mainly through the testimony of the said bishop, who knew Bernard well—the writ declared—it had been established that at no time did the accused adhere to Clement, the anti-pope. The king thereupon ordered the constable to release Bernard immediately.[2] Six weeks later Chamberlhac, too, was set free after having furnished caution money.[3]

The second case worthy of mention concerned William Buxton, a Dominican friar who had become titular Bishop of Maragha in Persia. Once again, Clement chose an Englishman to try his luck and it appears that this friar sincerely believed in the legality of Clement's position, having been misled by the Cardinal of Albano at the court of Avignon. Upon his

---

[1] *Foedera, loc. cit.,* 98.

[2] *Calendar Close Rolls,* vol. i, p. 301, membr. 10. He became later counsellor of the French king, see Valois, *op. cit.,* vol. iv, p. 248 note 3, after having been emissary for Clement, Valois, vol. iii, p. 179 note 6.

[3] *Cal. Close R.,* vol. i, p. 386. membr. 1d.

arrival towards the end of June, 1384, Buxton was immediately arrested on a charge of treason against the statute of Gloucester. After imprisoning him in Blackfriars the English informed Urban VI of the new attempt at " subversive activity " and the friar had to await the pope's decision as regards his fate.

The official report of the proceedings against William Buxton has been preserved.[1] According to this document, entitled " Instrumentum super examinatione fratris Willelmi Buxton, schismatici, coram rege et aliis facta ab archiepiscopo Cantuarensi ", the court met on 19th November, 1384. Its members, Courtenay presiding, were the Duke of Lancaster, the Earl of Buckingham, John Montacute, the royal seneschal, Ralph, son of the Earl of Stafford, Thomas Montacute, a legal expert, Thomas Crocer, the rector of the Church of Bocking, and John Beauchamp, the king's equerry. The proceedings took place in an underground room beneath the King's Chambers at Westminster, in the presence of the king himself.

The trial was opened by Courtenay, who related that William Buxton had been taken prisoner by command of the king,[2] on the ground of his being a schismatic ; he had frequently slandered the one true Pope, Urban, and had, at the same time, tried to further the cause of the anti-pope Robert of Geneva. Thereupon the archbishop impeached William and asked him there and then whom he thought to be the true Pope, Urban or Clement, and whether he had preached in this kingdom. Buxton replied, unperturbed and fearlessly, sometimes interspersing his answers with phrases such as " Honour ye the King " or " Further ye brotherhood ". To the question itself he replied that he had not preached publicly that with which he was charged, but that he came tardily to England for the sake of the salvation of his own soul, in particular to avoid a mortal sin, and for the sake of the king's honour and the salvation of his country, so that he might inform the clergy and the people upon important matters.

Upon this evasive reply William was reproached by

[1]Wilkins, tom. iii, p. 191.

[2]Perroy is not exact in his brief review when he says that Buxton was imprisoned by command of the archbishop, see Wilkins, tom. iii, p. 191, col. 1 : " De mandato regis ".

Courtenay as well as by the king and the Duke of Lancaster who all tried to obtain, by " rationibus coloratis et fortibus argumentis ", a more definite reply. In the course of this cross-examination there arose a certain altercation. William was prevailed upon to speak freely, without quibbles and without subterfuges. He then said that, having heard, on the one hand, the story from the Archbishop of Cashel and other friends of Urban, and having read the opinion of John de Lignano, and, on the other hand, having been informed by the Cardinal of Albano and other cardinals on the side of Clement VII, he had come to the conclusion that Clement was the true Pope. William, furthermore, said that he would say this before clergy and people everywhere, and he then produced the written testimony of the Cardinal of Albano,[1] to which we will return shortly. Upon the retort of the archbishop that William should consider the fact that the cardinals had treated Urban as true Pope during their stay in Rome as well as in Anagni, where they could not maintain that they acted under compulsion, William replied that, if the truth of this could be proved, he would consider himself as condemned without any further trial. After further debate William declared that he would submit to the verdict of his judges. A discussion by William of the case itself was forbidden by the archbishop, in order to avoid any doubt being cast upon the statute of Gloucester, which was the law of the land. William thereupon objected to being tried by certain Urbanist prelates, but declared that he would willingly submit to the judgment of others. King and prelates then appointed a small committee consisting of the Bishops of Ely, Rochester and Salisbury, to conduct the trial, to which procedure William Buxton *gratanter* agreed. On the suggestion of the archbishop, the king " willed and ordered " that William should be kept in prison, until the Holy See had determined his further fate (Wilkins, iii. 192).

Besides these two cases there were, of course, a number of others reported more cursorily by chroniclers. One doubtful

---

[1]He may have produced the *Certificatio Collegii Cardinalium nomine Cardinalis Albanensis*, printed by Martène and Durand, *Thesaurus Novus Anecdotorum*, tom. ii, cols. 1128-9. The cardinal expressly refers to the query of William Buxton. The declaration is dated 23rd June, 1384.

case was that of Raymond Pelegryn, a citizen of Aquitaine, thus once again a subject of the king, who was arrested on 10th July, 1380, in Oxfordshire by an order of the king to his serjeant-at-arms, John Morewell[1], and thrown into the Tower of London ; his goods, too, were confiscated. But by 29th August, 1380, he was released[2] and later, on 24th January, 1381, instructions were given by the king to " restore to Master Raymond Pelegryn all his goods, chattels, beasts, corn, jewels, etc."[3]

In view of the influence exercised by Angelicus Grimoard, the Cardinal of Albano, and because of the confidence which some contemporaries, such as William Buxton, placed on his statements, it may be worth while to review briefly the activities of this cardinal, who had received his hat from the hands of his brother, Pope Urban V. He had preferred not to accompany Gregory XI on his journey to Rome and was one of the cardinals who had never left Avignon. Of the events during the election he was informed only by reports of his colleagues, who had been the electors. It will be recalled that he was a signatory of the letter which the Avignonese cardinals had sent to Urban offering him their felicitations and paying him homage. Furthermore, together with another cardinal, he also signed the letter of 3rd July, 1378, in which the garrison of St. Angelo was instructed to hand over the castle to Urban.[4] As late as 3rd July, then, this cardinal addressed the pope as *dominus noster*, as *sanctissimus pater*, and the like. Now this last mentioned letter was written when all the French cardinals had already settled at Anagni—the place chosen by them as a safe place. As soon as they had issued their famous *Declaratio* of 9th August, this cardinal joined forces with them and became one of the fiercest supporters of Clement VII. This quick and curious change of mind is certainly remarkable, since in fact nothing had happened to justify this swing-over : unlike the other cardinals, he did not even attempt a justifica-

---

[1]*C.P.R.*, i. 574.   [2]*Calendar Close Rolls*, i. 406.

[3]*Ibid.* On the very interesting mission of Aymard Broutin, called Talebart, and on his conversation with Richard II, see Valois, vol. iii, pp. 617–23.

[4]See Martène and Durand, *Thes. Nov. Anecd.*, tom. ii, cols. 1073–5, and Raynaldus, *loc. cit.*, p. 315, col. 1.

tion of his change of mind. The plea of the cardinals that they were forced to write letters favourable to Urban lost whatever force it ever had as soon as they arrived at Anagni ; their excuse for writing begging letters to Urban from Anagni, i.e., that nobody else should receive benefices, etc., may have the shadow of a despicable excuse : but they were in no way debarred from a free intercourse with their colleagues at Avignon. This is all the more revealing as it was precisely at this time that they were in touch with the French court. This particular instance only goes to prove our suggestion that effective steps against Urban were not contemplated before Charles V showed himself favourable to the rebels' cause. The most natural reaction would surely have been to inform the colleagues at Avignon of the " true state of affairs " as soon as the opportunity offered itself. The reasons which had prompted the Cardinal of Albano to go over into the camp of the rebels were not made public by him, but we may surmise that they did not differ so very greatly from those which motivated the other rebellious cardinals. His declarations, avowals and " confessiones " could not have failed to produce astonishment, even amongst his most uncritical readers. In the *confessio* issued at Avignon on 9th May, 1380, the cardinal, weak in body but healthy in mind, avowed that Clement VII was the only true, canonically elected Pope : not being a witness of the events in Rome, what value could he himself have attached to his *confessio* ? His declaration of 23rd June, 1384, makes still stranger reading. In it he related how he was asked by the Englishman, William Buxton, his opinion as to who was the rightful pope. The cardinal, seeing the bishop's painful state of uncertainty, replied : " We confess according to our conscience and we are anxious to state this before the Supreme Judge that we believe Clement to be the rightful and true Pope : he was elected by the unanimous consent of the cardinals of the Holy Roman Church and is consequently the only head of the militant Church and her pastor." A little later the cardinal maintained : " The cardinals have never elected anyone else since Gregory's death. And since it is a mortal sin not to believe what the Holy Father wants you to believe, we urge you, in this cause of God, if you want eternal salvation, to believe and to hold that the present Pope

Clement VII is the rightful Pope."[1] Nevertheless, all the persuasive powers of the cardinal failed to have the slightest effect upon the English attitude. It is difficult to estimate the misleading influence of these " confessiones " on the rest of Europe : chroniclers do not actually record any change of opinion as the result of this cardinal's persuasive efforts.

Whilst the rebel pope's banner was thus upheld by this cardinal, the cause of the rightful pope found a powerful ally in the English " arch-heretic ", as St. Thomas More once called Wyclif. To him Urban was a providential confirmation of his charges against the papacy. The cardinal in the camp of the rebels—the heretic in the fold of the pope, assuredly an ironical combination of circumstances. Fate had played into Wyclif's hands. Although during Gregory's lifetime there was no marked antagonism between him and Wyclif— on the contrary the latter was favourably inclined towards this pope and viewed his return to Rome as a favourable omen —after his death he became the target of Wyclif's most vituperative outbursts : a " horrible fiend ", an " abiding heretic ", meeting his death without the slightest sign of repentance for his devilry, favouritism and butchery of thousands of victims—there is no need to dwell on the stream of abuse poured upon the dead Gregory XI. The violent reaction against the dead pope was caused by his promulgation on 22nd May, 1377, of the Bull to the University of Oxford,[2] of the three Bulls to the Archbishop of Canterbury and the Bishop of London[3], and of the letter to King Edward III.

[1]Baluzius, tom. ii, cols. 915–20.

[2]Forbidding the dissemination of Wyclif's erroneous teachings ; ordering the arrest of Wyclif and his delivery into the hands of the Archbishop of Canterbury.

[3]In one Bull the pope ordered that if Wyclif cannot be arrested, they should cite him to Rome within three months after the English publication of the Bulls (Walsingham, i. 349). In another Bull the order of arrest was repeated, but here the pope declares that they should also try to obtain a confession from Wyclif, which should not be made known to anybody and forwarded to the pope personally ; Wyclif was to be kept in prison until his further fate had been decided upon. It is interesting to note here that the pope expressly cancels the provisions of Boniface VIII as to the arrest and imprisonment of clerics, see Walsingham, i. 351.

The pope did not mince his words in his condemnation of the heretical character of Wyclif's doctrines—but by a coincidence of events most favourable to Wyclif these Bulls were published in England at a time when they were far less harmful to him than they would have been if their publication had not been delayed. It was not until 18th December, 1377, that Sudbury and Courtenay considered the publication of these Bulls advisable.[1] In the meantime Edward III had died, parliament had been dissolved and the danger of a serious quarrel between England and Rome appeared to have diminished. The University of Oxford was duly informed of the other papal Bulls by the two prelates who issued instructions to the University to investigate whether Wyclif had actually spread the incriminating theses and, furthermore, to tender a citation to Wyclif to appear before them at St. Paul's in London within thirty days. It is not difficult to see that the prelates had considerably modified the pope's demands, which expressly ordered the arrest of Wyclif. Oxford arrived at a compromise : not wishing that an English subject should be arrested by command of the pope, the congregation ordered the house arrest of Wyclif at Black Hall.[2] As to the theses themselves, the Oxford Masters declared that " they were true though they sounded badly to the ear."[3] Wyclif scorned the citation for St. Paul's, and it is possible that he appeared at Lambeth before the papal commissioners. By the intervention of the king's mother the court at Lambeth was prevented from passing judgment upon Wyclif and his theses.[4] But even this shadow trial—for what else was it, if the court was not allowed to pass a condemnatory sentence ?—was brought to a speedy end : citizens of London had *impudenter*[5] broken into the chapel

[1] See Workman, vol. i, p. 305.

[2] *Continuatio Eulogii*, vol. iii, p. 348. The text of the resolution is given by Workman, vol. i, p. 306. See also the decision as given by Mansi, in his *Sacrorum Conciliorum . . . Collectio*, tom. xxvi, cols. 721–2.

[3] Workman, *loc. cit.* ; Wyclif was not at all pleased with this decision and retorted that Catholic truth should not be condemned because it sounded badly.

[4] Walsingham, i. 356, says that she " (pompose vetantis) ne praesumerent aliquid contra ipsum Joannem sententialiter definere."

[5] Walsingham, *loc. cit.*

at Lambeth, where the bishops and Wyclif had gathered ; the citizens violently supported Wyclif, so that the latter— a *pseudopropheta et verus hypocrita*—once again escaped his judges.[1]

Before any effective steps could be taken, Wyclif was once more favoured by fate. The " horrible fiend " died on 27th March, 1378. There was no decrease in the Londoners' esteem of Wyclif, nor did the crown show any cooling in its affection for him whose counsel it would soon need, and Oxford University was as little inclined as before to condemn one of its members. The violation of sanctuary rights in Westminster Abbey on 11th August, 1378—the infamous Hauley-Shakyl affair—brought the conflict between Church and State to a head and inflamed the passions of the populace to such a high pitch that an open breach between Rome and England was considered, at the time, as more than an academical possibility. That it did not occur was partly due to the moderating policy of Sudbury, partly due to the preoccupation of the country with a very difficult financial situation and with the Duke of Lancaster's adventures. The news of the election of the Archbishop of Bari was warmly welcomed by the " arch-heretic ". In the elevation of the Italian he perceived a providential sign that his charges against Gregory XI were approved by God. Little imagination was needed on the part of this zealot to attribute all the corruption at the papal court, all the avarice and bribery of the cardinals and everything he thought abhorrent in the papacy, to its complete dependence on France and on the French monarchy. Now the advent of an Italian, who would not go back to Avignon and who appeared to have the firm intention to reform the ecclesiastical hierarchy, would eradicate all the evils from which the papacy had been suffering in recent years. No better proof of Wyclif's feelings can be adduced than his letter to the pope, in which he offers his apologies for not going to Rome : Gregory's citation, it must be borne in mind, was not cancelled and Wyclif was still under the papal injunction to appear personally before the pope.[2] The importance of this letter justifies its literal translation:

[1]Walsingham, *loc. cit.*

[2]Although the *Fasciculi Zizaniorum* give the date of the letter as 1384, Workman (ii. 315) has put forward good reasons for dating the letter 1378.

" I am glad to reveal my faith fully to everyone, especially to the Roman pontiff, because I submit that, if it is orthodox, he himself will condescendingly confirm it, and if erroneous, he will correct it. Indeed, I submit that Christ's gospel is the body of the divine law, but Christ, who directly inspired the gospel, I believe to be true God and true Man, and that, in this, the gospel surpasses all parts of Holy Writ. Again I submit that, since he is Christ's foremost vicar on earth, the Roman pontiff be of all travellers most specially bound to that law of the gospel. For the majority of Christ's disciples are judged, not according to worldly greatness, but according to their imitation of Christ in their moral conduct. Again, according to the true spirit of the gospel I plainly infer that, at the time of His earthly life, Christ was the poorest of men, declining all worldly rulership. This follows from the gospel, Matt. viii. 20 and 2 Cor. viii. 9. From all this I deduce that none of the faithful should imitate the pope himself or any of the Saints, unless he were thereby imitating the Lord Jesus Christ. For, by aspiring at worldly dignities, Peter, Paul and the sons of Zebedee, brought that mode of imitation into disrepute : therefore, they are not to be imitated in their errors. From this I deduce, merely as a counsel, that the pope should deliver the temporal power to the secular arm ; and that thereunto he should efficaciously admonish the clergy. For in this way Christ has expressly acted through His apostles.

" If I should have erred in these matters, I am humbly willing to be corrected, if it need be by death. If I were free to travel at will, I would have liked humbly to visit the Roman pontiff. But God had forced upon me the opposite course : and He has always taught me to obey Him more than men. But since God has given our pope true evangelical instincts, we are bound to entreat that these instincts may not be exterminated by deceitful counsel and that pope and cardinals may not be moved to act against the law of the Lord. Therefore, let us beseech God, the Lord of everything created, that He may continue to inspire our Pope Urban VI as he has hitherto done, so that he together with his clergy may imitate the Lord Jesus Christ in their moral conduct and that they themselves may teach the people to imitate them faithfully therein. And let us pray from the depths of our souls[1] that our pope be spared malicious counsel, for we know that a man's enemies are of his own household, and that God will not suffer man to be tempted beyond his powers of endurance."[2]

As counsellor of the crown at the parliament of Gloucester, Wyclif was present at the English hierarchy's public denunciation of the cardinals' behaviour, and he appears to have warmly welcomed the spirit of reform which was to animate Urban's policy.[3] The Hauley-Shakyl affair was the chief topic of discussion at Gloucester, and Wyclif was called upon to give his opinion on the case. Wyclif, it appears,[4] in agreement with other doctors of theology, did not condemn the procedure adopted by the excommunicated Sir Alan Buxhill in killing Hauley during mass at Westminster : they urged that in this case there was no violation of the right of asylum, because Hauley and Shakyl were not criminals, but merely debtors who fled into the abbey to escape their creditors. Though no parliamentary decision was arrived at in this affair, it was nevertheless plain that Wyclif enjoyed the confidence of king and parliament alike. After this discussion on the rights of sanctuary, the legates of the two rival popes appeared : at once Wyclif found himself in the company of Sudbury—against whom he had argued only a few days before and who had excommunicated Buxhill in whose defence Wyclif rose. In *De Ecclesia*, the tract which Wyclif wrote before the end of the year, he sharply contrasts Gregory XI and his successor : the one is stigmatized as anti-Christ, as a simoniac and as a servant of the devil under whose regime all evangelical precepts had fallen into abeyance.[5] Urban, on the other hand, had revealed the crimes of Gregory XI to the faithful. In the warmth of his approval of Urban Wyclif even went so far as to declare him a man of the gospel, a humble servant of Christ, well fitted to carry out the necessary reforms within the Church. Clement VII was branded as the Vicar of Lucifer

[1] " Spiritualiter ", and not as Workman, i. 310, seems to read, " specialiter ".
[2] *Fasciculi Zizaniorum*, pp. 341-2.
[3] Cf. *De Veritate Sacrae Scripturae*, i. 407-8.
[4] Workman, i. 321.   [5] *De Ecclesia*, 366.

(p. 352), to whose adversary the English had rightly vowed their allegiance. In another tract, the De Potestate Papae, Clement VII was characterized as one ignorant of the law of Christ, a pugnacious, arrogant and licentious man (p. 223).

It would be perhaps an over-statement to term Wyclif's support of Urban enthusiastic—since Wyclif was always too hot headed to do anything by halves.[1] But it is undeniably true that Urban's election met with his warm approval, whilst Clement's intrigues and the Avignonese court life considerably strengthened his conviction of the worldliness and depravity of the contemporary papacy. That he was guided in his considerations more by religious convictions than by political motives is a conclusion which follows from a close perusal of his contemporary writings and which at the same time raises him above the level of his fellow countrymen, motivated as they were mainly by political antagonism to France, as whose pliable tool the Avignonese papacy certainly appeared to them.

This warm approval of Urban by Wyclif was soon replaced by an attitude of indifference and then, as a result of Despenser's missionary and military campaign at home and abroad, by one of open hostility to Urban and the cause for which he stood. In particular, the sale of indulgences by Despenser and others aroused the fury and the " most savage attacks " by Wyclif,[2] who ranked all those partaking in the crusade among the servants of the devil.[3] It is probably true that Wyclif at this time welcomed the Schism.[4] Both popes were " devils " and " anti-Christs " and only a general council of the Church could clarify the real position of the pope. Without any apparent knowledge of Wyclif, Gerson and d'Ailly arrived at the same conclusion, and their efforts, in common with those of Cardinal Zabarella, led to the Council of Constance, at whose commencement three popes claimed to be the true vicars of Christ.

The unquestioned authority of Urban in England and the equally unquestioned contempt for Clement are faithfully reflected in the English chronicles. Indeed, to judge by the

[1] Wyclif's enthusiasm is the keynote of M. Perroy, p. 67.
[2] Workman, ii. 82. [3] Cf. his De Cruciata, and De Dissensione Paparum.
[4] Workman, ii. 81.

reports of chroniclers, the English public was never properly informed of the details of the occurrences before, during and after the election in April, 1378. Urban enjoyed undisputed authority. Chroniclers, either deliberately or through lack of knowledge, painted a picture of the events in black and white without the necessary intermediate grey. In political as well as religious matters, everything and everyone associated with Clement appeared in the blackest shade, whilst Urban and his cause were given a halo of sanctity, purity and utter blamelessness. In short, Clement was the scoundrel, Urban the saint. And nowhere can we find the slightest doubt expressed as to the validity of Urban's election. For the English chroniclers and contemporary historians the very fact that he was unanimously elected was sufficient proof that the election had proceeded canonically : there was no mention of the intrigues before the conclave, of the discord amongst the Gallic cardinals, of the request of the city officials, of the fraud with the Cardinal of St. Peter, of the cardinals' flight from the palace, or of the tumult outside the conclave. On the other hand, these historians refer to the fact that the cardinals had assisted the pope after his coronation, and—if any explanation is attempted, as is not the case in Walsingham or the *Chronicon Angliae*—their secession was said to have been caused by the greediness and avarice of the cardinals, who were confronted with a strong and saintly reformer, resolved to make them renounce their former luxurious mode of life. A feature common to all chroniclers was the great emphasis they gave to the corruption of the court at Avignon and to the bribery and venality of the cardinals in particular. Urban was presented as a saintly pope deserted by wicked underlings.

A notable exception, however, is the *Continuatio Eulogii* (iii. 341). Its author explains that the defection of the cardinals was due to the alleged compulsory election of Urban. Without examining this plea in the light of the known facts, he continues by saying that the cardinals had robbed the curia of many valuables. Though not giving any authority for this possibly legitimate charge, the author maintains that the cardinals had sent a large sum of money to the French king. Whilst not reporting this transaction, Walsingham and *Chronicon Angliae* record a factor which must have considerably discredited in

English eyes the Clementines and the French aristocracy. They maintained that Robert was a blood relation of the French ruling house.[1]

As to the juristic refutation of the cardinals' plea, the author of the *Continuatio* brings forward a very interesting consideration. He records the view of *sapientes* (their identity is not revealed) that a papal election need not be free in every respect, so far as freedom in the canonical sense is understood. The Romans could very well have compelled the cardinals to a certain mode of action, provided that a just cause existed, because every community is entitled to exert pressure upon a superior for the sake of the common good and the public weal. Although the election might suffer from formal defects, the cardinals had no right to secede for this reason alone.

The story of this phase of the English reaction would be incomplete if we did not try briefly to review the all-important but vexatious problem of foreign prelates holding English benefices. We have already touched upon the intertwining of questions of nationality with those of ecclesiastical incomes : and we said that the statute of Gloucester gratified the English, not because it forbade the export of ecclesiastical revenues, but because it forbade their export to supposed enemies of the country. This irksome problem of foreign benefice holders certainly assumed a different aspect in later years, but at this time we can detect no hostility towards foreign benefice holders as such, but only to those whose nationality or inclinations associated them with England's enemies.[2]

This thesis can be corroborated by the policy pursued by England in the years immediately following the drastic measures of confiscation decreed at Gloucester. It will be recalled both that the king confiscated all the goods, revenues and incomes belonging to the seditious cardinals, and that, on 9th November, 1378, Urban VI addressed to the king a Bull in which he suggested confiscation of two thirds for the curia and that the remaining third should be left for the upkeep of the benefices. At first there was no reaction towards this Bull—after all, king and parliament had only just decided

[1]Walsingham, i. 382, *Con. Eul.*, iii. 213.

[2]It is a truism that the overwhelmingly French nationality of the benefice holders gave rise to the statute of *Provisors* under Edward III.

that these goods and incomes should be confiscated for the benefit of the king's treasury. But very soon there came a reversal of the policy initiated at Gloucester. On 6th July, 1379, the king issued a writ which was to change it entirely and to be the first step towards considerable concessions. In this writ (*Foedera*, iii. 87) the king recalled that, by the law of the land, the " benefices of all Gallic cardinals or of cardinals otherwise in any way adhering to our enemy France " were confiscated and handed over to the royal fisc. But later, the king continued, it had been made clear to him, by his ambassadors returning from Rome as well as by papal Bulls, that Urban VI proposed a distribution of their revenues at a ratio of two-thirds for the curia and one-third for maintenance. Now it is interesting to note that Urban's Bull of 9th November, 1378, gave no reasons for this somewhat unusual distribution of the revenues hitherto enjoyed by cardinals. In his writ the king expressly stated that Urban's demand was prompted by necessitous circumstances—" propter ipsius indigentiam ". Therefore, the king went on, since on the one hand he had very much at heart the needs of the pope and since, on the other hand, the confiscated incomes of the rebellious cardinals, the allies of France, were legally his property (*nobis sunt de lege*) and, furthermore, since the king was desirous to come to the help of the pope in " such a moment of need ", he had accordingly decreed " by special grace " that the papal collector might, without hindrance by royal officials or ministers, freely dispose, for the benefit and use of the pope, of the fruits of benefices formerly enjoyed by cardinals revolting against the pope and hostile to the king. The king expressly reserved for himself the supervision and administration of the goods. All public officials were instructed not to interfere with the activity of the papal collector, Cosmato Gentilis, or his subordinates who were engaged in the exaction of revenues. " This gracious concession ", however, was to come to an end by the feast of St. Michael, 29th September of the following year, 1380. On 14th July, 1379, Master John de Thelewall, a clerk, was given royal protection as deputy of Cosmato Gentilis.[1]

It must have been immediately after the receipt of this royal writ that the pope formally appointed Cosmato Gentilis

[1]*C.P.R.*, i. 374.

as his collector. For as early as 9th September, 1379, Urban issued his instructions to Gentilis :[1] all previous nuncios and collectors were recalled and removed, and Gentilis was made both nuncio and collector in one. Peter's Pence especially was to be exacted. The pope conferred upon the collector the plenary faculty and power to hear and to examine the accounts of collectors and sub-collectors and to compel payment of the dues by ecclesiastical censure without appeal, by excommunication, citation to the apostolic see, and invocation of the secular arm. Delay for more than two years was not to be tolerated, and accounts were to be rendered biannually.[2]

But the papal collector appeared unable to harvest all outstanding dues within the period allotted ; he consequently proposed to the king a prolongation of the time limit. On 18th September, 1380, the king issued a new writ, identical with his previous one as to the reasons and the extent of his concession, but which declared that, upon the testimony of Cosmato Gentilis, a trustworthy man, it had not been possible to collect most of the fruits by 29th September (*Foedera*, iii. 106-7). Since, as the king averred, owing to his " zeal of faith " and " his sincerity of pious devotion to the most holy father ", he was more than ever desirous to help the pope " who is sweating in these stormy times to steer St. Peter's bark, now being thrown hither and thither " by the waves ; consequently, in accordance with the advice and assent of the council, he decreed a prolongation of the time limit until Easter, 1381, with the same reservations and provisos as previously.

Upon the application of the papal collector the king decreed on 8th May, 1381 (*Foedera*, 118-9; *Cal. Pat. R.*, i. 546) that certain specially named prebends and archdeaconries should also be

---

[1]*Cal. Pap. Reg. Letters*, iv. 257.

[2]The powers of Gentilis were enlarged in the following year, 15th May, 1380 (*Cal. Pap. Reg. Letters*, iv. 258–9), when he was given faculty " to compel all preachers and publishers of the proceedings lately made by the pope against the anti-pope and his followers in England, Scotland and Ireland, to assign sums received and to be received to the society of Guinisii, citizens of Lucca, dwelling in London. . . ." As papal nuncio he had to admonish the archbishops of York and Canterbury to pay their triennial visitation-dues " in consideration of the needs of the camera ", *Cal. Pap. Reg. Let.*, iv. 262.

made accessible to the collector. This order was to expire on All Saints' Day, 1381.[1] A further prolongation was achieved on 26th February, 1382, when the king ordered an extension for a further period of two years, ending on All Saints' Day, 1383 (*Foedera*, 135).[2]

By royal warrant of 4th May, 1382, the customs officers and emigration authorities in the ports of Bristol and Southampton were instructed to let the papal collectors proceed without hindrance and to charge no duty upon the articles specifically enumerated in these writs.[3] These concessions to the pope

[1]To judge from the instruction given to the collector, the financial situation at Rome cannot have been too gratifying ; and it appears that the papal income from the English benefices was one of the main, if not the only, source of income. For on 18th February, 1381, Gentilis was ordered (*Cal. Pap. Reg. Let.*, iv. 262) " to pay and assign out of sums collected by him to Jacobus Matheoli (called Cachiatus), butcher, a Roman citizen, 1,000 gold florins of the camera, due to him for beef, pork and mutton for the papal palace and members of the papal household."

[2]See also *C.P.R.*(Richard II), p.108, membr. 21, and p.99, membr.28.

[3]*Foedera, loc. cit.*, 138. *Bristol:* The articles named were 6 pieces of green tapestry covered with roses ; one large curtain of serge of the same colour ; 2 blue-dyed bench covers of tapestry work ; 5 identical sheets and 2 blankets for one bed ; bed sprays of blue colour ; one big bed cover and 6 cushions for the papal chamber ; 5 pieces of bed covers for beds of deer skin colour ; 2 large long pieces of red cloth for the decoration of the papal chamber, as well as 2 of a smaller type ; 2 large pieces of red serge for the decoration of the hall bearing the arms of the pope, king and Church ; several bench covers for the hall of the same colour and material ; one piece of tapestry cloth, in red and black ; 5 cloaks of Irish cloth of various colours ; 3 covered beds complete with canopies ; some more pieces of cloth of various shapes and colours ; one coat of mixed colour, furred with vair, together with a sur-coat and hood, all lined with fur ; another mantle in grey with sur-coat and hood ; still another one of calaber ; one garment without arms, lined with fur and lambskin ; one fur coat ; several garments of Norfolk cloth ; and a number of caps and hoods of various sizes, cloth and colours ; and lastly 30 books and booklets. *Southampton:* 3 pictures of alabaster, one representing Mary, another St. Peter, and the third St. Paul ; a small picture of the Holy Trinity, kept in a cask ; old curtains and appurtenances of moderate value ; 6 large vases ; 24 chalices ; 24 patens ; 24 cups of larger sizes ; 13 candelabra of brass ; 3 baptismal fonts of brass ; 5 pairs of stockings ; 2 pairs of big carving knives.

himself were accompanied by concessions to the newly created cardinals. The drastic change which English ecclesiastical policy underwent so swiftly after the draconian statute of Gloucester, is perhaps best reflected by the new conferment of a great number of benefices upon Urban's own cardinals. And this reversal of policy only corroborates our thesis that *the confiscation of benefices belonging to Clementine cardinals was not, in itself, an anti-clerical measure, but one caused and conditioned by the nationality of their holders* and their antagonism, supposed or otherwise, towards England. As early as 23rd May, 1380, Richard II gave licence to the Cardinal of Alençon and his protectors to collect the profits (*Foedera*, iii. 99) of the archdeaconry of Exeter, the reason being that, in this case, the cardinal was a kinsman of the king and that he had always shown great affection and concern for the king and his country.[1] And, in 1381, when the archdeaconry of Suffolk became vacant through the death of its holder, the king conferred it, by request of the pope, upon the Cardinal of Alençon on 4th August, 1381. By licence of Richard II the Cardinal of Ravenna received the profits of the chancellorship of the Cathedral of Lichfield and a prebend at Chester within the diocese of Lichfield.[2] By royal licence of 20th June, 1380, the Cardinal of Corsica enjoyed the profits of a prebend in Stranshale in the diocese of York,[3] whilst by writ of 13th June, 1380, the Cardinal of Naples obtained the profits of the archdeaconry and treasureship of Dorchester in the diocese of Salisbury as well as the prebend of Coringham in the diocese of Lincoln ;[4] on 26th February, 1383, the same cardinal was able to add to his benefices the profits of a prebend in Sutton and of the archdeaconry of Taunton in the diocese of Wells.[5] The pope's relative, Cardinal Nicholas, drew profits from the prebend of Thame in the diocese of Lincoln, as from 6th July, 1380.[6] Cardinal Ranulph of St. Pudentiana was provided with

[1] *Foedera*, 99, *C.P.R.*, i, 497.
[2] This archdeaconry belonged to Cardinal de Vergne.
[3] *Foedera*, 101, *C.P.R.*, i, 497.
[4] *Foedera*, 101, *C.P.R.*, i, 501.
[5] *Foedera*, ibid., *C.P.R.*, i, 502 and 505.
[6] *Foedera*, 148.

the archdeaconry of Bath on 28th August, 1380.[1] Barely eight
weeks later, on 19th October, Cardinal Agapito de Colonna
was in possession of the profits of the archdeaconry of Durham,[2]
which formerly belonged to the Cardinal of Albano. The
latter's profits from the deanery of York went to the Cardinal
of Ravenna, who also received the archdeaconry of Durham
after Cardinal Colonna's death.[3] In all these cases the reason
given by the king was that the cardinal had proved to be a
devoted friend of England, for which friendship he merited
reward.[4] This list could easily be continued, since benefices
were granted throughout the following years.

[1]*Foedera*, 104, *C.P.R.*, i, 520.
[2]*Foedera*, *loc. cit.*, *C.P.R.*, i, 536.
[3]*Foedera*, 108, *C.P.R.*, i, 549.
[4]*Foedera*, 111. In a mandate to the chapter and canons of York,
(*Cal. Pap. Reg. Let.*, iv. 262), the pope orders them to assign to
Gentilis all fruits of the deanery, formerly held by rebel cardinals
and confiscated for the camera : from " certain frivolous causes "
the chapter and canons of York had pretended that these fruits
belonged to themselves, which was not true, the pope reminds them.

VIII

THE OPINION OF LEGAL EXPERTS

D W E L L I N G remote from the turbulent and exciting political arena, the jurists were less swayed by religious or political passion. Though showing a certain sense of loyalty towards the contemporary holder of St. Peter's chair, they nevertheless tried to guard themselves against adopting any spirit of partisanship. Two leading lawyers of the time gave their verdict on the burning question of the day ; both were laymen, neither of them was officially consulted by the pope, and both, quite independently of one another, arrived at the conclusion that Urban VI was the true canonical pope. The *Consilium* of Baldus de Ubaldis is of especial interest as it was written at a time when there was as yet no visible breach between pope and cardinals : it was written as early as July, 1378, but was not published at the time. The avowed purpose of the *Consilium* was to prevent a schism which threatened Christendom twice within the second half of the century, and also to prove by purely legal arguments that any attempt on the part of the cardinals to question the validity of Urban's election was doomed to failure. Another element which makes this first legal verdict so remarkable is that Baldus arrived at this conclusion on the basis of the facts as described by the cardinals.[1] Baldus wrote another *Consilium* in 1380, this time basing his opinion upon the presentation of the facts as supplied by Urban's *Factum*. The second of these lawyers was Joannes de Lignano, who also wrote two tracts, the one in 1379, the other a few years later—its date is not certain.

Baldus was, after the death of his illustrious teacher, Bartolus de Sassoferrato, perhaps the greatest jurist of the late fourteenth century. His fame and reputation attracted students from all over Europe, and his influence continued until the sixteenth century. Even Rashdall, who showed very little

[1] The *Factum Urbani* was not yet made public.

appreciation for the achievements of medieval jurisprudence,[1] was bound to admit that Baldus was " the most famous jurist of the day."[2] His juristic genius revealed itself already at the age of fifteen when he held a *Repetitio* at the University of Bologna.[3] He received his degree Juris Utriusque Doctor at the University of Perugia on 28th June, 1344, when Bartolus himself, this giant of juristic thought, was his *promotor*.[4] In the same year Baldus transferred to Bologna, where he became teacher, not only of civil, but also of canon law. It was at this University that he held a public disputation with Bartolus on 16th November, 1344, lasting over five hours.[5] He moved, three years later, to Perugia, afterwards to Pisa, Florence, Padua (1376-1379), Perugia and lastly to Pavia, where he died at the age of seventy-two years on 28th April, 1400. A devout admirer of St. Francis, he expressed the wish in his last will to be buried in a Franciscan Church. This wish was fulfilled and he lay buried in the Church of St. Francis at Pavia until the nineteenth century, when his tomb was removed to the Aula of the University. During his long academic life

[1] Rashdall, *The Universities of Europe in the Middle Ages*, ed. F. M. Powicke, vol. i, p. 258.

[2] Rashdall, *op. cit.*, vol. ii, p. 37.

[3] His brother, Angelus de Ubaldis, reports this astounding feature, see Angelus de Ubaldis, *Commentaria ad Digestum Vetus*, 3, 1, 1 : " Nota filium Nervae in XVII anno respondisse de jure publico . . . audio, quod Bartolus similiter fecit. Baldus in XV anno repetiit legem ' Centum Capuae '."

[4] Cf. Baldus, C. v, 7 : Bartolus dixit scholaribus in scholis : ego volo, quod pro nobis scribatis benedictionem, quam dedi domino Baldo, qui recepit insignia doctoratus A.D.1344 mensis Julii in vigilia SS. Petri et Pauli, see also Savigny *Geschichte des Roemischen Rechts im Mittelalter*, vol. vi, p. 214, and Angelus de Ubaldis, *op. cit.*, 12, 4, 4 : this passage in Roman law was one of the examination questions put by Bartolus to Baldus. Part of Bartolus's speech is transcribed by Panzirolus, *De Claris Legum Interpretibus*, p. 163.

[5] See Baldus, *Practica Judiciaria*, Rubr. De Quaestionibus circa appellationem. Qu. 1 : Praedicta disputavi in civitate Senarum anno, quo studium meum complevi et fui doctoratus: postea Bononiae ivi causa legendi. Et quia etiam illic venit Bartolus, ipso ibidem praesente . . . quaestionem disputavi, qui strictissimis articulis mecum bellavit ab hora XVI usque ad XXI die XVI Novembris A.D.1344, quo die a magnis doctoribus et scholaribus reportavi victoriam et honorem . . . unanimes doctores ipsi laudaverunt praedicta decisa et per me conclusa.

he naturally became the teacher of many famous jurists, amongst whom Pierre Beaufort de Roger, the later Pope Gregory XI,[1] and Cardinal Francis Zabarella, the great canonist at the turn of the century, were outstanding examples ; mention should also be made of lay teachers of civil law who once were disciples of Baldus : Paulus Castrensis, later professor at Avignon, Joannes de Imola and Franciscus Aretinus. In political respect he was an imperialist.[2] Baldus produced voluminous writings, not only on all parts of Justinian's *Corpus Juris Civilis*, but also on the *Liber Feudorum* ; moreover, there is also an important tract from his pen on the peace of Constance.[3] As he was also a teacher of canon law, he had an opportunity to write on topics of canon law, such as his *Lectura super decretalibus*, in which the first three books of the Gregorian collection are treated. The frequent consultation of this great jurist on many controversial legal points produced five large folio volumes in which his *Consilia* are preserved. Lastly, there are a number of writings on procedural points.[4]

It has already been mentioned that, during the critical period, Baldus was at Padua, and it was here that he wrote his important *Consilium*, in July, 1378, before the actual break had occurred. Urban VI requested the city of Perugia, where Baldus had betaken himself in 1379, to give permission for him to travel to Rome.[5] Here he wrote his second *Consilium*, in 1380,[6] and it was here that he met Joannes de Lignano.[7] It was quite obvious that the extraordinary weight which

[1] There is a report by Panzirolus, *op. cit.*, 1. 164, which bluntly states that Baldus was instrumental for Gregory XI's return to Rome from Avignon, but I found nowhere any corroboration of this report.

[2] Some of his legal and political theories are treated in my *Medieval Idea of Law*, pp. 51, 95, 103, 178.

[3] Contained in the so-called *Volumen Parvum*.

[4] Above all, his annotations of the *Speculum Judiciale* by G. Durantis, and his own work, *Practica Judiciaria*.

[5] See Vermiglioli, *Biografa degli Scrittori Perugini*, p. 124, where the decision of the Senate, 2nd July, 1380, is printed.

[6] The MS. of this *Consilium* is preserved in the Library of Lucca, see Vermiglioli, *loc. cit.*, p. 123.

[7] See Baldus, *Commentaria ad Codicem*, C. vii, 39, 2: " Dum ego essem coram Urbano papa VI cum domino Joanne de Lignano, eramus in verbis. . . ."

learned circles attached to the opinion of a jurist of Baldus's standing, did great harm to the cause of the Clementine party. Indeed, malicious slander soon became active : it was asserted—without any shadow of proof—that Baldus had later written a *Consilium* in favour of Clement VII's position. The originator of this slanderous attack was the Carthusian monk, Boniface Ferrer, who, like his fiery brother, St. Vincent Ferrer, belonged to the party of Clement VII. This alleged *Consilium* was never produced by any Clementine follower[1]—

[1]Boniface Ferrer himself did not say that he ever had seen the *Consilium* of Baldus in favour of Clement VII. This slander by Boniface was first produced in 1409, thus some 30 years after Baldus was supposed to have written the opinion favourable for Clement. Boniface Ferrer first mentioned this slander when he wrote his tract *Pro Defensione Benedicti XIII*, which was finished on 5th January, 1409. This tract is printed by Martène-Durand, *Thesaurus Novus Anecdotorum*, tom. ii, 1436–1529, and the attack on Baldus is in cap. 46, col. 1468. Here Boniface merely said this: " Sunt inventae allegationes contrariae factae ab eodem solemnissimo doctore super eadem vel simili quaestione infra duos menses vel tres, datae et cum sigillo proprio illius doctoris signatae, quod illa erat veritas cum copiosissimis allegationibus in utraque. Ita audivi, cum eram in Perusiis, de D. Baldo solemniore doctore juris utriusque quam esset in tota Italia, et de nonnullis aliis, forte obliviose et inadvertenter et non malitiose vel fraudulenter . . ." Boniface was full of hatred against the jurists (as he hated everything and everyone not Spanish) whom he charged with partiality according to the social standing and financial position of the parties concerned: when the parties were poor, he said, the jurists were ready with their answer and pompously declared: " Ista est veritas et absque omni dubio." But if the same juristic problem arose with wealthy and influential people, then the watchword was : " Ubi est majus periculum, ibi cautius est agendum." And what would have been plain and beyond any doubt in the case of poor parties, suddenly became difficult and intricate. " Et quae (scil. quaestio) prius erat indubia et clarissima ex parvitate personarum et rerum, nunc effecta est difficillima et intricata," cap. 46, col. 1467. And it was in this context that Boniface wanted to quote Baldus as a particularly good example for the " varietas, inconstantia et instabilitas naturae humanae in magnis clericis, doctoribus et juristis ". Nor did the medical profession come any better off in the tract of this zealot. The richer the patients, the more dangerous was the illness: the doctors of medicine paid due regard to the purses of their patients. " Idem omnino faciunt medici, qui secundum pinguedinem bursae infirmantium, aggravant infirmitates, et asserunt eas periculosas, non leves," cap. 47, col. 1469.

Effigy of Baldus de Ubaldis, in the University of Pavia

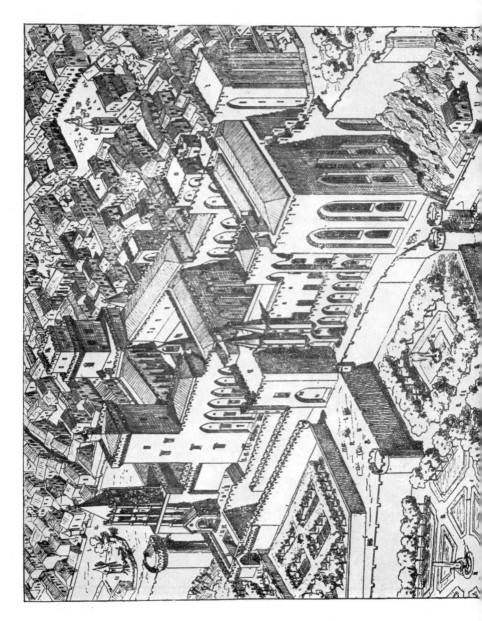

Avignon: The Palace of the Popes, about 1400
(*from " Album Historique, La Fin du Moyen Age ", by F. Lavisse and A. Parmentier*)

and what would have been more effective than to produce the actual document ? More than that : the Carthusian monk maintained that when Baldus was later confronted with this double-crossing, he was supposed to have replied : " Remember in whose territory I was staying when I wrote the *Consilium* for Urban."[1] This charge therefore implies that Baldus wrote whilst he was at one of the universities of the papal states. Now, it is a proven fact that Baldus, in 1378, was at the University of Padua and did not transfer to Perugia before 3rd November, 1379. But Padua was not in papal territory, and thus the remark attributed to Baldus lacks all foundation : whilst in Padua, Baldus was perfectly free to express his opinion, since this town was outside papal territory. Moreover, Clementine adherents never stated the reasons which led Baldus to assume the legality of Clement VII's position. Nor did they ever refer to facts : the whole charge was based on hear-say and rumours, without the slightest factual basis. There is no trace of any writing from the pen of Baldus for Clement VII— and surely the latter's followers would have given the greatest publicity to any writing of Baldus that would have supported their case ?[2] Panzirolus, who was favourably inclined towards Clement, did not even mention the slanderous statement of Boniface Ferrer ; on the contrary, Panzirolus stated that " Baldus luculento responso probat electionem Urbani nullo justo metu factam validam fuisse."[3]

The second of these lawyers belonged to the law school of Bologna. Joannes de Lignano is mainly remembered for what is called the first systematic treatise on international law,

[1] See Mansi in Raynaldus, *loc. cit.*, p. 321 note (1), quoting from Ferrer: " Narratur, quod dominus Baldus, quem opportuit deserere civitatem Perusii propter illas partialitates Italiae, et cum legeret duodecim aliis civitatibus Italiae et fuissent sibi ostensae allegationes contrariae per eum factae, in negotio primi schismatis, respondit : ' Considera, in cuius dominio eram, quando feci, et sic erit tibi soluta admiratio '."

[2] The profound researches of Noel Valois, *La France et Le Grand Schisme*, 4 vols., did not bring to light any incriminating evidence, see vol. iv, p. 76 note 2. It is therefore astounding that a judicious historian, such as Creighton, can reproduce the slander without however adducing one single proof in support of it, see Creighton, *History of the Papacy*, vol. i, p. 424.

[3] *Loc. cit.*, p. 161.

his *Tractatus de Bello, Repressaliis et Duello*, written in 1365. In politics he stood in the camp of the papalists, and was fiercely opposed to the imperialistic idea of the State.[1] In 1358 he was appointed professor of civil law at the University of Bologna, which professorship was followed by that in canon law in 1364. It was said that he taught also natural philosophy and that he had studied medicine and astronomy before he devoted himself to law.[2] He enjoyed great authority in ecclesiastical circles, as is evidenced by the fact that it was he, a layman, who gave the funeral oration for Urban V on behalf of the University of Bologna. Gregory XI appointed him there *vicarius generalis in temporalibus* in 1377. Amongst his pupils two canonists became very famous, the later Cardinal Francis Zabarella and Joannes de Imola. Lignano wrote a number of tracts on canonical and ecclesiastical topics, and commentaries on the *Decretals* of Gregory IX. His reputation was great—" interpretum juris pontificii princeps habitus est," says one writer on the medieval jurists,[3] whilst another calls him " summus et illustris capitaneus canonum et legum et philosophiae."[4] His two tracts on the Schism gave rise to a number of Clementine writings.[5] He died in 1383. In spite of the very favourable judgments by medieval chronologers, his illustrious pupil, Francis Zabarella, had formed an opinion on Lignano which, we believe, deserves mentioning, because it points out the weakness of this scholar very clearly. Zabarella thought that Lignano had studied too many things at one and the same time ; the result, as Zabarella not incorrectly observed, was a certain immaturity of judgment and shallowness of thought noticeable in all writings of Lignano. He had not the

[1]A few of his political ideas are treated in my *Medieval Idea of Law*, pp. 173 ff.

[2]See Panzirolus, *loc. cit.*, p. 344.

[3]Panzirolus, *loc. cit.*, p. 345.

[4]Quoted after Catellianus Cotta, *Tractatio de Jurisperitis*, in Panzirolus, *loc. cit.*, p. 526.

[5]The counsellor of the French king, Jean Le Fèvre, replied to Lignano in 1379 on the traditional Clementine lines. The title of his reply was *De Planctu Bonorum*, of which some MSS. are still extant (Vat. Libr. 4153 and 5668, and Bibl. Nat. 1469 and 1472, see Salembier, *Le Grand Schisme d'Occident*, p. 89 n. 1).

necessary detailed knowledge of the law and of its literature.[1]

Mention should also be made of a *Consilium* written by Bartholomeus Salicetus, yet another of the great jurists of the century, and a colleague of Joannes de Lignano at Bologna. But his *Consilium* is preserved only in manuscript.[2]

In the July of 1378 Baldus was asked, whilst in Padua, by a cardinal, whose identity he never revealed, to give his opinion on the legal position of Urban VI. He embodied this *Consilium* in his commentaries on the *Codex*,[3] where it was first published. This *Consilium* consists of two parts : the first reporting the facts, called the *punctum*, the second containing his own juristic opinion on Urban's position. Now, in appraising this juristic verdict one must bear in mind that Baldus wrote it before the cardinals had issued their famous *Declaratio* on 9th August, and, secondly, that he was supplied with the presentation of facts, which, only a short while afterwards, proved to be the Clementine version. Despite this, Baldus concluded that Urban was the rightful pope. The second *Consilium* was based on the *Factum Urbani*. It deals with certain improbabilities and incompatibilities from which the *Declaratio* suffers and then gives twenty reasons, purely legal, if not legalistic, why Urban

---

[1] See Francis Zabarella, *Commentaria in Clementinas*, Venice, 1602, fol. 2, col. 2 : " Subinde dominus meus multos ex praemissis in unum collegit, quos saepe nimium decurtavit, sed quod magis improbatur a compluribus, non apto retulit ordine, ita ut a paucis eius lectura commendetur et huic diligentia defuit, non probitas. Fuit enim omnium sui temporis longe princeps. . . ."

[2] The MSS. of this *Consilium* are, according to Fantuzzi, *Scrittori Bolognesi*, vol. vii, p. 278, in the libraries of Venice and Lucca ; another MS. is in the Vatican Library (Cod. Vat. 2660, fol. 240). Hitherto unnoticed by historians and legal historians are three *Consilia* contained in the collection of *Consilia* by Paulus Castrensis : they deal with the legality of a General Council convened by cardinals, i.e., pars i, *consilium* no. 419, fols. 216–7 (of the edition Lugdunum, 1548) by Castrensis himself ; No. 420, fols. 217–8, by the famous canonist Antonius de Butrio ; and, lastly, No. 421, fols. 218–218 *verso*, by Matthaeus de Matasselis, a civilian and pupil of the last-named canonist.

[3] See Baldus's *Commentaria in Codicem*, C. VI, fols. 117–121, also Raynaldus, *loc. cit.*, pp. 613–631. A slightly different version of this *Consilium* is in Abraham Bzovius, *Annalium Ecclesiasticorum Tomi XV*, tom. xv, pp. 62, col. 1–70, col. 2.

was the true, and Clement the false, pope.[1] As to the juristic value of the verdicts, the opinion of Baldus stands on a far higher level than that of his Bolognese colleague, Joannes de Lignano. The purely legal arguments are much more trenchantly put forward by the Paduan professor, although the tract by the Bolognese contains the more persuasive arguments and puts some very awkward questions to the cardinals.[2] Joannes's tract says more for the sincerity of his mind than for the correctness of his legal opinion, and exasperation at the division of the Church is more evident than the cool, dignified detachment of the juristic expert. He concludes his lengthy tract (52 folio columns) with an appeal to the cardinals to answer some of the embarrassing questions he had posed. He was, he stated, only a simple layman (" simplex laicus idiota ") and had not given his juristic opinion or asked them to answer questions because he wanted high honours or a fat living or any mundane favours, but simply because he wanted to set his mind at rest. His only purpose in writing his tract was to challenge the cardinals, in order that he might receive instruction in these matters.[3] Such was the naïveté (or the sarcasm ?) of Joannes, whose juristically valuable arguments we will set forth in conjunction with those of Baldus to which we now turn.

The legal issue was this. Did the fear the electors experienced invalidate the election ? That the cardinals consented to the election was never denied by them, but they maintained that it was through fear that they had given their consent. Now, argues Baldus, from their own description fear could not have had an invalidating effect upon their consent : if the fear had been as strong as they had made out, their immediate reaction would have been to raise a formal protest against such a procedure. The cardinals, said Baldus, were highly educated

[1]Raynaldus, Appendix, pp. 613–631. The first of Joannes's tracts is printed, in the form of an extract, by Raynaldus, pp. 318–21, and the second in his Appendix, pp. 631–57.

[2]One might be tempted to detect a certain partisan spirit in Joannes, whilst Baldus shows a striking degree of legal detachment. Baldus was an imperialist, whilst Joannes was a papalist, though in our present problem this political outlook cannot have affected their opinions to any appreciable degree.

[3]Raynaldus, loc. cit., p. 657.

men, holding the most dignified ecclesiastical offices, men who knew well the legal safeguard against fear. They themselves never said that they were so restricted in their movements that they could not have sent for a notary and two witnesses, as soon as circumstances permitted. This was the only way in which, from a purely legal point of view, they could express their dissension, a course surely familiar to them, trained as they were in legal practice and theory. But, Baldus continues, quite apart from this formal requirement, precisely on account of the cardinals' elevated position, they could not be judged by normal criteria applicable to the average man. Occupying as they did the highest offices in the ecclesiastical hierarchy they could not be presumed to have been intimidated by clamourings of the people outside the conclave. " Cardinals are not effeminate creatures easily intimidated by popular pressure." They are not " naturae fragilis et caducae."[1] Moreover, they must be presumed to have at least the same firmness of mind, courage, and fortitude as secular soldiers have who must not shun the danger of death.[2]

Both jurists point out that the assertion of fear made by the cardinals was incompatible with two unquestionable facts. The first was the solemn declaration made by all the electors when casting their votes that " the Archbishop of Bari be true pope ". This declaration was made when the cardinals were alone and could not be heard by the mob standing outside the palace. Moreover, these words were spoken, as Baldus said, in a deliberate and mature manner : one can surely not presume that words like these were uttered without due seriousness by cardinals, all honourable, extremely learned and wise men, " viri solennissimi et literati, utique boni et disciplinati ". So, if they had simply yielded to popular pressure, no explanation could be found for their declaring their intentions to make him " true pope ". On the contrary, these words

---

[1]Raynaldus, *loc. cit.*, p. 628, col. 1.

[2]" Praesumitur enim in eis et animi fortitudo et debent esse audacissimi . . . si enim in militibus saecularibus praesumitur animi magnitudo . . . scil. quod non evitant mortem pro republica . . . magis arbitrandum est de cardinalibus, quod non fragiles, et quod inter quaecumque pericula libere eligant, quod credunt expedire ecclesiae sanctae Dei ", Raynaldus, *loc. cit.*, p. 620, col. 2.

indicated a free election, as Lignano pointed out.[1] The second factor incompatible with their basic assertion was the alleged re-election of Urban. This fact, too, was not denied by the cardinals. Here again, the rule is that he who does something twice, or oftener, appears to will it and that he cannot construe anything against it afterwards. According to general legal principles, wherever a second consideration of the matter comes into play, full deliberation must be presumed. If, as they say, the whole election was staged, no reasonable explanation could therefore be furnished for the repetition of Urban's election.

Baldus declared that the description of events with which he was furnished not only failed to prove the case of the cardinals, but, on the contrary, enabled him to deduce their real motives in electing Urban. They had, Baldus said, examined the person and character of the man elected. Since, as Aristotle said, all men strive after the good and since, furthermore, the cardinals were intelligent men, they had elected him for the sake of the common good after due consideration of his merits. " It is impossible that he who has intelligence and judgment, cannot consent to that which he believes to be good." Could one really believe, Baldus sceptically asks, that the cardinals had willed something different from what they expressed in words ? " One would not even credit the most naïve of mankind with this." And if it were said that the cardinals did not believe that these words had any effect, reference must be made to the legal rule, namely that the mere belief that one's action is invalid does not necessarily render it so (D.29.2.96).[2] Furthermore, Baldus very rightly draws attention to the belated publication of the result of the election : the result was not published until the morning after the election. This undisputed fact shows quite plainly, Baldus observes, that they were afraid of letting the populace know of the election of the Archbishop of Bari ; they did not want to offend the crowds whose wishes

---

[1] Raynaldus, *loc. cit.*, pp. 640 col. 2, 642 col. 2, 654 col. 2.

[2] " Quis enim est tam insanus, qui arbitretur dominos cardinales aliud voluisse quam verum, aut aliter locutos esse quam de mente, quod etiam in vili homuncione credendum non esset . . . et si dicatur, domini non putabant ista verba valere, respondeo imo accidit, quod quis putat se nil agere, tamen valet, quod agit, ff. de acquir. haered., l. qui se pupillum." First *Consilium*, fol. 120, Nos. 13–14.

were not met. Speaking of the possibility that the nationality question might have been of some importance, Baldus maintained that the occupant of the papal throne should be considered neither as an *ultramontanus* nor as a *citramontanus* : these differentiations between various nationalities were unknown to God—" non erat apud Deum differentia nationum "—because He created all nations out of nothing : " quia ipse fecit omnes nationes de nihilo."[1]

Now, as Baldus very succinctly points out, it is very doubtful, apart from any previous consideration, whether the election of Urban can be said to have been brought about by fear : for the Roman people would scarcely have been enthusiastic about a man who, though born on Neapolitan soil, was wholly French by education, upbringing and outlook. His election, Baldus maintains, was merely a compromise ; the Italians voted for him on account of his Italian extraction, the French because of his manners and habits. The wishes of both parties had thereby been fulfilled.[2] When Baldus had the *Factum Urbani* before him he referred once again to this point, and said that the motives of the cardinals in electing Urban could be clearly discerned : they elected him because he was a *vir bonus, practicus et notus*.[3]

Joannes de Lignano devotes much space to the consideration of the exact degree of weight to be attached to the statements of the cardinals. He bluntly asks this question : " Can one believe the cardinals ? " " I reply by referring the question to their own consciences : they can be believed if they live a holy life, if they bear themselves like prophets, if they preach

[1] Baldus in the first *Consilium*, as printed by Bzovius, *loc. cit.*, p. 67, col. 1, no. 29.

[2] " Praeterea videamus, si iste dominus Urbanus debebat dici Italicus, quod si populus fuisset interrogatus de eo, qui sola nascendi causa erat Italicus, populo Romano nec gratus nec ingratus, an opinionem habuerit clamandi pro isto, cuius mores inter Gallicos sunt formati et qui nutritus est in Gallia et transformatus in mores eorum et de ipsorum appendicibus . . . non igitur iste fuit Italicus simpliciter, sed mixta ratione naturae et moris, electus, ut utriusque partis opinio salvetur . . . ex quibus apparet manifeste, quod domini ultramontani seipsos propter consuetudinem, et domini citramontani seipsos propter naturam considerantes, vota ad invicem miscuerunt." First *Consilium*, fol. 120 *verso*, no. 20.

[3] Raynaldus, *loc. cit.*, p. 628, sect. xxix.

in an apostolic manner, if they raise their voices in evangelical tones, if their labour is sufficient to meet with the approval of holy men."[1] It is worth while recording Lignano's own private opinion of contemporary cardinals, which he finds an opportunity of introducing at this point. Real cardinals are ministers of a divine and majestic hierarchy, but those (" hi ") who consort with the soldiery are pseudo-clericals who escape and shirk every difficult issue: here one can find haughtiness, pride, large households, magnificent horses, glittering harnesses, hunting falcons, a splendour of clothing unsurpassed by women : they celebrate pageants of superb meals and, veiled in hypocrisy, spend nights and days in drinking and sumptuously eating in their palaces, and make a cult of wealth and riches ; they promote not according to merit, but according to degree of kinship or of amounts paid ; therefore, many become impoverished ; here are leaders of the Church exploiting and strangling laymen, widows and orphans ; wholly devoted to worldly pursuits, betraying holy religion and dealing most tyrannically with humble and poor religious ; maliciousness is made a virtue ; they spread heresies by distorting Holy Writ with their logistics and juvenile sophisms and they elevate numbers of quite unsuitable individuals to the priesthood ; the filthiness of their vices and a mass of scandals sprout forth throughout the Church. Witnesses of such characters, Lignano concludes, do not merit credibility— " fidem non facient ".

Returning to the problem of fear, Baldus argues that even those cardinals who, according to their own statements, had not intended to vote for Urban, returned to the palace of their own free will and assisted in the performance of various ceremonies. They must be presumed to have reversed their intention. Moreover, any irregularity which may have occurred was remedied by the coronation, where no popular riots or clamourings were recorded or alleged by any one : here the motive of fear cannot have been effective, if ever it had been previously.[2] After all, says Baldus in his second *Consilium*, there must be some reason for a coronation: " Certum est, quod solemnitas coronationis supponitur pro aliquo, non pro nihilo."

[1] Raynaldus, *loc. cit.*, p. 636, sect. x.
[2] Second *Consilium*, Raynaldus, *loc. cit.*, p. 630, sect. xxxii.

And Baldus believes the function of a coronation to lie in that it takes the place of a confirmation. Even if, Baldus argues, the election were null and void, coronation would bestow the title of the position to be conferred, provided the individuals who perform the ceremony of the coronation have the power to do so.[1] The cardinals certainly have this power, Baldus says, but by no means have they the power to deprive the coronation performed by themselves of legal effects. It is possible, according to Baldus, that an individual can be enthroned by force, but he cannot be crowned by force, because the act of coronation entails many formalities and actions, and because every cardinal becomes active in it.[2] When the cardinals arrogate to themselves this power, it would be fitting to quote the law from which they derive it, Baldus counsels, and exclaims : " Adducant sacros canones eis permittentes hoc." But they can never adduce any law of this kind.[3] In this context Baldus comes to speak of another legal argument and says that during their stay in the castle of St. Angelo they had signed the document with their own hands, just as they had signed letters to the princes : it is an old-established legal rule, Baldus reminds the cardinals, that no testimony is admissible against signatures and official seals solemnly affixed to documents.[4] Apart from the fact that they sent petitions to the pope from Anagni, a safe place, they also received many privileges during their stay at Anagni. The cardinals, so Lignano declares, cannot even pretend to have acted from fear whilst in that place. And if they knew that Urban was not true pope, how could they suppose that he could validly confer upon them benefices and grants ? This latter point is also touched upon by Baldus in his first *Consilium*. Here he says that not every fear deprives an action of its validity, but only that which is the *causa*

[1] He continues : " Habetur loco confirmationis ; si vero nulla praecedit electio vel titulus, dat ex se titulum et habet vim collationis, dummodo investitens potestatem habet conferendi . . . sed cardinales habent potestatem conferendi pontificatum."

[2] " Nam potest quis inthronizari per vim absolutam sed coronari non potest per vim absolutam, quia coronatio habet in se multas sollenitates et unusquisque cardinalis ibi aliquid operatur et loquitur."

[3] " Sed numquam hoc invenient canonibus tantum, quod corona possit auferri de capite coronati per ipsos."

[4] Raynaldus, *loc. cit.*, p. 626, sect. xxiv.

proxima of the action in question. Now, although it is true that there was some *impressio* on the part of the Roman people, yet so far as the cardinals were concerned their election was free and deliberate : they failed to prove that the events outside the conclave had caused them to vote for the Archbishop of Bari. The election should not be annulled " sub velamento compulsionis,"[1] particularly with reference to the legal maxim that he who receives something from another has no right to make an objection alleging nullity : the cardinals received from Urban absolutions and graces as if from a true pope.[2]

Both jurists deal at length with the authority of the cardinals over the pope, and both reach the conclusion that cardinals have no jurisdictional powers over a pope : they cannot be accusers, witnesses and judges in one. No legal rule can be shown which would confer upon them any power in this respect. All disputes concerning intentions, motives and will must be decided by a judge : but who should be the judge in this case ? Certainly nobody else but a general council of the whole of Christendom ; this council could be lawfully summoned only by the contemporary holder of St. Peter's chair, that is, Urban VI.[3] The only passages in canon law upon which they might conceivably base any legal claim to judge the pope, are *Dist.* xxiii. 1, and *Dist.* lxxix. 9. The first merely gives cardinal bishops the power to elevate the elect to the papal throne. Nor is the second passage more relevant. As both jurists correctly interpret it, this merely states that if someone has been enthroned by bribery or favouritism or by popular or military upheaval, *without* previous canonical and concordant election, the man enthroned is not an *apostolicus*, but an *apostaticus*. In this specific case alone the law gives to cardinals, and to laymen also and God-fearing clerics, the right to proceed with anathema, and to depose the individual, if need be by

---

[1] First *Consilium*, fol. 120 *verso*, no. 4.

[2] " Et valde facit contra cardinales, qui ab Urbano susceperunt absolutiones et gratias tamquam a vero papa," first *Consilium, loc. cit.*

[3] " Omnis quaestio voluntatis in aestimatione judicis est (C. vi, 42, 7) ; quis ergo de hac causa cognoscere possit, non exstet, cum dominus Urbanus sit in possessione, nisi forte esset sacrum consilium totius mundi legitime congregatum, quod tamen congregari non potest, nisi per dictum Urbanum, qui est in possessione papatus et sedit super cathedram S. Petri." First *Consilium*, fol. 119 *verso*, no. 2.

force. Now, none of these legal requirements is fulfilled in the present case. If they had any jurisdictional powers, Lignano says, they had it, not on account of their own functions, but because derived from the pope. At the time, however, when they claimed this power, they also claimed that the apostolic see was vacant—consequently, they could not have derived any authority from a non-existing superior.[1] But even if a vacancy had arisen, the Sacred College had no jurisdictional powers. Baldus supports this opinion by a reference to *Clem.* I. iii. 2, which passage expressly lays down that during a vacancy the Sacred College cannot exercise papal jurisdiction, nor can the cardinals change the constitution of the Church.[2] In short, the cardinals could not be the *definitores justitiae* in their own cause, because they could have powers only in so far as the law conferred powers upon them. Baldus refers us to a commentary of Innocent IV (on *Decretales Gregorii IX,* v.40.23) in which this pope said that nobody could try or sentence a pope for any crime committed by him in any circumstances

[1] Raynaldus, *loc. cit.,* p. 637, col. 1.

[2] *Consilium primum,* as printed by Bzovius, *loc. cit.,* p. 64, col. 1. This was the view generally entertained, see, e.g., Joannes Teutonicus (wrote about 1215) in his gloss to *Dist.* lxxix, c. 7, and Joannes Andreae in his *Glossa ad Sextum,* v. 3. 1, fol. 134 *verso* : " Collegium cardinalium sede vacante non fungitur jurisdictione papae . . . dici posset, quod cardinales habent potestatis plenitudinem habitu tunc in quantum Romana ecclesia censetur, quae non moritur." Cf. also Joannes de Imola, *Super Clementinis* I, iii. 2. fol. 17 : " Vacante sede papali coetus cardinalium non succedit in potestate aut jurisdictione papae, nisi quatenus apparet expressum."

The main parts of *Clem.* I, iii. 2 were embodied by Pius X in his *Vacante Sede Apostolica* (25th December, 1904), I.i.§1, iii. §§ 1, 2; II.i.§ 29, etc.

It was a controversial point in the older doctrine whether all the cardinals formed the head of the Church in case of a real vacancy of the papal throne (death). The glossator Laurentius who finished his gloss about 1210 (see J. F. v. Schulte, " Die Glosse zum Dekret Gratians " in *Denkschriften der Kaiserl. Akademie der Wissenschaften,* phil. hist. Cl., vol. xxi, p. 69) maintained that the cardinals *obtinent vicem curiae* ; the Archdeacon (Guido de Baysio) in his *Rosarium,* Dist. 79, c. 7, declared that certain canonists " dicunt, quod cardinales sunt caput, quod non est verum ". Huguccio said that " cardinales funguntur vice capitis ". He finished his *Summa* 1188–90, see Kuttner, *Repertorium,* p. 158, and " Bernardus Compostellanus Antiquus " in *Traditio,* vol. i, p. 283.

whatsoever except those mentioned below.[1] Moreover, Baldus continues, canon law expressly states that nobody shall try a pope.[2] On the contrary, canon law lays down the dictum that in doubtful situations the man elected has to be held as pope—*Dist.* lxxix. 8. Thus, Baldus concludes this argument, " non habemus legem neque instrumentum legis in hoc casu."

These considerations lead Baldus to touch upon a legal point which shows that the question of deposing a validly elected pope has also aroused his interest. When writing the second *Consilium* Baldus does not seem to have had much doubt about the undignified and harmful impetuosity of Urban's behaviour. But Baldus, guided solely by legal considerations, and not by those of expediency or policy, reached the conclusion that there was no means by which a pope could be legally deposed from the chair of St. Peter.[3] The cardinals, says Baldus,

[1]There were, however, canonists who did not adhere to this point of view, though they certainly were in a minority. The famous glossator of the twelfth century, Huguccio (who died 1210, was a bishop of Ferrara and a teacher of Innocent III), wrote in his gloss on *Dist.* xxi, c. 7: " Sed ecce papa confingit novam haeresim, aliquis vult probare illam esse haeresim, papa dicit non esse haeresim, sed fidem catholicam, estne recipienda eius probatio ? Credo, quod non . . . . simplices et idiotae facile sequerentur illam haeresim, cum crederent non esse haeresim ; sed si papa committit simoniam vel fornicationem vel furtum et huiusmodi, sibi soli videtur nocere, cum omnes sciant, quod nulli liceat fornicari vel furari etc. Ego autem credo, quod idem sit (i.e., the same as heresy, see *infra*, p. 159); de quolibet crimine notorio papa possit accusari et condemnari, si admonitus non vult cessare."

[2]*Causa* ix, *quaestiones*, 13 and 14.

[3]Although this was the general opinion, there were some canonists, notably Huguccio, who held that the Sacred College could depose a pope, see the report of the " Archidiaconus " in his *Apparatus ad Sextum*, V.2.4, fol. 113 *verso*, no. 2.

The famous canonist of the fourteenth century, Joannes Andreae, denies the possibility of a deposition of a pope by the cardinals : since the papacy is, in his opinion, of divine origin, God alone is in a position to depose a pope. See his *Novella in Sextum*, I.7.1, no. 2, fol. 31 *verso* of the edition, Lyons, 1550 : " Papatus a solo Deo est, et quae a Deo sunt vel committuntur, ab inferiori tolli non possunt . . . papalem auctoritatem nullus conferre potest nisi Deus, ergo nec eam auferre . . . ergo remotio papae ab officio, quia papatus omnes dignitates excellit, per solum superiorem, scil. Deum fieri potest . . . nec papa nec tota universitas creaturae posset facere, quod non sit pontifex."

by their consent to the election of a certain individual as pope, thereby remedy every defect which would otherwise make the elect unfit or unsuitable for his office, even if he were excommunicated or a notorious concubinary priest or an infamous murderer. " The apostolic see either makes holy or it receives a holy man."[1] Accordingly, there is no doubt that the cardinals have it in their power to clear the candidate of all irregularities—except one, and that is persistent heresy. And even here, if this defect is *occultum vitium*, that is, not generally known, the cardinals have no power to cancel the election or to depose the elected man. Only when the heresy is notorious, so Baldus's argument runs, that is, when the fact of the pope's heresy has become *communis opinio*, can he be deposed, and not even then by the cardinals, but only by a general council (with a reference to *Dist.* lxxix. 8, and *Dist.* xxii. 5).[2] The pope is not, however, obliged to summon a council except in cases specified by the law, i.e., when questions of the faith itself are at stake.[3] This, Baldus declares, is the only

[1] " Nam quod volunt, efficiunt, etiamsi electus esset excommunicatus vel notorius concubinarius, vel notorius homicida, quia cathedra apostolica aut sanctum facit aut sanctum recipit."

[2] This was the common opinion, see, e.g., Bernardus Papiensis, in his *Summa Decretalium*, V, i, where he says: " Sunt autem quidam, qui omnino accusari non possunt propter excellentiam summae dignitatis, ut apostolicus et imperator, qui super se judicem non habent, nisi solum Deum . . . nisi in crimine haeresis." Identical was the opinion of Innocent IV in his *Commentaria in Quinque Libros Decretalium;* V, 40, 23, fol. 567, no. 2, and Joannes de Imola, *Commentaria in Decretales*, I. 33, 16, fol. 230, no. 3: " Licet papa sit maior omnium . . . tamen condemnari potest a concilio." Others went further and maintained that occult heresy, too, was a reason for deposition, cf. *Glossa ordinaria* ad *Dist.* xl, c. 6 (" Etsi occulta esset haeresis, de illa posset (scil. papa) accusari, sed de alio occulto crimine non posset "), Joannes Andreae, *Novella in Sextum*, V.2, 5, fol. 103 no. 2 (" Papa etiam de occulta haeresi potest accusari, 40 dist. si papa, et de tali occulto loquitur, quod probari possit . . . quandoque dicatur occultum, quod quinque sciunt "), and the " Archidiaconus " (Guido de Baysio) in his *Rosarium seu in Decretorum Volumen Commentaria*, ad *Dist.* xv, c. 2.

[3] " Non tenetur (papa) ad concilium convocandum, nisi in casibus expressis de jure, ubi de fide agitur ", with a reference to *Dist.* xix, c. 9. Baldus seems to have adopted, at least by implication, the prevailing view that namely in matters of faith the general council was above the pope. The glossator of the *Decretum*, Joannes

case, when a council can judge a pope : " Hoc enim solo casu concilium potest judicare de papa, quia de fide."[1] According to Baldus, then, there is no legal possibility of deposing an unsuitable pope, unless where matters of the faith itself are concerned : in this case alone a general council has authority to decide the pope's fate. Since this contingency had not arisen, canon law did not entitle the cardinals to proceed against the pope.

[1]Baldus carefully avoids the question—irrelevant in the present instance—of what is to be done if the pope refuses to summon a general council. According to Cardinal Zabarella, the illustrious canonist at the turn of the century, it was the emperor who was to convene the council. See appendix. The extreme papalist, Alvarus Pelagius, in his *De Planctu Ecclesiae*, lib. I, cap. 34, states that if the heretical pope should not abdicate, the cardinals may and should " ab eo recedere et alium eligere," because a heretical pope is to be treated as a private individual. According to Alvarus, no synodal sentence is necessary, though it may be advisable, because a pertinacious heretic is *ipso jure* deprived of all benefices. That proceedings before a general council are not necessary follows from the pope's plenitude of power which also comprises the power of the general council.

Teutonicus, wrote in his gloss to C. xxiv, q. i, c. 6: " Arguo, quod sententia totius ecclesiae praeferenda est Romanae, si in aliquo sibi contradicant " ; gloss to *Dist.* xix, c. 9 ; " Videtur ergo, quod papa tenetur requirere concilium episcoporum, quod verum est, ubi de fide agitur, et tunc synodus maior est papa." The " Archidiaconus " (Guido de Baysio) in his *Rosarium*, on *Dist.* xix, c. 9, fol. 23 *verso*, no. 2, said : " Nimis periculosum erat, fidem nostram committere arbitrio unius hominis . . . et synodus causam fidei papae committit."

IX

THE CHARACTERS OF THE TWO CONTESTANTS

THE OFFICIAL position which Bartolomeo Prignano occupied in the curia in Avignon and his post of vice-chancellor at Rome[1] would not of themselves have equipped him to fill the vacancy caused by Gregory XI's death. Nor can our assumption be lightly dismissed that he could not himself have seriously aspired to the throne of St. Peter. That he was no cardinal would have been of less importance[2] than the fact that he was socially inferior to the cardinals, and was regarded as such by them. The traits of his low birth can be clearly discerned throughout his pontificate. His descent from a poor Neapolitan family was of the first importance for those cardinals who could boast of distinguished ancestry. Moreover, Urban's cultural background compared very unfavourably with that of his environment in Avignon and Rome. In all likelihood the cardinals appreciated the competency and efficiency of this *curialis*, but further than that their appreciation did not go : he was never considered as one of their own set. The very fact that he spent fifteen years in the service of the curia and was, all this time, hierarchically subordinated to the cardinals and, to a certain extent, socially inferior to them, largely explains Urban's mentality as it explains much of the cardinals' attitude towards him as pope.

The cardinals came from the upper classes, and they had all the advantages of close association with the ruling circles, especially of France. By upbringing, education, training and

[1] See *supra*, chap. II. On the importance of this office, see G. Mollat, *Les Papes d'Avignon*, pp. 318–25.

[2] Two of the Avignon popes were not cardinals : Clement V was Archbishop of Bordeaux, and Urban V was a Benedictine monk.

ecclesiastical position they were thoroughly versed in the usages of diplomatic intercourse, language and skill. This necessitates self-control in behaviour as well as in the written and spoken word. In short, theirs was the bearing of the grand-seigneur, where dignity, splendour, grandeur, nobility, combined with sagacity, shrewdness and calculation, designed to maintain a proper balance between the demands of self-interest and the exigencies of the Church. We shall look in vain for anything resembling asceticism or austerity—either in their own private lives or in their conceptions of their office. Grandeur is perhaps the best symbol of their mentality : surrounded by a magnificent entourage, living on princely incomes and exhibiting manners appropriate to their social standing, they necessarily looked upon their offices and functions as sources of worldly pleasure and preferred to distinguish themselves in mundane greatness rather than in spiritual and moral leadership in dealing with others. Ruthlessness was a feature common to all ranks of medieval society. The cardinals' disregard of the most primitive precepts of human morality, and particularly their disregard of the common people, was only the reverse side of the medal. To illustrate this we only need very briefly review the conduct of the future Pope Clement VII when, as cardinal-legate in February, 1377, he was personally responsible for the bestial slaughter of the citizens of Cesena, who had killed some of the Breton garrison. Robert, assisted by the English mercenary captain John Hawkwood, ordered all the citizens to lay down their arms.[1] Then, having made sure that the citizens were defenceless, he dispatched both his Breton and English mercenaries into the city, with strict orders to spare neither sex nor age. The massacre was indeed horrible ; the Bretons went wild, and slaughtered " most cruelly a wretched and harmless mass of people." The English, under Hawkwood, had more feelings of humanity than the cardinal, and advised the citizens to flee—if they could find a way of escape. The Bretons, on the other hand, behaved in an unspeakably cruel manner : they tore babies from the breasts of their mothers, battered them against the

[1]Raynaldus, *op. cit.*, p. 281, col. 1—p. 282, col. 1. This order was instantly obeyed. " His verbis confisi, Cesenates arma deposuerunt."

walls or killed them by strangling or stabbing, throwing their corpses on the thresholds of the houses. Men and women, young and old, were massacred in the blood bath, and as one of the chief reporters of the scenes, St. Antonin, Archbishop of Florence, states : " The streets were full of blood and corpses." The number of killed is uncertain ; the lowest estimate was 3,000, the highest 8,000.[1]

This was the deed of the man who, 20 months later, claimed to be the true pope and head of the Church. We shall certainly join in the condemnation of this butchery by John of Jenzenstein, the then Archbishop of Prague and imperial chancellor :[2] "Sed quod horrendum est auditu et lamentabile dictu, universos civitatis huius habitatores et incolas feritate sua crudeliter interemit."[3] This cold-blooded disregard for the fundamentals of human morality is in striking contrast with the attitude to life to be expected of a prince of the Church—and yet so very medieval. The arrogance of this man was stressed by all who knew him, and this feature very well accords with his personality in general. He appears to have been completely devoid of moral and religious scruples—yet never, as cardinal or pope, did his typical medieval dignity desert him. Such was the personality of this shrewd and insinuating man, this tall, handsome ecclesiastical dignitary,[4] always, in his bearing, an imposing, aristocratic figure.[5] Nevertheless, he was no more than a symbol of a society which had degenerated morally : he was no isolated figure in his fourteenth-century milieu, and the defects of his character are only the more

[1]The details are described by Raynaldus, *loc. cit.*, mainly on the basis of Antonin's report. Robert never even attempted to deny his personal responsibility or to put forward extenuating circumstances.

[2]See Eubel, *Hierarchia Catholica*, tom. i, p. 429.

[3]Cod. Vat. 1122, fol. 45 *verso*, Vat. Libr., quoted by Pastor, *op. cit.*, vol. i, p. 112 note.

[4]Muratori, *Rerum Italicarum Scriptores*, tom. xv, p. 920. Dietrich of Niem described him as fat, squat, but eloquent; see also Workman, *John Wyclif*, vol. ii, p. 59.

[5]He was a cousin of the French king ; his brother was the Duke of Geneva and his mother the Duchess of Boulogne. At the age of 26 he became Bishop of Therouanne and held the bishopric of Cambrai from 1375, see Salembier, *Le Grand Schisme*, p. 63.

glaring, because so particularly unbecoming in a cardinal or a pope. The same moral and spiritual decay can be observed elsewhere in his surroundings.

Wholly different was the personality of Bartolomeo Prignano; here there were none of the signs of decay exhibited by the " upper class ". His long service in the curia, his close association with the cardinals and his ensuing opportunity to observe them most intimately, were bound to have influenced strongly his opinion of their inner worth. The very fact that he rose so high in his official career speaks for his tenacity, industry, efficiency and ability. And no one was in a better position to judge Prignano than Dietrich of Niem : according to him, Urban was entirely free from the great vice of his time— simony, and he did not know what avarice was.[1] A recognized expert in canon law, modest, humble and just, never accepting gifts, but yet ever ready to listen to flatterers, such is Dietrich's description of Urban VI. He always appreciated the company of educated and cultured men and his mind was agile through constant study of the Bible and the canon law. Like many conscientious and reliable high officials, he was one of those who never idled away their time. Pomp and ceremony were alien to him ; when he travelled it was always without ostentation—a mule for him and a horse for his companion were adequate means of transport. He was, in short, an ascetic and austere man, devoted to his office and ecclesiastical function.

We need little imagination to perceive how the cardinals would regard Prignano ; no doubt, they recognized and valued his efficiency and labours, but on the other hand he was a mere *curialis* with neither a glorious ancestry to boast of nor even enough of the culture typical of his time to have enabled them to consider him as one of themselves. His attitude towards them was characterized by a curious mixture of servility and contempt. His intense religious fervour could not but make him despise the worldliness clearly manifested in the cardinals' conduct. Any respect for their dignity as cardinals was entirely lacking : officially and externally he recognized his inferiority, but internally he felt himself their superior, precisely owing to his zeal for spiritual and moral

[1] *De Schismate,* lib. i, cap. i.

issues, which his masters and superiors had long since ceased to consider of more than secondary importance. With some exaggeration we might well characterize the relationship between the *curialis* and the cardinals as that of the feudal servant to the feudal lord.

And now his totally unexpected elevation to the highest office within the Church put Prignano into a place for which his previous existence had afforded no preparation. His election was unquestionably a means to achieve a compromise between the three conflicting parties in the Sacred College. The *curialis* was elevated to an office through which he received the *plenitudo potestatis*—complete, uncontrollable, and unfettered mastery over his former masters. Few human beings, surely, could effectively adjust themselves to this situation, unless gifted with rarer qualities than Urban ever possessed. An ordinary human being, he no longer attempted to suppress his contempt for the cardinals, and this now manifested itself in an almost morbid self-assertiveness. In other words, his previous feeling of undeserved inferiority rapidly gave way to one of superiority, tinged with no small streak of vindictiveness. Dietrich's observation of his weakness for flattery is as accurate as it is corroborated by experience. This self-assertiveness can be seen in all Urban's relations with his cardinals. His undignified outbursts are typical of the man who is bent on asserting his worth by any means at his disposal, relying upon sheer power instead of the force of personality or of reason. These outbursts amply prove that he felt the necessity of convincing his subordinates that he was really master ; but they also show—and this, perhaps, is more pertinent—his need to use drastic methods to convince himself also of the fact. His rudeness to secular princes reveals the same traits and the same psychic mechanisms. And worse cases were to follow.

Precisely because of what he had observed at Avignon, and because of his own unworldliness, Urban was convinced of the need of ecclesiastical reform, particularly amongst the higher clergy, for he had himself seen to what depths the leaders of the Church had sunk. Hence his almost passionate zeal for reform—reform at any price and cost. There can be no doubt that the pope was earnestly bent upon introducing reforms, but when we come to look at those actually envisaged and carried out by him, we cannot but conclude, regretfully, that they were few and superficial. For that the cardinals should have only one course at meals, that they should lead more arduous lives, and the like, was certainly desirable, but there were other matters far more urgently in need of alteration. Nevertheless, these partially completed measures reveal both his tendency to self-assertiveness and his lack of any objective conception of reform. Moreover, the manner in which they were put forward was in any case tactless, and, considering the special circumstances, particularly calculated to exasperate and irritate the cardinals to a quite unnecessary degree. It is only too evident that, seeing in him merely their own creation, they strongly resented his brusqueness, pugnacity and tactlessness. From this point of view, Urban, for them never more than a mere *curialis*, sank even lower in their esteem. They considered these outbursts merely as the expressions of a coarse, uncivilized boor. The uncouthness of Urban's manners damaged his cause and lowered him in the eyes of the cardinals : the reply of the Cardinal of Amiens that the *archiepiscopellus* lies in his throat, and the bold retort of the Cardinal of Milan that three warnings must be given before excommunication, are but two examples of the scant respect of the cardinals for their master. To them all his rebukes and reproaches were the caprices of a pusillanimous official who, in their opinion, had speedily revealed himself as an unsuitable tenant of the papal office.

Urban's bad government as pope was the result, not so much of vanity, as is often maintained, but rather of his native incapacity to cope with the admittedly difficult situation, demanding as it did extraordinary capabilities which he certainly was far from possessing. Choosing to crush the cardinals' pride and vanity, he pursued as pope the worst possible policy. In short, the cardinals became convinced that they had made a blunder in electing Prignano. Having recognized this, they proceeded to withhold their allegiance from the unsuitable occupant of St. Peter's throne. A careful reading of their testimonies goes to show that the plea of a forced election was merely a pretext put forward to nullify their own lawful choice, and that the real cause of their secession was their conviction of his unsuitability. Our thesis is perhaps best corroborated by an almost identical situation only a few years later, to which we will now give our attention.

In no other field did Urban show his innate self-assertiveness more blatantly than in his relations with the kingdom of Naples. The early years of his pontificate saw the creation of a great number of cardinals, many of whom were quite unworthy individuals.[1] We have already referred to Urban's dealings with Charles of Durazzo, whom he made King of Naples and from whom he exacted a promise to hand over certain Neapolitan territories to his nephew, Francis Prignano. But as soon as the pope had conferred the Kingdom of Naples upon him, Charles clearly showed that he meant to delay the fulfilment of his undertaking. This aroused the wrath of the pope. Furious, and " blazing like a lamp ", as usual he disregarded the counsel of his own new cardinals who had cautioned him against forcible action against Naples. Nothing could stop Urban from going to Nocera, and once again the undignified behaviour of the pope made him an object of ridicule. Four times a day he went to the battlements of the castle in which he had taken refuge from the Neapolitan army and with bell, book and candle he solemnly excommunicated the besiegers. The cardinals—who, it must be borne in mind, were all of them of his own creation—saw themselves in the very same predicament as their seditious predecessors of 1378. Realizing the damage their master was inflicting upon the prestige and authority of the Church, they consulted a canonist of repute, Bartolino of Piacenza, as to what legal proceedings could be taken against a pope who showed himself incapable of governing the Church. Though canon law had undoubtedly not provided for such a contingency, the canonist, by subtle and sophisticated reasoning, concluded that it did allow the establishment of a council consisting of the cardinals to exercise guardianship over a pope incapable of ruling : to this council papal decisions would be submitted, before they were put into execution. Through someone's indiscretion, probably an information from the Cardinal of Manupello, Urban heard

[1]Dietrich said that he had heard Neapolitan ladies who knew the new cardinals say to their friends : " I hope I may see your husband a cardinal " ; see also Jacob, *Essays in the Conciliar Epoch*, pp. 30–1.

of this proposal and immediately interpreted it as a plot against himself. The cardinals he suspected, including the Cardinal of England, Adam Easton, were imprisoned, put in chains and tortured : confessions were extorted from them and admissions that they had conspired against Urban. All these cardinals, except Easton, afterwards mysteriously disappeared.[1]

Urban's self-assertiveness was now accompanied by a strong vein of sadism, as is shown by the primitive enjoyment he derived from the tortures of the old Cardinal of Venice. At the time fixed for the torture of this dignitary the pope stalked up and down the garden beneath the window of the cell in which the cardinal's torture was administered, reciting his office, according to Dietrich, to drown the old man's screams. But this cardinal had more dignity than his master, and each time he was flung against the ceiling, he cried out : " Christ suffered for us."[2] The pope's crime was adequately described by the Augustinian general, and cardinal, Aegidius of Viterbo, as " scelus nullo antea saeculo auditum."[3] The death in 1389 of Urban VI, " this small, stout man with a yellowish face,

[1] For a description of these events, see Raynaldus, pp. 481–3. The English cardinal was deprived of his hat and of all his dignities by Urban, but was restored to his rank in 1390 by Boniface IX, see Walsingham, *Historia Anglicana*, vol. ii, p. 197. It was upon the intervention of his king, Richard II, that Adam Easton was saved further humiliation, see Valois, *La France et Le Grand Schisme*, vol. ii, p. 116.

[2] He, together with his colleagues, suffered the death of a martyr, see Dietrich, *op. cit.*, lib. i, caps. 45, 46, 47, 50–3, 57, 60, 61, etc.

[3] Bibl. Angel., Cod. C. 8. 19, quoted by Pastor, *op. cit.*, vol. i, p. 137. Salembier, *op. cit.*, p. 110, makes the futile attempt to vindicate Urban for his treatment of these cardinals ; but he is rightly censured by Leclercq, who says that Salembier gives " une solution empirique imaginée pour dégager la responsabilité d'Urbain. Celui-ci donnait le spectacle affligeant de continuelles violences ", see Hefele-Leclercq, *Histoire des Conciles*, vol. vi, part 2, p. 1109. Cf. also Valois, *op. cit.*, vol. ii, p. 113, and, for reports, Dietrich, *op. cit.*, lib. i, caps. 41–4 (Dietrich was a member of the commission appointed by Urban to investigate the plot of the cardinals, see caps. 46, 47, 49, 50 seq.), Gobelinus Persona, *Cosmodromium*, pp. 300–1, *Chronicon Siculum*, pp. 54–5, and Muratori, *Rer. Ital. Script.*, tom. xviii, referring to the *Chronicon Regiense*, and Raynaldus, pp. 481–2.

this choleric individual, who became red with anger and hoarse with rage ", was no loss to the Church.[1]

Such then were the personalities of the two men who dragged the whole of European Christendom into an abyss of religious hatred, deepened by national animosities and rivalries. Can one wonder that masses of Christians not only doubted the very fundamentals of Christianity, but were also morally repelled by both the contestants ? Were the people at large in any position to draw the correct, though subtle, distinction between the papacy as a divine institution and the personal character of the actual occupant of the papal throne ? A tragedy the Schism certainly was. But did the tragic element lie merely in the two personalities, or did the Schism dramatically and symptomatically reveal some serious constitutional crisis ? Was the Schism a purely personal issue, or the manifestation of an idea ? To these questions we will try to give an answer in the next chapter.

[1]See Dietrich, *op. cit.*, lib. i, caps. 1, 9, 45, and also Heimpel, *Dietrich von Niem*, p. 207. His epitaph is in Dionysius, *Sacrarum Vaticanae Basilicae Cryptarum Monumenta*, Rome, 1773, p. 149 ; see also Muratori, *Rer. Ital. Script.*, tom. xxii, p. 196. For the memorial erected to Urban in St. Peter's, see Hefele-Leclercq, *op. cit.*, vol. vi, part 2, p. 1113, note 3.

CONCLUSION

THE OVERRIDING question which besets the historian is not so much, who is to be blamed for this disaster, but rather, why did it arise ? What was the cause of the Schism ?[1] That racial and national questions played an important role in the whole affair is only partly true : no doubt, at the beginning of his pontificate Urban VI correctly perceived his cosmopolitan mission, but it is equally true to say that questions of nationality became important only when the idea of a break had found a ready response. It was only when the cardinals saw that Urban would not abdicate that they turned to an unenthusiastic French king, and remembered their national ties with the French monarchy. The grouping of Europe around the rival popes was certainly based upon national animosities and alliances, or the advantages to be derived from adherence to the one or the other pope : but all that was *post factum.* The nationality question was not in itself a cause of the outbreak of the Schism : it became decisive when the break had already occurred, and the break was, in a sense, contributory to it. Thus we are thrown back to the question : Why was there a break at all ?

A second road to a solution that offers itself is to maintain that the wickedness of the cardinals would not admit of a pope sincerely bent upon reform. But, although this consideration had undoubtedly some bearing upon the secession of the cardinals, it must be kept in its proper place : it was merely contributory and ancillary to the eventual rupture. The further history of the Schism clearly bears out that the pontificate of Urban VI failed to distinguish itself by any real

[1]In spite of Noel Valois's statement that " la solution du grand problème posé au XIV siècle échappe au jugement de l'histoire " (*La France et Le Grand Schisme,* vol. i, p. 82), we will try to give an answer to this question.

reform measures. Urban's own nepotism in his dealings with Francis Prignano, his favouritism towards Neapolitan aspirants to the cardinalate, his mandate to Bishop Despenser, his private handling of the cardinals at Nocera, and many other items of a questionable character, prove amply that not a single step did he take in the direction of radical reform. The cardinals themselves could not fail to see that Urban's avowals of reform were not to be taken at their face value, since they themselves greatly benefited from privileges granted by Urban in open contrast to the repeated declarations of intended reforms.

The third way to explain the break would be to accept in its entirety the plea of the cardinals, namely, that Urban's election was caused by fear of the people. But this, beyond all doubt, is the weakest explanation of all. The weakness of their case has been so frequently demonstrated that any further refutation would be tedious. But another question arises in this context : Could the cardinals really assume that they would be believed ? Could they, on the strength of the facts known to all concerned, honestly believe that credence would be given to their later statements, which either wholly deny previous actions or palliate them by sophistical arguments ? Even the most uncritical observer must have noticed the inconsistencies and improbabilities of their claims. One can have little respect for the cardinals, yet their outstanding diplomatic abilities, their shrewdness and intelligence cannot be denied. Bearing all this in mind, we can only assume that they themselves could not really have attributed to the faithful the amount of credulity and fatuity which their statements about the election unquestionably presuppose in them. The haughty cardinals might certainly have credited the faithful with even less critical ability than they really possessed, but their declarations, memoranda and statements presuppose on the part of the faithful a really gross stupidity. Moreover, it was not the faithful as such who really counted, but the rulers and princes. Would the cardinals attribute this degree of stupidity to them also ?

This question can safely be answered in the negative. And this answer excludes any further doubt as to the legality and lawfulness of Urban's election. Urban was the rightful and lawful pope. But this still leaves unanswered the fundamental question, Why did the cardinals break away? Now to understand their ways of thinking we must try to align ourselves with them and put ourselves into their position. The election of Prignano was a stop-gap, brought about first to achieve some sort of compromise between the contending factions in the Sacred College itself ; to pacify the Roman officials and to avoid a protracted conclave in a city obviously not amicably disposed towards the cardinals ; and thirdly, because no better candidate was available at the time. Prignano was an efficient and reliable, but otherwise colourless official, whom they all knew and whom they expected to find easy to handle. He was for them, so to speak, a figurehead. But his overbearing attitude disappointed their expectations, and his behaviour proved repulsive to them. To all this must be added that the cardinals lacked just that degree of inner respect for Urban which was necessary to ensure obedience. Moreover, they demanded from him that he meet them with precisely that degree of respect and honour with which they were treated by former popes. Thus, they not only had little respect for him, but they also demanded more respect from him. The remark of Robert of Geneva on the occasion of one of the brawls between Urban and the Cardinal of Amiens inevitably comes to one's mind.

After their treatment of Urban in Rome and at Anagni, the cardinals cannot possibly have doubted that he was legally pope, that is, that he was pope officially, as formal head of the Church. But this formal recognition by no means implied an internal recognition of Urban's superiority. Pope though he was, they still thought of him as the Archbishop of Bari whom they had as a matter of form elected into this office, and who did not of course command their unquestioned obedience. To Urban, however, there was nothing merely formal—in this sense—about his election : he made it amply clear that he intended to be pope in the full meaning of the term. When we keep in mind this formal role assigned to him, and set it against succeeding events, we may well imagine that the cardinals became gradually convinced not only of having made a big blunder, but also of having elected a totally unsuitable head of the Church. Whether their conclusion was already justifiable, is of no concern : it suffices that they had this conviction—in which they would have been entirely justified a few years later. Thus we must keep apart the (objective) incapacity of Urban to be a ruler of the Church, which incapacity was fully established within a few years, and the cardinals' (subjective) conviction of this incapacity at a time when, as yet, there was no sufficient justification for the conviction. Whatever few objective criteria they may have had during those few months, they were certainly strengthened in this conviction by personal considerations : to them it was unbecoming for a pope to live in a city of misery and poverty ; he should be surrounded by glittering splendour and the magnificence which could be found only in Avignon (and had they not already persuaded Urban's predecessor, Gregory XI, to return to the city on the Rhone ? The reasons for his decision to go back were no less cogent in the case of Urban) ; above all, a pope, in their opinion, should listen to the cardinals and should act according to what they thought best for the Church ; Urban, in particular, was to be merely a figure-head in the Church. Such purely personal considerations as these strengthened them in their conviction that he was unsuitable. A careful reading of their numerous statements abundantly bears out our assumption that what these were really trying to express was the *unsuitability* of Urban as pope. Perhaps this emerges most clearly in a statement of the Cardinal of Glandève.[1] This cardinal declared that Urban would have been pope if he had been prudent enough and known how to rule : " Certe si Barensis fuerit prudens et sciverit facere, poterit esse papa." A little later, in the same statement, the cardinal quite plainly expressed his opinion as to the unsuitability of the pope. They had recognized him as stupid (" habebant eum tamquam fatuum "); if he had been suitable— " si fuisset aptus "—he would have been acknowledged pope. " In no way was he apt to govern the Church " —" nullo modo erat aptus ad gubernandam ecclesiam "—and consequently they maintained " quod erat non papa." Not less illuminating is a statement by Cardinal Peter de Luna, the later anti-pope Benedict XIII.[2] He freely admitted that he had voted for Urban, but

[1] See Baluzius, vol. i, cols. 1079 and 1080 (ed. Mollat, vol. ii, p. 600).
[2] Raynaldus, p. 318, col. 1.

had later seen his mistake : " If he had not behaved in this manner, we would all still be with him, but he turned everything upside down through his violence."

Now, as canonists, they knew that a deposition of a pope by the cardinals was an impossibility. The only way out was to invoke the one regulation in canon law which gave them some faint hope of success, and that was *Distinctio* 79, *canon* 9 : the election of a pope under the impulsion of fear was null and void. But, quite apart from other considerations, there arose immediately the question : Who was to decide whether unjustifiable fear had caused this particular papal election ? And the cardinals maintained that the decision of this question lay in their own hands—a point of view which has no support in canon law. Having gone so far, they arrogated to themselves the further right to depose the pope. This too was canonically illegal. All this must have been known to them, trained as they were in canon law. But the whole procedure had at least the semblance of legality, and that was sufficient for them.

Strangely enough, the conviction of the cardinals as to Urban's incapacity was proved right by subsequent events. Their original suggestion, however debatable it may have been at the time, later years proved true. This was a complication and a new situation which was insoluble on the basis of existing canonical regulations. The real problem which the Schism brought to light so clearly was this : What is to be done with a pope who is incapable of governing the Church ? Urban's incapacity was first only subjectively conceived, but later it proved to be objectively true. In other words, this problem concerned first the cardinals only, later the whole of Christianity. The fundamental character of the problem was the same in 1378 as it was in 1385, where no possible doubt about Urban's incapacity could exist. The same holds true of the legal position : there was no legal remedy to curtail or depose an incapable pope, and all the actions of the cardinals were illegal, considered from the point of view of positive law.[1]

The question underlying all contemporary discussion was

[1]With all due respect, Trevelyan's statement that the cardinals were " the most conservative body in Christendom " must be considered inaccurate, see his *England in the Age of Wycliffe*, p. 310.

therefore : How *ought* the law to settle a problem of this magnitude ? The question was not one *de lege lata*, but one *de lege ferenda*. For, considering the immense papal power, the problem was indeed one which affected the whole existence of the Church : according to the strict letter of canon law and according to the constitution of the Church, a pope, once elected, enthroned and crowned, was beyond control of any power. Incapacity or any other defect which would have clearly been an impediment to the government of any secular ruler did not count in the case of a pope, concentrating as he did the spiritual, and partly also the temporal, plenitude of power over all Christians. However much this question was considered from the purely theoretical point of view, the law, as it stood at that time, did not provide for this contingency. What, therefore, *ought* the law to be ?

This was the crucial problem that confronted thinking men as soon as the incapacity of Urban was an established fact. Is it right that an incapable pope should have all this power ? —that was the problem besetting all scholars and thinkers who had the fate of Mother Church seriously at heart. All proposals to end the Schism concentrated on the solution of this problem. In other words, they were legislative and constitutional measures intended to modify the existing law. The Schism, stripped of its confused mass of details and facts, charges and countercharges, was a purely legal and constitutional problem. The actions of the cardinals constituted a revolt against the existing constitutional law of the Church ; this revolt took the form of a personal issue. The later writings—and actions— of theologians and thinkers presented proposals for a change in the Church's constitutional law. The cardinals initiated a revolution, the writers an evolution, with their idea that the pope should be under the control of a constitutional body. In most of the schemes which were later put forward, this body was to be a general council—that is why this ideological movement came to be called the " Conciliar Movement ".

Nevertheless, it was a fundamental axiom of canon law that the only legislator to promulgate binding rules was the pope. But now there were two popes— which of them could, then, issue binding rules, supposing he would have assented to a curtailment of his powers and to submitting them to control ? The history of the Schism shows that none of the popes—of either line—would even consider such a curtailment. Thus, from whatever angle one looked at the needed legal reform, the power which was to be controlled had first to give its consent and actually carry out the reform. And whatever proposals were made, they were palpably against the law and against the dogma—ironically enough, the Schism ended by a disregard for law and for dogma, for it was a council that put an end to the Schism and a council that was originally summoned by an indisputably illegal pope (John XXIII).

It was reflections such as these on the constitution of the Church which prompted Conrad of Gelnhausen, the Parisian theologian and later provost of Worms, to compose his treatise *Epistola Concordiae*, in May 1380.[1] This treatise marks a turning point in the history of the Schism, and we may well try to summarize its main contents. This letter was the first systematic exposition of what came later to be called the " Conciliar Theory ". In support of his postulate for a General Council, Conrad of Gelnhausen spared no pains to quote lavishly from the Fathers, such as St. Chrysostom, St. Augustine, St. Jerome, St. Isidore, St. Cyprian, and so on, as well as from such commentators on the canon law as Innocent IV, the *Archidiaconus* (Guido de Baysio), Hostiensis (Henry of Segusia), and Joannes Andreae ; nor did he omit to quote St. Bernard's *De Consideratione ad Eugenium Papam* and to refer to the *Summa* of St. Thomas Aquinas. There are two main lines of thought upon which Conrad's advocacy for a General Council rests. They are, firstly, a late fourteenth-century conception of the *ecclesia* and her relationship with pope and cardinals, and, secondly, an interpretation of canon law on the basis of extra-legal criteria. In other words, Conrad's conception of dogma and interpretation of law are the main pillars for his proposals.

He distinguishes clearly between the Church universal on the one hand, the pope and cardinals on the other. It is one of his axioms that the former is superior to the latter. For the Church founded by Christ Himself cannot deviate from her path and cannot commit any crime : popes and cardinals can commit crimes and are quite capable of deviating from their

---

[1] Contained in Martène and Durand, *Thesaurus Novus Anecdotorum*, tom. ii, cols. 1200–26.

prescribed path. A glance at the history of the popes confirms for Conrad that there were heretics amongst popes, such as Anastasius II, idolaters such as Marcellinus, and that even St. Peter committed a crime by denying his Master three times. Moreover, as St. Jerome once said,[1] the world is greater than the city—*orbis maior est urbe*. That the Church universal is superior to pope and cardinals follows also from the statement of Boniface VIII in *Unam Sanctam* that, namely, there is *nulla salus extra ecclesiam*. But there can very well be salvation outside the college of cardinals : " Salus potest esse extra cardinales et papam."[2] The Church is constituted by the pope *and* the faithful. The power of salvation no more rests with the pope than with the humblest layman. The pope is only a secondary head of the Church, her primary and principal head being Christ Himself. In spite of the Schism Christ still reigns over Christianity : the pope may die or be killed—and Christianity lives ; and even if there were no pope at all, the body and members of the Church would continue to exist : " Nihilominus corpus et membra vivunt."[3] In short, the congregation of all Christians is superior to the pope.[4] And every dispute must be submitted to a " superior " for jurisdiction. Consequently, the whole of Christianity is the only rightful judge who can terminate the present dispute.[5] Furthermore, the

[1] In the letter *Ad Evandrum*, see col. 1210.

[2] Col. 1208. Here, without referring to Ockham, Conrad uses precisely the same words as Ockham, see *Dialogus*, pars i, lib. 5, cap. 7 and cap. 10, p. 477, al. 61 and p. 481, al. 1, in Goldast, *Monarchia*, tom. ii.

[3] Col. 1215.

[4] This is in literal agreement with John of Paris, a forerunner of Marsiglio of Padua, in his *De Potestate Regia et Papali*, in Goldast, *Monarchia*, tom. ii, p. 139, al. 56. On John's theory cf. Scholz, *Die Publizistik zur Zeit Philipps des Schoenen and Bonifaz VIII*, pp. 275–332, Riezler, *Die Literarischen Widersacher der Paepste zur Zeit Ludwig des Baier*, p. 145, Finke, *Aus den Tagen Bonifaz' VIII*, p. 162, A. J. Carlyle, *History of Political Thought*, vol. v, pp. 422–37, and above all, Rivière, *Le Problème de l'Eglise et de l'Etat au Temps de Philippe le Bel*, Louvain (1926), pp. 281–300. On John of Paris's predecessor, see my paper, " A Medieval Document on Papal Theories of Government", in *English Historical Review*, 1946, pp. 180 ff.

[5] " Nec est in terris alius superior, ad quem in hoc casu haberi valet recursus," col. 1208.

whole of Christianity is torn asunder and the issues involved concern every single Christian and, therefore, " quod omnes tangit, ab omnibus vel vice omnium tractetur."[1] This way is not only the safest to arrest the spread of heresies, but is also in the public interest and for the good of mankind, in short *pro bono publico*. Whilst a provincial synod deals only with provincial matters, a General Council is concerned with affairs which are of vital interest to everyone. For Conrad, then, the Schism can be brought to an end only by the summons of a General Council to depose both popes.[2]

This proposal is not so new as might at first sight appear, Conrad is at great pains to show. In primitive Christianity the synodal system was quite a common institution : these early synods, in fact, prevented or healed schisms, heresies and the like. Although after Constantine the Great the general councils were not so frequent as before the official recognition of Christianity, there were nevertheless four great councils, according to St. Gregory, St. Isidore and Bede, that is to say, those of Nicea against the Arians, of Constantinople under Pope Damasus, of Chalcedon under Leo I, and of Ephesus under Celestine I.[3]

Yet the great obstacle to a convocation of a General Council lay in the law, as Conrad is well aware. Papal authorization of any General Council is the necessary prerequisite for the validity of its decrees and decisions. But who should convoke the Council, asks Conrad, since there are two popes ? And it is quite contrary to dogma that there can be two pontiffs. Neither of the two popes can say of himself that he enjoys

[1] The same phrase occurs also in Ockham's *Dialogus*, lib. 6, cap. 85, and *ibid*. " *Secundus tractatus*," lib. 3, cap. 6 (in Goldast's *Monarchia*, tom. ii, p. 604, al. 26, p. 934, al. 18). It should be noted, however, that the original phrase is contained in Roman law, see C.V., 59, 5, and was also used by Boniface VIII in his *Regulae juris*, regula xxix (*Sextus*, V. 12).

[2] The deposition of the pope by a general council was one of the main ideas of John of Paris, who saw in it the embodiment of the popular will ; he often used " people " when he meant a general council, see *loc. cit.*, e.g., p. 127, al. 5 and 10, p. 130, al. 37, p. 144, al. 57, p. 146, etc.

[3] Here the resemblance of Conrad and Marsiglio is striking. The latter also referred to these four Councils to prove the historical justification for the synodal system, see *Defensor Pacis*, Dictio Secunda, cap. 20.

Tomb of Anti-Pope John XXIII, in the Baptistery of Florence

FRANCISCVS · ZABARELLA
I. C. Pat. S. R. E. Cardinalis ↄ.

Cardinal Zabarella

undisputed authority in every part of the world.[1] Accordingly, one cannot say that there is a legitimate authority to sanction the convocation of a General Council. But Conrad somehow feels the weakness of his point of view, as the arguments upon which he bases his constructive proposals quite plainly reveal. For these arguments are all of an extra-legal nature, and he studiously avoids dealing with the positive law. If, he says, Paris were beleaguered by a hostile army and the king were away, would the citizens have to wait for the *licentia* of the king before they could lawfully rise against the attacker?[2] Neither for material nor for formal reasons is there any need for a papal authorization.

In this connexion another typical medieval argument emerges, the argument, namely, that it is lawful to resist an unjust ruler. Citizens, Conrad holds in agreement with medieval lore, are allowed and obliged to resist the government of a ruler who, instead of promoting, would destroy the unity of the citizens within the State. The ruler would not be resisted as a ruler, but as the enemy of the people. The Schism is, in the opinion of Conrad, a case like that of an unjust ruler, and it should be treated on the same principle : " Simili modo in materia proposita est censendum et posset haec solutio in simili declarari."[3] These ideas Conrad transplants to the field of ecclesiastical government. If, for instance, the pope persisted in heresy, proved incorrigible and would not consent to the convocation of a General Council, Christianity would be entitled to summon a Council *against the will of the pope*, who could and should be indicted in this Council.[4] The same applies to a pope who is a notorious criminal and whose papacy means scandal for the Church. This is the view, Conrad declares, of the gloss to *Dist.* 40, cap. 6. There can never be any

[1] " Nullus pro tali concorditer habetur, nec cuiquam ut papae ubilibet per Christianitatem paretur," col. 1213.

[2] Col. 1216.

[3] Col. 1222 ; the whole passage runs thus : " Nam etsi rex vel princeps vellet rempublicam et civium custodiam destruere et vastare, ad cuius conservationem et custodiam est deputatus, subditi possent, immo tenerentur, efficaciter sibi resistere. Nec se tunc opponerent regi, sed poenis, hosti et regni persecutori. Simili modo . . ."

[4] " Nihilominus posset et debet eo invito convocari, in quo et posset accusari et judicari," col. 1217.

papal authorization in a case like that envisaged by him. Furthermore, if all the cardinals had been killed during an election, or
had all died, no other way would be open to elect a new pope
except by a General Council : this, Conrad maintains, is the
considered view of such eminent canonists as Joannes Andreae
and Hostiensis. Thus, there can be a General Council without
papal authorization. The pope's consent to a General Council
is therefore not a formal requirement for its validity : " Non
est de formali ratione concilii generalis, ut per papam con-
vocetur."

It is quite true, Conrad argues, that positive law requires
papal authorization, but one cannot and must not take a
narrow and purely legalistic view in these matters by simply
relying on the letter of the law. For legislators are concerned
mainly with those issues which occur frequently: "Legislatores
frequenter attendunt ad ea, quae saepe et ut in pluribus acci-
dunt." It is impossible, he says, to lay down binding rules which
are suitable for every case : " Non fuit possibile regulariter
leges et jura condere positiva, quae in nullo casu deficerent."
Referring to the simile of St. Augustine that just as the soul is to
be preferred to the body, in the same way the sense should take
precedence over the words of the law, Conrad coins a phrase
which betrays his legal training, understanding and acumen,
namely, that the law is not made for the sake of words, but for
the sake of things themselves : " Nec verbis, sed rebus lex est
imposita." The true interpretation of every law must proceed
upon the Aristotelian basis of *epieikeia*, that is, of equity, which is
the only adequate criterion for a satisfactory explanation of
positive law. Equity is that element which is best fitted to discover the *mens legislatoris*.[1] Although it is still true to say that the
pope must authorize a General Council, there are cases which
the legislator could not have foreseen, and which therefore are
outside the precincts of positive law. One of these cases is
" casus noster, qui a regula est exceptus juxta mentem condi-
torum." This view is supported by a reference to *Dist.* 17, cap. 1,

[1] This term played an important role with Marsiglio, see his
Defensor Pacis, Dictio Secunda, cap. 12. Whether or not Conrad
borrowed the concept from Marsiglio, Conrad was at any rate
the first to apply it to the solution of this legal problem, see also
Kneer, *Die Entstehung der Konziliaren Theorie*, p. 52.

which says, *inter alia*, that " synodum congregare non potestis regulariter." Consequently, the legislator implicitly admitted that there are cases which are outside the general norm. And for these cases the law does not provide. They must be decided on the basis of generally valid principles. In conclusion, there is, according to Conrad of Gelnhausen, no legal obstacle to the convocation of a General Council without papal authorization.[1]

Akin to these considerations of the provost of Worms were those of another theologian of the University of Paris, Henry of Langenstein, who wrote in 1381 : " If the cardinals should have chosen a pope, *who does not suit the Church*, she has the right to revise the work of her agents and even to deprive them of her commission."[2] And : " The criterion by which

[1]How strongly Conrad was influenced by Ockham, may be seen from a comparison of the definitions of a general council as given by Conrad, cols. 1217-8, and Ockham, *Dialogus*, in Goldast, *Monarchia*, tom. ii, p. 603, al. 61.

Ockham : " Illa igitur congregatio esset concilium generale reputanda, in qua diversae personae gerentes auctoritatem et vicem universarum partium totius sanitatis ad tractandum de communi bono rite conveniunt, nisi aliqui noluerint vel non potuerint convenire."

Conrad : " Concilium generale est multarum vel plurium personarum rite convocatarum repraesentantium vel gerentium vicem diversorum statuum, ordinum, et sexuum, et personarum totius Christianitatis, venire aut mittere valentium aut potentium, ad tractandum de bono communi universalis ecclesiae in unum locum communem et idoneum conventio seu congregatio."

With Conrad one might detect a certain influence of Marsiglio's *pars valentior*, cf. his ideas on the composition and nature of a general council in his *Defensor Pacis*, Dictio Secunda, cap. 22. Neither Ockham nor Conrad stated who should convene the general council. Ockham, in a somewhat hazy manner, seems to think that it is the *universalis ecclesia*, cf. *loc. cit.*, e.g., pars i, lib. 5, cap. 84, p. 603, al. 23, 24, and pars iii, lib. 3, cap. 13, p. 829.

[2]Cf. *Consilium Pacis*, in v. d. Hardt, *Concilium Constantiense*, tom. ii, cols. 3 seq., but without the first two chapters, which are contained in Hartwig, *Henricus de Langenstein*, Marburg, 1857, vol. ii, pp. 28 ff. Henry's *Epistola Pacis* appeared very shortly after Conrad's *Epistola ;* there are excerpts of it in Bulaeus, *Historia Universitatis Parisiensis*, tom. iv, pp. 574 ff. As a vice-chancellor of the University of Paris he recognized Urban VI as a rightful pope as early as September, 1378, see also Valois, *loc. cit.*, vol. i, p. 123 note 2, pp. 356-8. About his importance for the University of Vienna, see *supra*, p. 92, n. 3,

all acts of Church and State are to be judged is whether they do, or do not, promote the general good. A prince," Langenstein continued, " who, instead of promoting the State, would ruin and betray it, is to be resisted as an enemy; the same course should be pursued in the Church." Cardinal Zabarella, a canonist of glittering renown, developed a similar line of thought.[1] Still more radical, however, were the proposals of Dietrich of Niem, who said that if the Church were in danger, she would be dispensed from the observation of the moral law. " The end of unity (*scil.* of Christendom) sanctifies all means : craft, deception, violence, bribery, imprisonment and death. For all law is for the sake of the whole body, and the individual must give way to the general good."

As a glance at the canon law confirms, all these proposals, however ingenious they may have been, were—from the point of view of positive canon law—illegal : it was only through what nowadays would be called a normative-teleological interpretation that theologians and canonists were able to deduce conclusions which seemingly harmonized with the spirit of the law ; no other than this extra-legal, meta-juristic method of explaining canonistic enactments, would have yielded the desired result.

The appeal to *epieikeia* was bound to fall on fertile soil.[2] In spite of some divergences, one element is common to all

[1]See Schard, *De Jurisdictione . . . Imperiali et Potestate Ecclesiastica*, Basle, 1566, p. 706 and the Appendix, pp. 190 ff.

[2]Nearly all supporters of a General Council referred to this panacea. Especially Jean Charlier de Gerson made great use of this idea, see also E. F. Jacob, *loc. cit.*, pp. 9–10, Valois, *op. cit.*, vol. iv, pp. 83–6, 229, 496–7. There was, it is true, some uneasiness about this kind of interpretation, as is clearly evidenced in the letter of the Patriarch of Alexandria, Simon de Gramando (Simon de Cramaud) to the Archbishop of Canterbury (in Martène-Durand, *Thesaurus Novus*, tom. ii, cols. 1230–61), in which the patriarch (at cols. 1255–6) advocates the deposition of the pope, though not strictly allowed by canon law, except for heresy, on grounds of the higher good for Christianity.

and about his views see also Mollat in *Cambridge Medieval History*, vol. vii, pp. 292 ff, E. F. Jacob, *Essays in the Conciliar Epoch*, p. 8, and Scheuffgen, *Beitraege zur Geschichte des grossen Schismas*, pp. 61–75, Aschbach, *Geschichte der Wiener Universitaet*, vol. i, pp. 371 ff.

these proposals : the restriction of the pope's plenitude of power and his subjugation to a body, be it the Sacred College or a General Council, which shall exercise control over his actions. But this trend of opinion was not only illegal ; it was, above all, against a fundamental article of Faith. And that is another strange phenomenon in the history of thought, namely, that measures palpably against law and dogma were thus propounded by canonists and theologians of the highest repute. Furthermore, not a single writing can be produced which would show that the illegal and anti-dogmatic character of these proposed measures was recognized. Anti-papalism became the watchword, defended by cardinals, theologians and canonists generally.

We may now briefly outline the dogma which was so openly violated and we may then ask : How can this change of opinion be explained ? The dogma was lucidly laid down by St. Thomas in his *Summa* (2ᵃ 2ᵃᵉ q.39, 1). According to him— and we may well add, according to the teaching of the Church —the unity of the Church is achieved, on the one hand, by the close interrelationship of the members of the Church and, on the other hand, through the subordination of all its members under one head. This head is Christ Himself, whose representative is the Roman pontiff. The primacy of the pope essentially consists in an omnipotent jurisdiction as regards everything spiritual. The pope is not a delegate of the Church, but her head divinely ordained. Consequently, everyone, including the cardinals, are subordinated to his power and jurisdiction. He, on the other hand, wields all power, precisely because he is the divinely ordained head and he cannot be subjugated to any body or power.

This dogma was fully expressed in the canon law also: the constitution of the Church, as set out in the canon law, does not allow any curtailment of the pope's all-embracing authority. As long therefore as there is no reason to challenge the power of the pope, this legal and constitutional principle works satisfactorily. But cardinals and others thought that Urban VI did not exercise his powers for the good of the Church. He was thus made a test case, not indeed in the sense that he created the problem, but that ideas which had been latent for a considerable time were at once thought to be applicable to this case. That brings us to the question which we have already asked, How can the change of opinion and temper be explained ?

Ever since the memorable quarrel between Boniface VIII and Philip the Fair, French political opinion had held that the pope must be curtailed in his powers. The most extreme exponents of this opinion were Marsiglio of Padua and Jean of Jandun, though they only brought to light ideas which were already more or less current in early fourteenth-century thought.[1] Applying his doctrine of the sovereignty of the people to the government of the Church, Marsiglio, in 1325, maintained that questions of faith are matters for a General Council and not for the pope. Moreover, the pope does not enjoy any supremacy in the ecclesiastical hierarchy ; his powers are derived from a General Council to which he is accountable for all his actions. Well may a distinguished historian write that Marsiglio's attacks upon the papacy " surpassed all preceding attacks in audacity, novelty and acrimony."[2]

Still more radical were the opinions of William of Ockham, who—in his system—hands the whole Church over to the Emperor : the pope was to be deposed by the Emperor, if he proved to be a heretic and if he involved the Church in a scandal. Neither pope nor a General Council is infallible. Infallibility is attributed to Holy Writ alone. Ecclesiastical institutions are merely expedients of policy and administration, but are not essential to Church government. Consequently, the pope is only an executive organ under the sway of the Emperor. Changed times call for changed institutions, is the keynote of Ockham's theses.

But apart from these extreme writers—to whom we might well add John of Paris and Michael of Cesena—there were some late thirteenth-century canonists who, long before the first anti-papalist writers came to the fore, propounded views on the curtailment of the pope's powers which were very similar to those so vociferously propagated by the publicists. Thus, Hostiensis (Cardinal-bishop Henry of Segusia), before

[1] See my paper, " A Medieval Document on Papal Theories of Government ", in *English Historical Review*, vol. lxi (1946), pp. 180 ff.
[2] Pastor, *op. cit.*, vol. i, p. 81.

1270, and Cardinal Johannes Monachus, about the turn of the century, taught that the pope should be ruled by the college of cardinals, that he therefore possessed no plenitude of power, and that decisions of the pope arrived at without consultation with the cardinals were null and void.[1] A great number of influential fourteenth-century canonists and glossators of the canon law accepted this point of view. Whether, however, these canonistic ideas were known to the publicists is a matter of conjecture ; in all likelihood they were not, but that these ideas had some influence on the cardinals of 1378 and on the theological writers of the time may well be presumed, although the writings of the publicists had gained far greater currency and were therefore far better known to men of letters than the somewhat recondite disquisitions of canonists. The former set forth revolutionary theories in a demagogic form, whilst the latter's views were known only to a limited circle of savants. The attacks against the papacy by the publicists were, for understandable reasons, answered by the popes with counter-measures.

The history of thought indicates that repressive measures against revolutionary doctrines can have only a delaying effect upon them. The very fact of their being propounded testifies

[1]Some of their theories are treated in the Appendix, pp. 206 ff. A close scrutiny of the relations between Boniface VIII and his cardinals would perhaps reveal tendencies amongst the latter not unlike those which led to the disaster of 1378. During the pontificate of Boniface VIII we find already the idea that an appeal should be made to a general council to protect the Church from the government of this pope : did not cardinals, such as Simon of Palestrina and Napoleon Orsini, try to persuade Philip IV of France to convoke a general council which was to sit in judgment on Boniface ? See Hefele-Leclercq, *Histoire des Conciles*, vol. vi, part i, p. 446. Moreover, were not the demands of Sciarra Colonna, put by him to Boniface VIII in Anagni during the assault, a clear indication that some prelates must have been implicated in the attack ? And an explanation may perhaps be found in the complaint of some cardinals that Boniface had not treated his cardinals with that respect which they had expected from him. On this suggestion, see Professor Henry G. J. Beck, " William Hundleby's Account of the Anagni Outrage " in *Catholic Historical Review*, vol. xxxii (1946), pp. 190–220, at pp. 201 and 211 note 18, and about the demands themselves, see P. Dupuy, *Histoire du différend d'entre le pape Boniface VIII et Philippe le Bel*, Paris 1655, p. 104, and p. 212.

to a change of tone and temper in society, perceived at first only by more sensitive observers. Though decades may pass before the revolutionary doctrines are accorded general recognition, very little can be done to check their career, and very few individuals appear to be immune from them—whatever the repressive measures applied. This truism can be clearly seen in the present case. Popes excommunicated revolutionary authors, and their writings were banned and burnt, but their mischievous doctrines spread. True, the views expressed by the few revolutionaries are usually handed down to the ordinary man in a diluted manner, so that what becomes later common property is merely a sediment or a residuum of the original idea. Whether as a direct result of the views set forth by Marsiglio and Ockham, or whether as merely echoing the general anti-papal tendencies of the age, cardinals, theologians and lawyers embodied these tendencies in their own thought. What cardinals tried to express, and what contemporary theologians did express, was anti-papalism pure and simple—anti-papalism, however, only in a restricted sense, in so far as the position of the pope as a leader with unfettered powers was no longer considered compatible with the function and position of the cardinals. They, in their turn, failed to concede to the pope the plenitude of power, and were desirous to govern the Church jointly with him. For the last seventy years they had taken a decisive part in shaping papal policy. And it was this attempt at a restriction of the cardinals' (unconstitutional) powers on the one hand, and the attempt at a strengthening of the (constitutional) position of the pope on the other hand, which makes the Schism understandable. Most significant in this respect is a casual remark of Cardinal Robert of Geneva, spoken to Urban in the heat of a dispute : "You are diminishing our authority and we will do our best to diminish yours." Bishop Alphonso of Jaën, whose deposition we have already reviewed, said as a witness before the tribunal sitting in Rome in 1379 that the cardinals had feared the loss of the supreme power they had enjoyed for so long.[1]

[1] "Cum cardinales intempestive dolerent supremum se imperium in ecclesiam universam, quo tamdiu erant potiti, amisisse," see the deposition in Raynaldus, *loc. cit.*, p. 380, col. 1.

The idea of controlling the pope's policy and actions became therefore determinative. The proposals of Marsiglio and Ockham aiming at a democratic government of the Church— all and everyone enjoying equal status—had been transformed into the idea of an oligarchic government of the Church, exercised by pope and cardinals jointly. Or, seen from a different angle, the cardinals of 1378 had adopted, without any explicit reference, the point of view as propounded by such eminent canonists as Hostiensis and Johannes Monachus. It was this changed opinion as to the relationship of the pope to his cardinals which was the underlying current of the Schism : this opinion was as contrary to law as it was in conflict with dogma, but neither of these defects was pointed out at the time. Nevertheless, the idea of an oligarchic kind of Church government was unfavourable to the idea of a more representative government, exercised for example, through a General Council and partly envisaged by Marsiglio and Ockham. Here is the reason why the cardinals, as the upholders of the oligarchic system, were never inclined to favour proposals for a General Council.

It is therefore necessary to distinguish between the early stage of the Schism and its final phases. The cardinals in 1378 were the protagonists of an oligarchic form of Church government ; this form of government found supporters only with the members of the Sacred College, as it was composed in 1378. But canonists, theologians and ecclesiastical writers who came to the fore in later years were as little inclined to adopt and propagate the cardinals' oligarchic system as the latter were to accept the Conciliar idea.[1] And, as the writers had a far greater influence upon shaping the minds of men than the

[1]Even as late as 1395 the cardinals on the side of the anti-pope, Benedict XIII, were still adamant in rejecting the Conciliar idea. This emerges quite plainly from the *Instrumentum* drawn up at Villeneuve, near Avignon, on 1st June, 1395 : all cardinals were asked which way appeared to them the safest, shortest and most practicable to end the Schism. And all cardinals—amongst them were the Cardinals of Florence, Amiens, Albano, Aigrefeuille, Pampeluna—replied that the *via cessionis* was the only method of bringing the Schism to a successful end. This *Instrumentum* is printed by Martène and Durand, *Veterum Scriptorum . . . amplissima Collectio*, tom. vii, cols. 466–72.

cardinals, it is understandable that the Conciliar idea gradually ousted the original oligarchic movement of the cardinals : this movement was then completely discarded and found no representatives.[1] Whilst, according to the cardinals, the *plenitudo potestatis* should rest with the pope and the Sacred College, it was the General Council, according to the later generally prevailing opinion, that should be the bearer of this plenitude of power.

It will be recalled that the first attempt to formulate the " Conciliar Theory " was made by Conrad of Gelnhausen in May, 1380. His *Epistola Concordiae* tries to prove that a General Council is necessary to establish the union of Christendom : he employs, as we have seen, all his dialectical acumen to make a case out for the convocation of a General Council, and that without papal authorization. It is from this date that the " Conciliar Theory " won adherents, so that, significantly enough, the acts of the Council of Constance contain no proviso for the Sacred College to act as a Council : power was given to the General Council, and not to the Sacred College.

Thus the history of the Schism and of the trend of contemporary thought (whose actuality coincided with the beginning of the Schism) shows that the existing constitutional and legal system of the Church was regarded by men as unsatisfactory. Considered in all its aspects, the Schism signified a crisis. And the strength of this crisis can be measured by the absence in this literature of any contemporary recourse to the traditional dogma, which theologians and canonists of the highest repute openly flouted. More than that : the idea that the dogma of the primacy of St. Peter was attacked in its most naked form failed to be recognized, since we cannot discover any theory

[1]This distinction between the two phases is usually not made, but it is, I think, necessary for an accurate assessment of the forces at work. The " Conciliar Movement " was but the offspring of the " Oligarchic Movement ". It is usual to present the whole trend of opinion, from the inception of the Schism in 1378 until its end, as the " Conciliar Movement ", see, e. g., McIlwain, *Growth of Political Thought in the West*, pp. 346–7, A. W. Dunning, *History of Political Theories*, vol. i, p. 258, and E. F. Jacob, *loc. cit.*, p. v : " The Conciliar Epoch is the period of the Great Schism and the General Councils of the Western Church (1378–1448)".

of the time which attempts to reconcile these heretical ideas with the teaching of the Church.

There is an observation which should not be omitted. The tendencies of ecclesiastical thinkers to curtail the pope's powers ran in a direction diametrically opposed to the tendencies which can be observed in the field of secular government. Whilst ecclesiastical scholars and thinkers were endeavouring to change the ancient constitution of the Church by basing her government upon a " broader basis ", secular scholars and thinkers were doing their best to strengthen the constitutional and legal position of the monarch, until, in the sixteenth century, there emerged the stark absolutism of the prince.[1] This sixteenth century was also the century of humanism, of the rebirth of ancient classical literature and art : the return to the classicism of antiquity became the hallmark of that age. The turn of the fourteenth and fifteenth centuries presents a similar attempt at a revival of " classical " institutions. For what else was the synodal system, so much trumpeted by contemporary theologians and canonists, if not a repudiation of papal authority and an avowed return to the primitive institution of a synod or a council ?

It was these illegal and anti-dogmatic views which eventually put an end to this European tragedy. The Council of Constance (1414) was, in the first instance, convoked by a pope who was to all intents and purposes an unlawful pope : Alexander V had been created pope by the Council of Pisa (1409), which was summoned by certain cardinals who had deserted the two rival popes, Gregory XII and Benedict XIII (Peter de Luna), and which Council declared both of them heretics and deposed them.[2] This Council of Pisa—the summoning cardinals were assuredly acting with the best of intentions—had, according to the law of the Church, no authority, because it was not summoned by papal order ; but it implicitly declared itself above the pope. A clearer instance of an illegal body

[1] I have tried to show in my *Medieval Idea of Law* that the absolutist tendencies current in the sixteenth century can be traced back to the middle of the fourteenth century, see pp. 54 seq., and 173 seq.

[2] The Council of Pisa deposed both popes, because they were " notorious schismatics ", see Mirbt, *Quellen zur Geschichte des Papsttums*, 4th ed., 1924, p. 227.

cannot be adduced. And yet, it was Alexander's successor, John XXIII, who, reluctantly yielding to the Emperor's demands, convened the Council of Constance. Accordingly, this council was summoned by a pope who lacked all authority to do so—deriving his powers as he did from an unlawful body. In order to prevent any further " lawful " session of the council, John XXIII fled from Constance under somewhat adventurous circumstances (20th March, 1415) and was " deposed " by the council some two months later (29th May, 1415). Thereupon Gregory XII, the Roman pope, stepped in : after promising to abdicate, he formally convened the council which had already been in full session and abdicated (4th July). This formality preserved the (further) legality of the council, which, in a lawful manner, disposed also of the third pope, Benedict XIII. It then elected Martin V, with whose election the Schism came to an end.

APPENDIX

CARDINAL ZABARELLA AND HIS POSITION IN THE CONCILIAR MOVEMENT

W E H A V E laid emphasis on the character of the Schism as a revolt against the existing constitution of the Church ; and we said that men came to consider the constitutional machinery of the ecclesiastical government as unsatisfactory for the solution of such a problem as the Schism. The proposals to end the Schism were, roughly speaking, of two kinds : that is, either of an ideological, extra-legal character, such as Conrad of Gelnhausen's *Epistola* or Langenstein's *Consilium*— a kind of literature we might classify as publicistic ; or, secondly, proposals in the nature of legal disquisitions— literature, that is to say, which tries to propound a solution that fits the existing law. To be sure, only the latter kind of literature could have any prospect of eventual success, however much more publicity was given to literary products of the first kind. But in an age of whose spirit the saying *nemo clericus nisi causidicus* is symptomatic, an age with whose character a great legal and constitutional crisis that touched the very foundations of the Catholic Faith was well in keeping, it is surely not surprising to find a constructive contribution to a solution of the burning problems of the day coming from a canonist : nor that it was this canonist's line of reasoning which, to a greater or lesser extent, was followed in the end.

The canonist was Cardinal Francis Zabarella, and his importance as the pioneer who paved the way for the Council of Constance is still not fully recognized. If any recognition has been accorded to him, it has been of a negative kind.[1] The cardinal is charged with adopting the well-known views of Marsiglio of Padua and William of Ockham, the obvious

[1]See Enrico Carusi in *Enciclopedia Italiana*, vol. xxxv, p. 858, following Pastor, *History of the Popes*, vol. i, p. 187, and A. Kneer, *Kardinal Zabarella*, p. 61.

hostility of whose ideas to the Church the cardinal was, apparently, unable to recognize.[1] Although F. J. Scheuffgen and A. Kneer have dealt, in a somewhat perfunctory manner, with Zabarella's opinions, they have represented his views as if they were just another product of the publicistic literature.[2] And we venture to add that it is this misrepresentation of the cardinal's theories which has given rise to the charge that he followed the heretical theories of Marsiglio and Ockham. None of the authors who have dealt with Zabarella's ideas has accorded him that position which he alone would have claimed, and which his contemporaries did accord to him, that is to say, high rank as a canonist—and not, what modern historians are wont to give him, as a publicist. No contemporary would have ranked him amongst the ideological and controversial writers. For this injustice committed against Cardinal Zabarel-

[1] See especially Carusi, *loc. cit.*, saying that Zabarella wanted to see the idea of the people's sovereignty applied to the government of the Church ; and Kneer, *op. cit.*, pp. 61–2. It is hoped that the following reconstruction of the cardinal's ideas will show that there is no trace of any " people's sovereignty " in his proposals : this charge could only be levelled by those who never took the trouble to study Cardinal Zabarella's thought and mode of his argumentation.

Ockham, perhaps the foremost of the exponents of popular sovereignty, stated that the pope is merely a representative of the whole Church : " Papa representat ecclesiam universalem et eius vices gerit, quia est persona publica totius communitatis gerens vices et curam," *Dialogus*, pars i, lib. 5, in Goldast, *Monarchia*, tom. ii, p. 494, al. 54–6. Cf., on the other hand, the statement of St. Thomas Aquinas, quoted *infra*, p. 221. Therefore, according to Ockham, the election of the pope should belong to the general council which is a truly representative assembly of the people, just like any other parliament, with which he compares the general council, cf. p. 603, al. 29. He even seems to imagine a general council " elected by the people ": this assembly does not need any further authorization. The members of the general council " vicem gerant totius communitatis aut corporis absque alterius auctoritate." Those elected in this way constitute a general council, " quia concilium generale non videtur esse aliud quam congregatio aliquorum, qui vicem gerant totius Christianitatis ; " therefore, the pope's authorization is not necessary. *Ibid.*, p. 603, al. 7–13, pars i, lib. 6, cap. 84.

[2] Reference is made to F. J. Scheuffgen, *Beitraege zur Geschichte des grossen Schismas*, Freiburg, Herder, 1889, and A. Kneer, *Kardinal Zabarella : Ein Beitrag zur Geschichte des grossen abendländischen Schismas*, Munster, 1891.

la's views—an injustice that necessarily entails a distortion of
his views—the two mentioned writers, the one a Catholic
historian, the other a Protestant writer, can chiefly be held
responsible.

At the turn of the century Francis Zabarella was the foremost canonist of the day, and his reputation was such that,
as Muratori reports the utterance of Michael Savonarola,[1]
without proper knowledge of the cardinal's writings no man
could have gained a degree in canon law : not to be familiar
with them would have proved the candidate an ignoramus.
And the Emperor Sigismund exclaimed, on hearing of Zabarella's death, " Hodie mortuus est papa."[2] The future cardinal
was born on 10th August, 1360;[3] he went at the age of sixteen
to the University of Bologna where he studied canon law under
Joannes de Lignano.[4] There he seems to have remained until
1385, when he transferred to Florence to receive the university's degree of *doctor utriusque juris.* Zabarella was, then,
witness, in his early youth, at the most impressionable stage
of his life, of the havoc wrought by the dual headship of
European Christendom. This impression of the disaster was
never to leave him. It broke through in his lectures on the
Sext and the *Clementines* which he gave as so-called *extraordinarius* at the age of twenty-five at the University of Florence.
The same impression can be gathered from his lectures on
the *Decretals* which he delivered after his appointment as
ordinarius at Christmas, 1386.[5] In 1391 he went to Padua

[1]Testimony of Michael Savonarola in Muratori, *Rerum Italicarum
Scriptores*, vol. xxiv, col. 1153 : " Tanta . . . ipsius scripta sunt
reputatione digna, ut quis decretorum doctor eis caruerit, veluti
ignorans habitus sit."

[2]Muratori, *loc. cit.*

[3]And not 1339, as Finke's researches have conclusively proved,
see Kneer, *op. cit.*, p. 45.

[4]See the passage transcribed by Schulte, *Geschichte der Quellen und
Literatur des Canonischen Rechts*, vol. ii, pp. 553 f.

[5]See Cod. chart. MS. lat. 5513, med. saec. XV in the National
Library of Vienna, fol. 200 : " Incepi legere Sextum et Clementinas anno aetis XXV 1385 in studio Florentino." Fol. 200 vo :
" Anno sequenti aetatis XXVI . . . tunc assumptus ad ordinarium
decretalium in sola lectura decretalium et sic habemus tres annos
completos," that is, autumn 1386–89. The difference between
professor extraordinarius and ordinarius is this : according to the

where, as professor *ordinarius,* he taught at the university for twenty years. Soon after his appointment as archpriest of the Cathedral of Padua, in 1397, he became the trusted legal adviser of two successive (Roman) popes—Boniface IX and Innocent VII—and then of John XXIII. It was the last-named pope who made him a cardinal in 1411,[1] although Zabarella had never received more than minor orders. The conferment of the cardinalate was probably an official recognition of his reputation as a canonist. Cardinal Zabarella was one of the ambassadors sent by John XXIII to the Emperor Sigismund to negotiate about the convocation of a general council. He died during the sessions of the Council of Constance, on 26th September, 1417 ; the whole council took part in his funeral. He now lies buried in the Cathedral of Padua. Amongst his pupils was Nicholas de Tudeschis, also called *Panormitanus* or *Abbas Siculus,* who became the great light of canonist scholarship in the fifteenth century.

The literary output of Zabarella consists of a huge commentary on Gregory IX's *Decretals* and also of a commentary on the *Clementines.* His activity as a public teacher at Padua made it inevitable that he was frequently consulted in all kinds of legal disputes, and his juristic replies are contained in a volume of *Consilia.* All his writings show a sound canonist scholarship, and in many cases a quite unorthodox approach to the problems arising out of various enactments in the canon law books. His literary output also proves him a man with whom the pursuit of serious canonistic scholarship was the dominant note of his whole life. Very aptly says one modern writer of him: " Mit Leib und Seele war er Jurist."[2] But he certainly was not one of those arid lawyers who clung only to the letter of the law ; quite on the contrary, he reveals in his writings an astonishingly wide knowledge of the theological and philosophical literature of his time ; he was also

[1] Eubel, *Hierarchia Catholica,* tom. i, p. 32.   [2] Kneer, *op. cit.,* p. 13.

---

curriculum in force at the medieval universities lectures were given on the *Decretum* and the *Decretales* in the morning ; as every student was bound to attend these lectures the professor was called ordinarius. The Lectures on the *Sext* and the *Clementines* and the *Extravagantes,* if there were any at all, were in the afternoon ; they were not compulsory and the professor was called extraordinarius.

well versed in the poets and historians. All his writings go to prove the strong impression which Florence, that citadel of the revived classical humanism, must have made upon him. Nor is it surprising to find reports which speak of the extreme kindness of this great teacher towards poor students at his university. His charity in personal relations was nothing but the concrete realization of the abstract idea of justice the scholarly elaboration of which is amply justified in all his writings. Charity and justice are virtues which epitomize perhaps best the character of the man and the scholar who was Cardinal Francis Zabarella.

That a man imbued with such a burning sense of justice and the desire to see the Church as a capable instrument of God's will could not stand aloof, indifferent to the sordid state into which affairs had drifted, is not indeed surprising. Having seen in his own youth how the cancer grew, he could not but devise his own remedy, and put forward his own ideas as to how best this miserable state where two popes contended could speedily be brought to an end. It was with this avowed intention that he wrote the now famous tract *De Schismate*. But before we enter into a detailed consideration of its leading ideas, it should be pointed out that this tract, as it is contained in the current printed versions,[1] consists, in fact, of three tracts, each written at different times ; the first probably finished on 30th December, 1403, the second under the pontificate of Innocent VII, and the third during the reign of Gregory XII. One part of the tract is to be found in the *Consilium* CL.[2] For our present purpose it will be sufficient if we rely on the version as given by Schard, and we shall analyse

[1] Schard, *De Jurisdictione, Auctoritate et Praeeminentia Imperiali*, Basle, 1566, pp. 688–711 ; it is also printed in Th. Niem, *De Schismate*, 1609, pp. 541–70, and inserted in Cardinal Zabarella's own *Commentaria in Decretales*, Venice, 1602, after *Decretales*, I. 6. 6, fols. 107–110 vo.

[2] I used the edition of his *Consilia*, Lugduni, 1552, CL. fols. 90 vo, col. 1—92 col. 2. Kneer, *op. cit.*, p. 57, divides the tract as printed by Schard, *op. cit.*, into three parts, relying upon a MS. at Breslau. But the tract which Kneer maintains to be the first tract is literally identical with that printed in *Consilium* CL, whereas the tract alleged to be the second differs only in its introduction of 8½ lines from the first, but otherwise is completely identical with the first. On the other hand, the version of Schard appears to have some

the tract as a whole, notwithstanding the fact that there are actually three tracts combined in one.

What first strikes the modern reader, and what must have impressed the medieval reader, is the sincerity of the author : his soul seems so torn by the disaster that has befallen the Church that his intellect often runs away with him, and arrives at conclusions which are sometimes highly unorthodox and fall just short of direct opposition to dogmatic teaching. And, we presume, it is this unorthodox character of some of his conclusions which brought him into bad repute ; and we presume, furthermore, that this adverse judgment passed on Zabarella has come from the neglect of the basis upon which he worked, that is, from the neglect to study the canon law and the canonist literature of the Middle Ages.

The tract *De Schismate* opens with the statement of the canon law[1] that all Catholics are bound to strive for unity within the Church, and that this duty is especially incumbent upon bishops and doctors of canon law. Unity in the Church is sadly lacking, he says, and, as a doctor of canon law, he is obliged to contribute to the establishment of the desired unity. For this reason— " qua de causa motus "—he had arrived at some conclusions as to how this " pestiferum schisma, quod est in Dei ecclesia " could be brought to a speedy end.

How, he asks, can unity be achieved so that one supreme pontiff rules over the Church, one to whom all Christians owe allegiance ? As he prepares to answer this question a host of others emerge, of which the first is : Who shall be the judge, if two contend for the papacy, each styling the other an *intrudor* and *invasor* ? The cardinal's laconic answer is : " Respondeo, quod concilium, ut notatur 79 dist.c.si duo, in glossa prima ". This passage—*Dist.* 79,c.8 (of the *Decretum* of

[1] C. xxiv, q. i, c. 18.

___

lacunae, especially after " per alios intentatum ", p. 695 (A), since the new paragraph starts off with " Secundus modus ", and a " primus modus " cannot be found in that version. Moreover, that the third tract should begin with " Alium et octavum modum ", and without any further introduction, is highly unlikely. One may be reasonably certain that there are three tracts, but where they begin and where they end cannot be ascertained with any degree of certainty. What is needed is a carefully worked new edition of these three tracts based upon the available MS. material.

Gratian)—speaks of the installation of two popes elected, and says that this election is null and void: but that he alone shall remain in the papal chair whom the *consensus universitatis* had elected. And the gloss of Joannes Teutonicus which came to be considered the *glossa ordinaria*[1] simply elaborates this passage and says that a general council has to be convoked. Zabarella, attempting to interpret the canonical term *universitas*, declares that it comprises the whole of Christendom ; his contention, however, is that the *ecclesia universalis* is quasi-vacant, as there is no pope who can claim the allegiance of all Christians. Consequently, the power which the pope usually combines in his person seems now to rest with the whole Church, which is the *fidelium congregatio*—a term used by Nicholas III in the *Sext* I.6.17.[2] In a similar way, Zabarella continues, the philosophers say that the government of the State rests with the *congregatio civium* or with the *pars valentior* of the body of citizens : this is, as Zabarella hastens to add, the view of Aristotle which he expressed in his *Politics*.[3] This idea can be transferred to the government of the Church : in the case of a vacancy of the headship the government rests with the universal Church, which is represented by the general council ; and in the council, again, the actual government rests with the *pars potior*, which Zabarella seems to identify with the *pars valentior*. For in a general council, in spite of its name, not all the Catholics of the whole world are assembled, but only *personae praecipuae*, such as bishops, abbots, rectors of great religious houses, in short the *pars idoneior*.

Now it is obvious that the employment of the term *pars valentior* would *prima facie* suggest that Zabarella had in mind

[1] Joannes Teutonicus held a position in canon law similar to that of Accursius in civil law. See Schulte, *Quellen*, vol. i, pp. 172–5, and Tiraboschi, *Storia della Letteratura Italiana*, vol. iv, pp. 304 f. Joannes died in 1245. He wrote his gloss about 1215.

[2] And *Decretum, De Consecr. dist.* i, c. 8, says : " Ecclesia, i.e., catholicorum collectio." Both passages are referred to by Zabarella who states : " Cum autem vacat ecclesia, quae est fidelium congregatio."

It is therefore quite wrong to attribute this definition to Ockham, simply because he also used it : *Dialogus*, pars I, lib. v, cap. 7 and cap. 12, in Goldast, *Monarchia*, tom. i, p. 477, al. 54, and p. 481, al. 39 ff.

[3] Lib. iii, cap. 8.

Marsiglio's *Defensor Pacis*, where the term is used in a very similar manner.[1] And it was, to be sure, this identity of the term used by Marsiglio and Zabarella which brought on the cardinal the charge that he had propounded the views of Marsiglio on popular sovereignty and transferred them into the realm of Church government.[2] But this purely external similarity of ideas, or identity of concepts, should not have led to such a condemnation of the cardinal, who himself is certainly not responsible for this confusion. For, in the first place, Zabarella uses the term *pars valentior* in the meaning of *pars potior* as well as in that of *pars idoneior*. Thus, Zabarella himself is not very consistent in the usage of the term. What seems far more likely is that he used William of Moerbeke's translation of Aristotle's *Politics*, without paying any attention to Marsiglio. But apart from this external similarity, canon law itself uses a term hardly distinguishable from *pars valentior*, that is, the term *pars sanior*,[3] in the case of the election of a bishop by the cathedral chapter. Moreover, the term *pars potior*, too, occurs in canon law, e.g., *Dist*.50, c.28, where it is laid down that, in cases of contradicting conciliar decrees, that decree should be adhered to which emanated from a council with *potior auctoritas*. And lastly, the idea, if not the term, of *pars idoneior* can also be found in Roman law as well as in canon law.[4] The charge levelled against Cardinal

[1] *Defensor Pacis*, Dictio Prima, cap. 12.

[2] Even McIlwain, *Growth of Political Thought in the West*, p. 304, n. 1, indicates that Zabarella had adopted the term *pars valentior* from Marsiglio.
That Zabarella knew Marsiglio's treatise seems certain, however, though strangely enough he thought that the author of the *Defensor Pacis* was not " Marsilius de Mendardino de Padua, non is, qui late scripsit in medicina, sed alius egregius doctor sacrae paginae. Iste namque adhaesit Bavaro . . .", see Zabarella's *Commentaria in Decretales*, I. 6, 34, no. 2 (fol. 149 *verso* of the edition, Venice, 1602).

[3] *Decretales*, I. 6. 22 and 57.

[4] C. ii, 59, 2, 1 and Dig. 35, 1, 97, and *Sext* I. 19. 9. This idea of a *sanior* or *valentior* pars is typically medieval, cf., for instance, the statutes of the Benedictines in England, year 1249, as reported by Matthew Paris, *Chronica Majora* (Rolls), vi, addidamenta, p. 183: " What touches all should be done by all or by their sanior pars." It will be recalled that this principle was not only contained in the *Decretum*, *Dist*. 61, c. 14, but also in the decisions of the Third Lateran Council (1179), *Decretales*, III. 11. 1, and repeated by Celestine III,

Zabarella that he had followed the notorious Marsiglian view of popular sovereignty cannot seriously be upheld, if one only attempts to follow the cardinal's own lines of thought. What Zabarella did, was simply to transfer the idea of the medieval cathedral chapter to the general council—a juristically tenable and canonically justifiable procedure, though one need not necessarily agree with it.

Perhaps the best criterion that distinguishes Zabarella from the publicists, including Marsiglio,[1] is that the pseudo-legal, meta-juristic panacea of *epieikeia* occurs not once in his tracts. This concept, as we have seen, assumed great importance in the publicistic literature which tried to introduce this compliant term in order to achieve the desired result. Zabarella is far too much of a jurist to operate with amorphous concepts such as *epieikeia*.

But in view of *Dist.* 17, c.4, which plainly lays down that the pope is above the general council, can one reasonably propound, as Zabarella does, that a general council should sit in judgment over a pope ? The cardinal's answer to this vitally important question is strongly in the affirmative. He does not try to minimize the canonical and dogmatic precept that the pope is superior to any assembly, however representative this may be : he knows canon law too well to overlook the legal axiom that councils derive their authority and force from the Church herself,[2] but—and here enters the argumentative and legal acumen of Zabarella—canon law rightly speaks of the pope only, not of the Church as a whole : in the present dispute it is not the pope or his position which is at stake, but the life of the whole Church. A clear distinction must be made, he declares, between the pontiff and the *sedes apostolica*—a dis-

[1] *Defensor Pacis*, Dictio Secunda, cap. 12. On Conrad's *Epistola*, see *supra*, pp. 176–81.

[2] " Concilia per ecclesiae Romanae auctoritatem facta sunt, et robur acceperunt," p. 700 (B).

---

ibid., III. 10. 6, and by Innocent III, *ibid.*, III. 11. 4. On this concept see also Gierke, " Ueber die Geschichte des Majoritäts prinzips " in *Essays in Legal History*, ed. Vinogradoff, pp. 312–27 ; A. Esmein, " L'unanimité et la majorité dans les élections canoniques " in *Mélanges Fitting*, vol. i, pp. 355–82, and also G. Post, " A Romano-Canonical Maxim . . . in Bracton " in *Traditio*, vol. iv, p. 232, note 180.

tinction upon which the law itself relies : the former can die, the latter never dies.[1] " Aliud autem papa, aliud sedes apostolica " maintains Zabarella, referring to the enactment in the *Sext.* For whilst the Holy See cannot err, the pope can very well be the victim of error and heresy. He points out that this is not a new idea at all, but one derived from the gloss on the *Decretum.* The glossator, Joannes Teutonicus, commenting on C.xxiv, q.i, c.9, says that *apostolica ecclesia,* as used in this particular passage, is infallible, whilst the pope can err: " Certum est, quod papa errare potest ".[2] According to Joannes Teutonicus the term *ecclesia* refers to the whole *congregatio fidelium,* and it is this body of the faithful which is incapable of error: God would not allow, says the glossator, in another passage,[3] that His Church could commit an error.[4] It is then only logical to say, the glossator points out, that in matters of faith the pope is subject to the authority and judgment of the general council. In his gloss on *Dist.* 19, c.9, Joannes Teutonicus says: " Videtur ergo, quod papa tenetur requirere concilium episcoporum, quod verum est, ubi de fide agitur, et tunc synodus major est papa "—a point of view which can be obtained from an interpretation of *Dist.* 15, c.2. In his gloss on the latter passage Joannes says that the pope cannot destroy the decrees of general councils, because *orbis major est urbe.* Nor was this opinion of Joannes Teutonicus unique. For example, the Wolfenbuttel MS. of the gloss on the *Decretum,* commenting on C.xxiv, q.i, c.9, maintained that " ecclesia numquam in universo corpore suo errat, licet quandoque in aliqua persona erret ". And to leave no doubt, this gloss, whose authorship is unknown, continues: " Licet papa erraverit, qui et per heresim judicari potest, non tamen ecclesia Romana sive apostolica errat."[5] In his commentaries on *Decretales* I.1.1, Innocent IV

---

[1] *Sext* I, 3. 5 : " Sedes ipsa non moritur," says Boniface VIII in this passage.

[2] Referring to *Dist.* 40, c. 6.   [3] C. xxiv, q. i, c. 6.

[4] "Arguo, quod sententia totius ecclesiae praeferenda est Romanae, si in aliquo sibi contradicant, arg. 93 dist. legimus, sed contrarium credo, arg. infra eod., haec est, nisi erraret Romana ecclesia, quod non credo posse fieri, quia Deus non permitteret."

[5] Quoted after J. F. v. Schulte, " Die Glosse zum Dekret Gratians " in *Denkschriften der Kaiserlichen Akademie der Wissenschaften* (phil. hist. Cl.), vol. xxi, p. 11. This gloss was written before Huguccio, but probably after 1179, see also Kuttner, *Repertorium,* p. 21.

declared that every Christian had the duty to believe whatever the Catholic Church believed—" credere verum esse, quicquid credit ecclesia catholica ". Baldus, writing a century after Innocent IV, interpreted this declaration of the pope as meaning that the pope too could err in matters of faith, although he was not presumed to fall into error: " Papa etiam potest errare in fide, ita notat Innocentius, c. 1 de trin., licet non praesumetur ".[1] A very similar line of thought can be detected with the famous canonist Guido de Baysio (commonly referred to as the Archdeacon), who in his commentary on *Dist.* 19, c.9[2] declares, obviously elaborating the dictum of the *glossa ordinaria*, that it would be too dangerous to leave matters of faith to the judgment of one man : therefore, when faith is at stake, the pope must be subjected to the general council.[3]

[1] He continued : " Et ideo non debet quis dicere, credo id, quod credit papa, sed illud, quod credit ecclesia, et sic dicendo non errabit," *Margarita Baldi Loco Repertorii Innocentii super Decretalibus.*

[2] Fol. 23 no. 3 col. 2 of the edition of his *Rosarium seu in Decretorum Volumen Commentaria*, Venetiis, 1577.

[3] " Nam nimis periculosum erat, fidem nostram committere arbitrio unius hominis . . . et synodus causam fidei papae committit, 21 dist. nunc autem." In his commentary on *Dist.* 15, c. 2, the archdeacon says that the pope cannot decree anything against the general council " in his, quae ad fidem pertinent, et salutem et generalem statum ecclesiae. In aliis potest contra concilii statutum venire."

It is worth while recalling the view of the greatest pupil of the cardinal, that is, Nicholas de Tudeschis (Panormitanus), a Benedictine, who was a professor of canon law at the universities of Siena and Parma, and Archbishop of Palermo, and who took a prominent part in the proceedings of the Council of Basle ; he was called " Bartolus inter juris pontificii professores ", see Panzirolus, *De Claris Legum Interpretibus*, cap. xxxii, p. 357 ; J. F. v. Schulte, *Quellen*, vol. ii, pp. 312–3, does not question the legitimacy of the " cardinalate " of Panormitanus, which was conferred upon him by the Duke of Savoy (anti-pope " Felix V "), cf. Panzirolus, *loc. cit.*, p. 356. According to Panormitanus, the council is above the pope ; which general statement this canonist considerably modifies in the course of his further discussion. He declares that the pope's view on a matter of faith in opposition to a general council should be adhered to, if the pope is moved by better reasons or better founded authorities than the council. For the council can err also, just as it erred in the matter of matrimony between the ravager

It is upon sayings such as these to which we have referred that Cardinal Zabarella bases his theory of the superiority of the council—sayings which are derived through interpretation of canon law by the thirteenth-century canonists. The step which Zabarella now takes in pursuing this fundamental thesis is that he presents the Schism as a matter of faith and thus has few difficulties in. applying the above dicta to the

---

and his victim. But this can not only be said of the pope, but of every individual, for in matters of faith the opinion of a single individual might be preferable to that of the pope, if the former's opinion is based on better reasons than that of the pope. Let us quote this important passage from Panormitanus' *Commentaria in Decretales*, Lugduni, 1512, 1. 6. 4, no. 2, fol. 85 vo. : " In concernentibus fidem concilium est supra papam, unde non potest papa disponere contra dispositum per concilium, c. Anast. dist. 19, hinc est, quod concilium potest condemnare papam de haeresi . . . puto tamen, quod si papa moveretur melioribus rationibus et auctoritatibus quam concilium, quod standum esset sententiae suae. Nam et concilium potest errare, sicut alias erravit super matrimonium contrahendum inter raptorem et raptam . . . nam in concernentibus fidem etiam dictum unius privati esset praeferendum dicto papae, si ille moveretur melioribus rationibus novi et veteris testamenti quam papa." This, no doubt, is an opinion as individualistic as it is truly courageous. The infallibility of the general council was denied by William of Ockham in his *Dialogus*, pars iii, tract. 2, lib. 3, cap. 13 (in Goldast's *Monarchia*, tom. ii, pp. 829–31). Furthermore, Ockham asserted that although pope, cardinals, the whole Church and clergy might err, the true faith, according to him, might survive in women and infants, *Dialogus*, pars i, lib. 5, esp. caps. 29–31, pp. 498–503 ; cf. also his *Breviloquium de principatu tyrannico*, ed. Scholz, 1944, lib. v, cap. 4, p. 175. It should perhaps be mentioned that, generally speaking, it was not only open heresy, but also occult heresy, which made the pope liable to be brought before the general council. See, e.g., the usually over-cautious Joannes Andreae in his *Novella in Sextum*, Lugd. 1550, V. 2. 5, fol. 103 no. 2: " Papa etiam de occulta haeresi potest accusari, 40 dist. si papa." Innocent IV, *Decretales*, V. 40. 23, no. 2, fol. 567, treats of open heresy alone as a possible charge against a pope, whilst the glossator, Joannes Teutonicus, stated that an occult heresy was also a reason for indicting the pope : *glossa ordinaria* on *Dist.* 40, c. 6.

Against these views should be set the opinion of Gregory VII. He maintained that although papal decrees may be against the law, and may even amount to heresy, yet no power on earth may judge him, not even a general council, see P. Jaffé, *Monumenta Gregoriana*, vol. ii, p. 175 (*dictatus papae*).

solution of the Schism. " Item in casu nostro," says our author,
" agitur de fide, quae periclitatur in hoc schismate . . . cum
autem agitur de fide, synodus est major quam papa, 19 dist.c.
Anast. in gl.15 dist.c. sicut sancti in gl. ult."[1] In order to fortify
his argument, the cardinal dwells upon the term *ecclesia* and
declares—referring to Joannes Teutonicus—that this term
means *sedes apostolica*, but the Holy See is, according to
Zabarella, not the pope, but is *constituted by the pope and the
cardinals* who become, metaphorically speaking, members of the
pope's body.[2] It is, however, interesting to see that the very
same metaphor was used by Panormitanus, the great pupil of
Zabarella, in an almost opposite meaning. In his commentary
on the *Decretals*[3] he speaks of the relations between pope,
cardinals and the body of the faithful, and says that the pope
as the head indicates the bodily movements.[4]

[1]P. 701 (A). Whilst Zabarella thus maintains, in harmony with
canonist doctrine, a superiority of the council in matters of faith,
Marsiglio, on the other hand, held that the general council should
always be above the pope ; moreover, Marsiglio wrote that the
general council should really be the instrument of Church government and administration, so, for instance, it should be in the
discretion of the council to confer benefices, to excommunicate,
to correct recalcitrant clerics, to canonize, maintain schools, levy
taxes, appoint notaries and, of course, legislate on all matters, see
Defensor Pacis, Dictio Secunda, caps. 17, 18, 19, 21, 22.

[2]" Ecclesia Romana, quae non censetur esse solus papa, sed ipse
papa cum cardinalibus, qui sunt partes corporis papae, seu
ecclesiae, quae constituitur ex papa tamquam ex capite, et ex
cardinalibus tamquam membris," *loc. cit.* This latter view had
already been propounded some hundred years earlier by Laurentius,
a canonist of the early fourteenth century in his commentary on the
Clementines iii, 14. 6 to which Zabarella refers us. The Church is
represented by the pope as the head of the " sedes apostolica " as
well as by the cardinals as the members of this " sedes apostolica ".
On the other hand, Guilelmus Durantis, in his *Speculum Judiciale*
(written before 1287), says laconically enough that " papa est sedes
apostolica ": I. De legibus, § 5, no. 1, fol. 213 vo, of the edition
Basileae, 1574.

[3]*Decretales*, I. 6. 4, fol. 85 vo.

[4]" Ipse (scil. papa) est caput ecclesiae, unde licet potestas fuerat
data papae et toti ecclesiae, papae tamen fuit attributa tamquam
capiti. Unde debet moveri corpus ad dispositionem capitis." With
Gerson the pope became merely *membrum corporis ecclesiae*, see
Goldast, *Monarchia*, tom. ii, p. 1515, al. 53. In spite of the immense

The foregoing considerations lead Zabarella to an investigation of the plenitude of power which the pope alone is supposed to enjoy. For if the cardinals are members of the pope's body, then they must be endowed with special rights and must stand above the ordinary clergy and, furthermore, must somehow partake in the pope's powers. Can this idea be upheld in view of the maxim, hitherto held unimpeachable, that the pope, and he alone, has the *plenitudo potestatis*?[1] Zabarella refers us to the writings of the canonist Joannes Monachus, also called Jean le Moine, who, a cardinal created by Celestine V on 30th September, 1294,[2] wrote the first gloss on Boniface VIII's *Liber Sextus*. Monachus died, as chancellor of the Holy Roman Church, at Avignon on 22nd August, 1313. This gloss on Boniface's law book has not frequently been printed, and it has, to all intents and purposes, been forgotten.

[1]The pope's plenitude of power was usually based on Matt. xxviii. 18 : the pope as Christ's vicar on earth was therefore invested with the same powers which Christ Himself wielded. The strongest protagonist for this plenitude was Aegidius Romanus who, in his tract *De Ecclesiastica Potestate*, written about 1301, elaborated this idea at great length, see pp. 73 f. of the edition by R. Scholz, Weimar, 1929. On the whole question, see Carlyle, *History of Political Thought*, vol. v, p. 405, Rivière, *Le Problème de l'Eglise et de l'Etat au Temps de Philippe le Bel*, Louvain, 1926, pp. 114 f. and also my paper, "A Medieval Document on Papal Theories of Government", in *English Historical Review*, 1946, pp. 180 ff.

[2]See Eubel, *Hierarchia Catholica*, tom. i, p. 11, and Panzirolus, *De Claris Legum Interpretibus*, p. 334. On the cardinal himself, see also H. Denifle, *Chartularium Universitatis Parisiensis*, II. p. 90, and F. Lajard in *Histoire littéraire de la France*, vol. xxvii, pp. 201–24. On the mission of Joannes Monachus to Philip the Fair on behalf of Boniface VIII, in 1302, see Hefele-Leclercq, *Histoire des Conciles*, vol. vi, part i, pp. 431–4. On some of the alleged ambiguities in the cardinal's conduct, see also H. Finke, *Aus den Tagen Bonifaz' VIII*, pp. 177 ff, R. Scholz, *Publizistik zur Zeit Philipps des Schoenen*, p. 194, and O. Martin, *L'Assemblée de Vincennes de 1329 et ses Conséquences*, p. 125, note 3.

---

powers which Gerson would have conferred on the general council, the laity, according to him, had only a consultative function in a council, see his *De Potestate Ecclesiae*, in Gerson's *Opera Omnia*, tom. ii, pp. 250 f. Nor was d'Ailly any more " democratic ", see Gerson, *Opera*, tom. i, pp. 661 ff.

A brief reference to the ideas expressed in the *Apparatus in Librum Sextum* may throw some light upon the conduct of the cardinals in their relation to Urban VI and also clarify Zabarella's position. The *Apparatus* is extant in MS form, of which there are several at Cambridge : two at Caius College and one at St. John's College.[1] That these MSS were written by English scribes cannot seriously be doubted, as they all substituted, in a somewhat high-handed manner, when copying the text of the *Sext, Oxoniae* for the correct word *Bononiae*.[2] None of the Cambridge MSS is complete : in the St. John's MS there are ten leaves of the fifth book missing,[3] whilst the Caius MSS show the text of *Apparatus* often in a curtailed form, so that only by comparing all three MSS can a somewhat reliable and satisfactory reconstruction of the gloss be obtained.[4]

[1]About the latter, see D. D. Egbert, *The Thickhill Papers and Related Manuscripts*, New York, 1940, pp. 117–20, 219.

[2]The proper initium of the *Liber Sextus* is : " Bonifacius, episcopus servus servorum Dei, dilectis filiis doctoribus et scholaribus universis Bononiae commorantibus, salutem . . ." Instead of " Bononiae " the three scribes put " Oxoniae ". It is, however, an established fact that the *Sext* was issued to the University of Bologna, see Potthast, *Regesta Pontificum Romanorum*, vol. ii, p. 1971, no. 24632, though a few months after its first promulgation it was also issued to the University of Salamanca, *ibid.* p. 1978, no. 24726. The edition of the *Corpus Juris Canonici* of Lyons, 1591, says, however, that there is one MS version of the *Sext* which has " Paduae " while another Vatican MS has| " Bononiae, Parisiis Aurelianisque commorantibus."

[3]The St. John's MS A. 4 shows the following omission : from V. 2. 20 . . . " advocatorum ac judiciorum " to V. 11. 6 ". . .— juriam se tueri."

[4]The year of the composition of this *Apparatus* is not quite certain. Schulte, *Quellen*, vol. ii, p. 192, maintains that it was written in 1308 : he relies on a Berlin MS which says at the end : " *anno di. m° cc° octavo.*" Schulte, in a very unscholarly manner, supplies another " c " and says : " Of course a ' c ' had been forgotten," and in this way he arrives at 1308. Against this must be set the fact that the Caius MSS 475 and 662, although written by two different hands, have both : " *explicit app. VI*[1] *li. dec. comp. et prom. p. ven. vir. Jo. Mo. tit. ss. Marcel. et Petri presb. card. an. di. m° cc° nonagesimo octavo.*" The *Sext* was issued on 3rd March, 1298, and it seems, therefore, unlikely that the date given by the Caius MSS is correct. Moreover, Joannes Monachus himself refers in his gloss to Benedict XI and thus at least parts of his gloss must have been written after 1304.

In the gloss on V.2.4. s.v. *Fratrum nostrorum* Joannes Monachus wrote that the pope could not enact anything without previous consultation with his cardinals. He said that the *plenitudo potestatis* of the pope was thus restricted in favour of the cardinals. " Scio," wrote Monachus, " quod Coelestinus pp. V multas abbatias, episcopatus et superiores dignitates contulit sine fratrum consilio."[1] Under his successor, Boniface VIII, the question had been raised as to whether this conferment by Celestine V was legally valid. He himself had been consulted on this point; and he had replied that just as bishops and abbots had to seek the advice of their chapters, in the same way the pope should consult his cardinals. As a result of his reply, Celestine's conferments were revoked. " Et scio, quod dictae collationes fuerunt cassatae praesertim, quia coetus cardinalium erat in hac positione, quod ardua negotia erant, quorum consilio tractanda et convocanda sunt." Joannes referred, furthermore, to " the many laws " which contain the phrase *de fratrum nostrorum consilio*. Joannes saw fit to draw a parallel between the pope and the emperor who both were said to be *legibus solutus*. But just as it is fit and proper for the latter to live according to the laws, in the same way it should be fit and proper for the former to consult his cardinals. This glossator quoted, as another instance of the restriction of the pope's powers, the case of Benedict XI, who cancelled certain statutes issued by his predecessor Boniface VIII without previous consultation with the cardinals. The glossator ends this discussion : " Nam defectus in persona facientis vel in modo necessario reddit factum inutile."[2] In another gloss Joannes came to speak of the relationship between the pope and the Sacred College[3] and here he bluntly declared that the pope received the right of canonical *administration* (!) from the cardinals: " Item canonica administratio data papae per cardinales non tollitur legitime." And that was the reason, Joannes continued, why the pope's relation to the Sacred College was exactly the same as that of *any other bishop* to his chapter; consequently, neither the bishop

[1] St. John's MS A. 4, fol. 69, col. 1, according to the pagination of Montague James.

[2] This conclusion is contained in the St. John's MS A. 4, but in neither of the Caius MSS.

[3] In his gloss on V. 3. 1 (*Ad succedendos*), s. v. " *collegium* ".

could legitimately do away with the jurisdictional powers of the chapter, nor was it permissible for the pope to curtail the cardinals' power. " Et papa sic se habet ad collegium cardinalium sic alter episcopus respectu sui collegii . . . episcopus non possit tollere administrationem legitimam sui capituli nec papae licebit."[1]

These views of Cardinal Joannes Monachus were later adopted by a great number of canonists, although there was already, before Joannes, some inclination to enlarge the powers of the Sacred College. The Archdeacon (Guido de Baysio), in his commentaries on *Dist.* 50, c.25, wrote that the cardinals could issue binding rules which had the force of law.[2] He relied, as so often, on the compilation, *Glossa Palatina*, which had declared that the pope could not issue a general law without the consent of the cardinals.[3] And more than an inclination towards this point of view can be observed in Hostiensis (Henricus de Segusia, Cardinal-bishop of Ostia, 1210-1271), though, strangely enough, none of the later canonists ever referred to his opinion on this point. In his *Summa Decretalium*, 1. 2, 4, he treated exactly the same problem as did Joannes Monachus some forty years later, and he concluded that the pope is ruled by the Sacred College.[4] He based this idea, firstly, on *Decretales* I. 6. 6, where Alexander III decreed in the Lateran Council (1179) the necessity of a two-thirds majority in papal elections and said: " De consilio fratrum nostrorum "; secondly, on *Decretales* I. 6, 55, in which passage Gregory IX, again " de consilio fratrum nostrorum," declared the election of a bishop null and void ; and thirdly, on *Decretales* I. 6, 57, where the pope used the same phrase when he declared another election invalid.[5]

[1] This gloss is missing in St. John's MS A. 4 and Caius MS 475, but is contained in Caius MS 662.

[2] Fol. 67, no. 4 : " Cardinales possunt jus constituere, cum aequiparantur senatui."

[3] See the Archdeacon, *Rosarium*, C. xxv, q. i, c. 6, no. 1 : he attributed this view to Laurentius, but see Prof. Kuttner, " Bernardus Compostellanus Antiquus " in *Traditio*, vol. i, pp. 290, 309, and *id.*, *Repertorium*, pp. 79, 87.

[4] Fol. 237 of the edition Coloniae, 1612.

[5] The passage in Hostiensis runs : " Nam sicut papa cardinalium concilio regitur, ut patet supra de el., licet, et cap. in gen. i. fi. et c. eccl. II, sic episcopi canonicorum concilio regi debent," *loc.*

The *glossa ordinaria* on the *Extravagantes Communes* III.10,[1]
dutifully referring to Joannes Monachus, said that the pope
should be ruled by the advice of the cardinals in the same way
as the bishop is ruled by his canons.[2] The position of Joannes
Andreae was not quite clear—he was an extremely cautious
writer and never wanted to offend anyone—in fact he left the
question open. After reporting the opinion of Joannes Monachus, Andreae somewhat ironically doubted the truth of the
cardinal's report about the alleged revocation by Boniface

[1]Fol. 27 of the edition Chappuis, Lugduni, 1517.

[2]" Quod papa regatur consilio cardinalium, probatur c. licet, et.
in c. in gen., et in c. eccl. II, i. fi. de elect., sicut episcopi consilio
canonicorum regi debent . . . et hoc servat consuetudo." Note the
wording and compare it with Hostiensis.
It should be pointed out, however, that it was after Hostiensis'
death (1270) that Nicholas III (1277–80) as supreme legislator
of the Church gave some indication as to the legal relations between
pope and cardinals. His dicta were taken into the *Sext* by Boniface
VIII, i.e., 1. 6. 17. One would have reasonably expected that those
canonists who wrote after the promulgation of the *Sext* would have
referred to this passage, but in fact none of them did. Here Nicholas
III spoke of the cardinals as *coadjutores* of the pope, whose counsel
he would be advised to seek. The modern *Codex Juris Canonici*,
c. 230, speaks of the cardinals as the pope's " praecipui consiliarii
et adjutores ".
Taking a broad view, it would appear that the rise in power, at
least of the Roman cardinals, can be traced back to the late eleventh
century, when the anti-pope Clement III (1080–1100) increased
the constitutional position of the cardinals ; see the penetrating
study by Professor Stephan Kuttner " Cardinalis : The History of
a Canonical Concept " in *Traditio*, vol. iii (1945), pp. 129–214,
at pp. 172–7. St. Peter Damian called the cardinals " spirituales
ecclesiae universalis senatores ", *Contra Philargyriam*, in Migne, *Patr.
Lat.*, vol. cvl, p. 540. The increase in the cardinals' power during
the eleventh and twelfth centuries went so far that " the original
meaning of the name ' cardinalis ' was definitely obliterated. The
name was now understood as expressing the participation of its
bearers in the primacy of Peter," Kuttner, *loc. cit.*, p. 176 and pp.
197–8. In fact, Cardinal Deusdedit, perhaps somewhat rhetorically,
likened the cardinals to the kings and considered them as the hinges
(cardines) who ruled God's people : " Sicut a basibus, quae sunt
fulturae columnarum a fundamento surgentes, basilei id est reges
dicuntur, quia populum regunt; ita et cardinales derivative dicuntur
a cardinibus januae, qui tam regunt et movent, quod plebem Dei,

VIII. " Hoc multum admiror et difficulter credo Bonifacium id fecisse."[1] But Petrus de Ancharano, a canonist at the end of the fourteenth century, stated in general terms that the pope was bound to consult the cardinals in all matters.[2] The teacher of the last named canonist, Dominicus de S. Geminiano, however, struck a more conservative note by relying on the older doctrine of the pope's plenitude of power which could never be curtailed. He referred to Huguccio (died 1210), who stoutly upheld the dogmatic point of view, declaring that the pope was above the council and there was no need for him to consult the cardinals. This older doctrine was adopted by Dominicus : he dismissed the theory of Joannes Monachus, whom he called biased in this matter as he himself was a cardinal and therefore wanted to enlarge his power as a member of the Sacred College.[3]

Such was the canonistic background against which Zabarella worked. He fully adopts the views of Joannes Monachus and of the gloss on the *Extravagantes Communes*, but he also raises the question—very topical and pertinent in the present case— what should be the procedure, if there is disagreement between pope and cardinals ? For in normal circumstances pope and cardinals will agree on most points, but what should be the

---

[1] *Novella ad Sextum*, V. 2. 4, fol. 103, adding that only if the letter of the conferment had still been in the papal chancery would he think the story credible. In his gloss on the *Sext*, however, Joannes Andreae, more youthful and less cautious, says that the Sacred College has that plenitude of power which the Church had conferred on it. Gloss ad V. 3. 1, fol. 134 vo : " Posset dici quod cardinales habent potestatis plenitudinem habitu tunc in quantum Romana ecclesia censetur, quae non moritur."

[2] *Super Sexto*, Bononiae, 1593, I. 7, 1, fol. 104 vo : " Debet papa omnia facere de consilio cardinalium ", see also his remarks to V. 4. 2, fol. 386.

[3] " Ad dictum Jo. Monachi hic posset responderi, quod sibi non sit credendum, quia cum ipse esset cardinalis, conabatur sustinere causam propriam ", Dominicus, *Super Sexto Decretalium*, Venice, 1578, V. 2. 4, fol. 269 vo.

---

ut superius diximus, doctrinis sanctis ad amorem Dei moveant . . ." W. Glanvell, *Die Kanonessammlung des Kardinales Deusdedit*, p. 268. Cardinal Deusdedit wrote his *Collectio Canonum* between 1085 and 1087, see also P. Fournier, " Les Collections Canoniques Romaines de l'époque de Grégoire VII " in *Mémoires de l'Académie des Inscriptions et Belles-lettres*, vol. xli, pp. 345-56.

principle, if there is a discrepancy between them ? " Quaero circa hoc," Zabarella asks, " si inter papam et cardinales surgit discordia, sicut nunc evenit ? " The only feasible remedy, according to the cardinal, lies in the convocation of a general council which should be composed of the whole congregation of Catholics, that is, the principal heads and prelates, " who represent the whole Church."[1] This, too, Zabarella is at great pains to emphasize, is not a novel idea at all, for we read in the Acts, xv.1-5, that the question of circumcision—hotly disputed at the time—was referred to " the apostles and presbyters " in Jerusalem : they held a great congregation and there they thrashed out the question, which was then finally decided, and the decision is still valid. We cannot do better, counsels Zabarella, than adopt this example, in which the Holy Spirit had worked miraculously and which we must believe was inspired by God Himself.[2] Nor can it be said that St. Peter had all plenitude of power, for there are numerous examples which go to show that he consulted the whole congregation in · difficult cases.[3] Afterwards, however, there were some pontiffs who tried to rule the Church on the model of earthly princes and never convoked a council, " ex qua omissione prodierunt multa mala."

The cardinal then advances to an interpretation of the term *plenitudo potestatis*. This, he says, rests basically and fundamentally with the whole congregation of Catholics and with

[1] " Dic, quod oportet congregare totam ecclesiam, i.e., totam congregationem Catholicorum, et principales ministros fidei, scilicet praelatos, qui totam congregationem repraesentant ", p. 702.

[2] " Quod enim tunc gestum est per illos, qui spiritum sanctum miraculose susceperant, debemus credere, quod Deo inspirante factum sit ", *ibid.*

Here one might find a parallel between Zabarella and Michael of Cesena : the latter, in his *Tractatus Contra Errores Papae* (John XXII, written 1331, and printed in Goldast, *Monarchia*, tom. ii, pp. 1236–1361, at p. 1360, al. 46), also chose this example to show that the first doubtful article of faith was decided by a council ; he expressly referred to the Acts. It would be merely guessing to assume that Zabarella was acquainted with the ideas contained in this piece of publicistic literature.

[3] " Et in hoc etiam apparet, quod licet fuerit princeps apostolorum, tamen plenitudo potestatis non fuit in eo solo, imo ut patet . . . et hinc mos antiquus habuit, quod omnia difficilia terminabantur per concilium et crebro fiebant ", p. 703.

the pope as the principal minister through whom this power is externally manifested. " Ex hoc apparet, quod id, quod dicitur, quod papa habet plenitudinem potestatis, debet intelligi non solus, sed tamquam apud universitatem, ita quod ipsa potestas est in ipsa universitate tamquam in fundamento, et papa tamquam in principali ministro, per quem haec potestas explicatur." Accordingly, the pope does not possess plenitude of power, as already Innocent IV had pointed out some one hundred and fifty years earlier, though in quite a different context. Innocent, speaking of the powers of the pope,[1] maintained, realistically enough, that although the pope possessed, *de jure*, supreme powers over everyone, whether Christians or not, he did not wield this power *de facto*. To possess full plenitude of power, however, so Zabarella's argument runs, it would be necessary that he wields it factually as well as in law.[2] It is idle to maintain, says Zabarella, that the pope has plenitude of power, if he cannot exercise it in fact. As a further proof for his correct interpretation of the term, Zabarella refers us to *Dist*. 93, c.24, where St. Jerome is reported to have said that the world is greater than the city. The *glossa ordinaria* of Joannes Teutonicus, indeed, maintained here, relying on the utterance of St. Jerome, that, in case of disagreement, the decrees of a general council must be preferred to those of a pope.[3] Finally, canon law in another

---

[1] Innocent IV's *Commentaria in Quinque Libros Decretalium*, Francofurti, 1570, II. 24, 18, no. 4, fol. 285 vo.

[2] The passage contained in the long commentary of Innocent IV runs : " Omnes autem tam fideles quam infideles oves sunt Christi per creationem, licet non sint de ovili ecclesiae, et sic per praedicta apparet, quod papa super omnes habet jurisdictionem et potestatem de jure, licet non de facto."

[3] *Glossa ordinaria* ad *Dist*. 93, c. 24 : " Statuta concilii praejudicant statuto papae, si contradicant ".
  The opinions on this point, however, were divided. Goffredus de Trano, who wrote the first *Summa* of the Decretals, states in his *Summa in Titulos Decretalium*, I. 2 no. 11, fol. 2 of the Venice edition, 1586, that " et in conciliis excepta intelligitur auctoritas domini papae ". The *glossa ordinaria* of Bernardus Parmensis (finished before 1263) on *Decretales*, III. 34. 4 stated that the pope could grant dispensations against the explicit decrees of a general council, because " papa major est quam concilium ", referring to *Decretales*, I. 6. 4.

passage explicitly lays down that Christ had bestowed upon St. Peter the plenitude of power *principaliter*, though not *totaliter*, which would have meant that others could not partake in this plenitude of power.[1] Thus, St. Peter as the prince of the apostles was resisted by St. Paul, because he was to be blamed.[2] If, Zabarella continues, St. Peter had been given plenitude of power by Christ, to the exclusion of everyone else, St. Paul would not have effectively withstood him. He would not have dared to do this, as St. Jerome said, had he not considered himself an equal of St. Peter.[3]

Since, therefore, fundamentally the plenitude of power rests with the general council, it is this body which has to correct a pope, if he errs: " Cum errat, habet corrigere concilium." If the pope should resist the decrees of a council, he would overthrow the structure of the Church,[4] a step against which Pope Sixtus II in his capacity as pope had warned.[5] All the foregoing Scripture and canon law passages should be borne in mind by those papal counsellors, says Zabarella warningly, who are so adamant in ascribing to the pope powers which he cannot possess : these writers had put into the minds of popes the idea that they could do as they pleased ; in this way many

[1]*Dist.* 19, c. 7 : " Dominus ad omnium apostolorum officium pertinere voluit, ut in beatissimo Petro, apostolorum omnium summo, principaliter collocaret, ut ab ipso quasi quodam capite dona sua velut in corpus omne diffunderet ". Zabarella says, p. 703 (A) : " Christus commisit salutem universitatibus omnibus apostolicis : ita tamen, quod in Petro principaliter collocavit. Ubi nota, quod non dicit totaliter, ut alii excludantur, sed dicit principaliter, ut sic plenitudo potestatis sit in universitate ipsa, et per singulos exerceatur, sed principaliter per Petrum."

[2]Galat. ii. 11.

[3]C. ii, 1. vii, c. 33 : " Paulus Petrum reprehendit, quod non auderet, nisi se non imparem sciret." We read the same in Gerson's tract : *Quomodo et an liceat in causis fidei a summo pontifice appellare* ? in Goldast, *Monarchia*, tom. ii, p. 1515, also *Opera Omnia*, tom. ii, p. 303. Gerson calls the action of St. Paul " public resistance ", (Goldast, al. 41), continuing that St. Peter " non recte ambulabat ad veritatem evangelii ". But Gerson did not refer to Zabarella.

[4]" Neque in hoc potest papa per suas constitutiones vel alio modo facere resistentiam, quia hoc esset subvertere ecclesiam . . . papa non potest immutare universalem ecclesiae. . . ."

[5]C. xxiv, q. i, c. 10. This passage appears to be taken out of the Forged Decretals.

errors were committed and many evils wrought.[1] Had not
God Himself come to the help of His Church, she would have
been destroyed.[2]

It is from yet another angle that Cardinal Zabarella tries
to tackle the problem of the pope's plenitude of power. The
power which the pope possessed is truly an emanation of the
divine law, proceeds immediately from God,[3] and cannot be
removed by man. But against this must be set the simple fact
that although the pope's power is derived from God directly,
he is elected by men, that is, the cardinals, and therefore can
be deposed by men.[4] For *omnis res, per quascumque causas nascitur,
per easdem dissolvitur*, as an old legal maxim runs.[5] But it does
not follow therefrom, Zabarella is anxious to add, that it is
the cardinals who could depose the pope :[6] logically there

[1] It is interesting to observe that the cardinals who wrote the
Consilium de emendanda ecclesia gave Pope Paul III the same warning
in almost the same words. I am grateful to Father Philip Hughes
for drawing my attention to this interesting fact.

[2] " Quae jura sunt notanda, quia male considerata sunt per multos
assentatores, qui voluerunt placere pontificibus per multa retro
tempora, et usque ad hodierna suaserunt eis, quod omnia possent et
sic quod facerent quicquid liberet etiam illicita, et sic plus quam
Deus. Et ex hoc enim infiniti sunt errores, quia papa occupavit
omnia jura inferiarum ecclesiarum ... et nisi Deus succurrat statui
ecclesiae, universalis ecclesia periclitatur," pp. 703 (B)—704 (A).

Already in his commentaries on the *Decretals* he showed himself
a firm supporter of the conciliar theory : he advocated that general
councils should fix the precise jurisdictional authority of the popes.
" Saepe dixi necessarium, quod in concilio generali fierent constitutiones ita regulantes potestatem papae, quod non absorberetur
potestas aliorum praelatorum. Per hoc enim ecclesiasticus ordo
confunditur ", *Commentaria super Decretales*, I. 34, 6, no. 4, fol. 314.

[3] This was an old established axiom and is also laid down in
civil law, see *Authenticum* " Quomodo oporteat episcopo ", *Collatio*
I, tit. 6.

[4] " Licet potestas papae sit a Deo, tamen quod iste sit papa, vel
iste, est immediate ab homine, scil. per electionem cardinalium.
Unde potest ab homine tolli," p. 708 (B).

[5] St. John Chrysostom, *Decretales*, V. 41, 1.

[6] This, however, was the point of view of Marsiglio's forerunner,
John of Paris. In his tract *De Potestate Regia et Papali* he explicitly
declares that the Sacred College is entitled to depose the pope,
because the cardinals act " vice totius ecclesiae ", see his tract in
Goldast, *Monarchia*, tom. ii, p. 146, al. 13 and al. 26.

would not be any objection because they represent the whole body of the faithful, but ecclesiastical and historical precedent stands against the acceptance of this logical sequence.[1] The historical argument proves that the deposition of a pope is a matter to be decided by a general council. " Collegium, licet possit eligere, non tamen deponere." Whatever opinion one followed—either that of Innocent IV, who said that the jurisdictional powers of a corporation were vested in its *rector* and not in the corporation itself or its members[2], or the view of Hostiensis, who taught a doctrine opposed to Innocent IV[3]—none of these opinions can be applied to the present case : for Innocent as well as Hostiensis considered a corporation which had a superior. This presupposition, however, cannot be said to apply to the Church as the body of the faithful, since this corporation has no superior except God alone, and the pope in a purely administrative capacity.[4] And the judgment whether the pope is a good or bad administrator must be left to the decision of the whole body of Christians. " Et de hoc, an bene vel male, habet ipsa universitas decernere."

Nor can it seriously be maintained that the body of Chris-

---

[1]*Loc. cit.* Nevertheless, the bishop and glossator at the turn of the twelfth and thirteenth centuries, Huguccio (whose pupil at Bologna was Innocent III, see Schulte, *Quellen*, vol. i, p. 158), taught that the cardinals were entitled to depose the pope on the ground of heresy. See the Archdeacon in his *Apparatus ad Sextum*, V. 2, 4, fol. 113 vo, no. 2, who reports that Huguccio expressed this opinion in the gloss on *Dist.* 63, c. 23 : " Cardinales possunt deponere papam propter haeresim." But the Archdeacon reproaches Huguccio for not quoting any law in support of his opinion : " Sed hoc jure aliquo non probavit, et ideo non recedo . . ."

[2]Innocent IV in his commentaries on *Decretales*, I. 2. 8, fol. 4, col. 2, no. 3 : " Et est notandum, quod rectores assumpti ab universitatibus habent jurisdictionem, et non ipsae universitates."

[3]Hostiensis, *Apparatus ad Decretales, ibid.*, fol. 2 vo, no. 5, referring D. 1, 3, 2, 6, and *Decretales* I, 31, 13 (§ Excessus) and I. 33, 14. See also his *Summa Decretalium*, I. 2, fol. 18 vo, no. 2, where he seems to come nearer to Innocent's view.

[4]" Quicquid sit de hoc, istud tamen locum habet in universitate habente superiorem, quod cessat in universitate totius ecclesiae, quae superiorem non habet nisi Deum et papam, cum bene administrat," *loc. cit.*

tians could transfer plenitude of power—resting as it does
fundamentally with them—to the pope. Here the cardinal
borrows an argument from political thought and secular
scholarship : there the question was as to whether the emperor
was given absolute powers by the Roman people in the famous
Lex Regia, or whether these powers of the emperor could be
revoked by the people at any time. The majority view amongst
the jurists was that the people had irrevocably entrusted all
powers to the emperor.[1] But Zabarella holds to the minority
opinion which considered that the people had a right to
revoke the mandate given to the emperor, whose powers are
less than those of the people as a whole.[2] This view of the

[1]Cf. Placentinus, *Institutiones*, Moguntiae, 1536, lib. i, p. 2.
" Populus in principem transferrendo communem potestatem
nullam sibi reservavit, ergo potestatem leges scriptas condendi."
Placentinus died 1196. On the similar opinions of Irnerius and
Rogerius, see Carlyle, *op. cit.*, vol. ii, pp. 58 ff. Bartolus, the giant
of juristic thought in the fourteenth century, held the same view :
" Hodie omnis potestas imperii est abdicata ab eis (scil. populo
Romano et senatu) ", lecture on C. i, 14, 11 nos. 2–4. On the whole
question see Gierke-Maitland, *Political Theóries of the Middle Ages*,
pp. 39 ff, Woolf, *Bartolus of Sassoferrato*, pp. 35–7, Rivière, *op. cit.*,
pp. 214 ff, and my *Medieval Idea of Law*, pp. 48–9.

[2]Zabarella refers to the Commentary on the *Codex* by Guilelmus
de Cuneo, but I was unable to obtain a copy of his commentaries,
which are extremely rare, see Savigny, *Geschichte des Roemischen
Rechts im Mittelalter*, vol. vi, p. 35, note (i). But we may quote the
opinion of another Frenchman, who also belonged to the minority
party and who declared himself very clearly on this point. Petrus
de Bellapertica (a bishop of Auxerre, later professor of civil law
at the universities of Toulouse and Orleans, and eventually chancellor of France, who died in 1308 according to Savigny, *op. cit.*,
p. 28, but in 1307 according to Baluzius, *Vitae*, tom. i, cols. 585,
587) may be taken as the originator of the minority opinion. In his
lectures on C. i, 14, 12, fol. 36 of the Paris edition, 1519, he said :
" Populus Romanus concessit imperatori potestatem imperii, sed
a se non abdicavit . . . credo, si imperator male egerit, posset
populus eum revocare . . . si populus voluisset a se abdicare, non
potuit, nam potestatem vel jurisdictionem sibi commissam non
potest abdicare quis a se, nisi in manu superioris . . . et populus
non habet superiorem."

There is a report of Guilelmus de Cuneo's doctrine in a lecture
of Bartolus, D. 1, 3, 8, no. 5, fol. 53, which seems to confirm that
Zabarella's quotation is correct.

legists Zabarella transfers to the government of the Church and declares that the general council cannot be subjected to positive law, as it has plenitude of power.[1] At this stage yet another argument appears that is borrowed from the legists, the argument, namely, that the prince (emperor) can confiscate private property, if he can adduce a just cause for doing so.[2] If, therefore, the ruler can dispose of a right that is derived from the *jus naturale* (or *jus gentium*), how much easier can the mere title of administration be revoked by a general council, which title is merely an issue of positive law : " Quanto ergo fortius potest auferri titulus administrationis seu praelaturae, qui est de jure positivo ? "[3]

[1] " Ipsum concilium non subjicitur juri positivo, cum habeat plenitudinem potestatis ", p. 709 (A). It should be noted here that the *glossa ordinaria* on the *Decretum* held a view that was not unlike that of Zabarella, who however makes no reference to it. The gloss goes even so far as to declare that the Roman Church receives her authority from the councils, whilst the emperor receives his power from the people. Gloss, s. v. " *Jussione* ": " Habet ergo Romana ecclesia auctoritatem a conciliis, sed imperator a populo." In his further disquisition the glossator modifies this point of view, mainly on account of *Dist.* 21, c. 3 and *Dist.* 22, c. 1, which laws plainly say that the authority of the Church does not rest on any synod but solely on the " evangelica vox Domini et Salvatoris nostri." (It is noteworthy that the gloss on these two laws does not contain anything relevant to the point in question). To reconcile *Dist.* 93, c. 24 with these two passages the glossator declares that, in the first place, the Church's authority rests on Christ, and in the second place on the councils: " Dic principaliter habuit a Domino, secundario a conciliis." It is therefore inaccurate to attribute the origin of this idea to d'Ailly, as Gierke did, see Gierke-Maitland, *Political Theories*, p. 155, note 183. D'Ailly used, without referring to the glossator, a phrase hardly distinguishable from that of the glossator: " Licet principaliter Romana ecclesia principatum habuerit a Domino, tamen secundario a concilio ", in Gerson, *Opera Omnia*, tom. i, p. 905. Gerson himself adopted the same opinion, see *Opera*, tom. ii, pp. 239 f.

[2] Zabarella refers to *Decretales*, i. 2. 7. The general consensus amongst the fourteenth-century legists was that the ruler could transfer property, if the transfer was based on a just cause, see my *Medieval Idea of Law*, pp. 100–3. But there were already voices which maintained that even without a just cause the ruler was entitled to transfer property, see Lucas de Penna, C. x, 31, 33, no. 42, and Cynus in his lecture on C. i, 19, 7, no. 12.

[3] P. 709 (A).

The clarification (or attempted clarification) of the relations between pope and cardinals, and of the function and position of the pope himself as regards the general council and his alleged plenitude of power, convinces Zabarella that the general council is, theoretically at least, the proper authority to judge the pope. This was laid down in canon law and acknowledged by all canonists as far as matters of faith were concerned. That the Schism, especially at the time of Zabarella's writing, that is, within the first decade of the fifteenth century, was an issue that touched the fundamentals of the faith, was, for the cardinal, a matter beyond all doubt. Whether or not this view of the Schism is correct, it is not our concern to investigate: the contemporary, especially if of a sensitive nature, like Cardinal Zabarella, who had witnessed the cancerous growth of the Schism from his early youth onwards, was not inclined to see in the Schism any transitional stage, but a struggle between two conceptions of Christianity, each headed by a pope claiming to be the rightful occupant of St. Peter's chair. To understand such ways of arguing as we meet in Cardinal Zabarella, we must try to put ourselves into the position of the contemporary observer. It is certainly easy, and it betokens complacency, to pour scorn on the man—however wrong he may have been. It was the sore and troubled state of affairs within Holy Church that led him to meditate on the remedies needed to bring to an end this sorrowful and unprecedented state of things : Zabarella's writings go to show how genuinely he had the earthly fate of the Church at heart. A man who had devoted his lifetime to the teaching of canon law and doctrine could not but look to his own subject for a solution of this disaster. The clue, if not more, was undoubtedly contained in canon law and theory—though, admittedly, a great number of the passages adduced and the dicta of famous canonists had been coined in totally different times and under totally different circumstances. In this application of laws and doctrines, *prima facie* inapplicable, lies perhaps the greatest weakness of Zabarella's argumentation. It was not, however, a weakness confined to the cardinal alone. It was perhaps the most characteristic feature of the legal and canonistic scholarship of the Middle Ages that the jurists tried to elicit general principles from terms and notions which their originators had perhaps not used with a generally applicable meaning. It must never be forgotten, in judging medieval scholarship, that these professors of law were the first to establish what we call nowadays legal science. The law, upon which they worked, was casuistic—and that applies to both the civil and the canon law ; but they tried to lay down generally valid principles, which they deduced from the casuistic, quite unscientific medley of positive legal enactments.[1] This, from the point of view of modern legal science, is certainly a grave defect ; but there would not have developed any modern science of law (or modern principles of legislation) had it not been for the medieval jurists working in the field of the civil and the canon law.

It is against this background that, in justice, one must view the ideas and the working methods of Cardinal Zabarella, so far as we have attempted to reconstruct these. And we need to apply the same standard of judgment to the answer he gives to the question, Who is to summon the General Council ? We have already said that he considered the Sacred College as invested with authority to summon a General Council, but immediately there arose the further question, Which of the two Colleges should summon it ? The obvious answer was of course, both ; but the story of the Schism showed that this proposal had little prospect of success, as neither of the two Colleges was, so far, ready to take this step. On the other hand, it was for every Christian a duty to do his best to achieve the sorely wanted unity within the Church. Zabarella, too, discusses the possibility of the two Colleges being the summoners of the council. But failing this, he says with an eye to the future, who should be the proper authority ? However startling, the answer he has at hand is : the Emperor.

History affords many examples, Zabarella declares, in which an emperor or king had convoked a general council. Thus the Emperor Constantine (Constantine IV, 668-685 :

---

[1] I have tried to show the working methods of the medieval legists in op. cit., pp. 2, 15, 35, 60 n. 2, 63 n. 2, 71, 184 n. 3, etc., to give examples how the legists generalized some seemingly insignificant concepts and remarks in order to achieve some system of legal thought. Mutatis mutandis the same applies to the methods of the canonists.

the Sixth General Synod is the Third Council of Constantinople, held in 680-681) had summoned the Sixth General
Synod, as canon law itself says in *Dist.* 16. c. 6 : " Constantinus,
qui eam (scil. synodum) congregaverat." Another passage, also
in the *Decretum* (*Dist.* 16, c.9), speaks of the Sixth Synod as being
called together by this Emperor. And this passage in fact
proves that many of the most important councils in the Church
were convoked by lay princes.[1] Moreover, C.xi, q.i, c.5 reports
that Constantine the Great (twelve years before his baptism)
presided over the Council of Nicea, and in yet another passage
we read that Charlemagne " constituit synodum cum Hadriano
papa."[2] These examples could easily be multiplied, Zabarella
says ; they suffice to show that primitive and early medieval
Christianity found it quite natural that an emperor should
summon a council, the decrees of which were binding on the whole
Church. At a later date it was decreed that the convocation
of a general council was to be the sole prerogative of the Holy
See—*Dist.* 17, c.1, and C.ii, q.vi, c.10.[3] But all this only applies
if there is one undisputed pope. Yet, the history of the Church
proves that a situation similar to the present one had already
arisen—namely, in the double election of Pope Symmachus
and Pope Laurentius, on 22nd November, 498.[4] Canon law,

[1] Zabarella furthermore refers to *Dist.* 15, c. 3, which says that
the Synod of Chalcedon was held "mediante Constantino Maximo."

[2] *Dist.* 63, c. 22 : Adrian I.

[3] " Postea constitutum est, quod ad solum Romanum pontificem
spectet talis congregatio, 2 q. 7 c. ideo (should be 6), 17 dist. c. 1,
et concilia, § hinc," p. 689. Here Zabarella commits a serious
historical blunder : the first quoted passage refers to Pope Marcellus
I (308-9), who wrote to the Emperor Maxentius that a synod of
bishops needs papal approbation and sanction, whilst the latter
passage refers to a decree of Pope Julius I (337-352) with similar
contents. Consequently, the first decree was issued before the
Council of Nicea, and both decrees well over 300 years before the
sixth oecumenical synod at Constantinople (Pope St. Agatho, 680)
—*Dist.* 16, c. 6.

[4] On this schism, see Stöber, " Quellenstudien zum laurentianis-
chen Schisma " in *Sitzungsberichte der Wiener Akademie*, vol. 112,
pp. 269 ff. Maassen, *Geschichte der Quellen des Kirchenrechts*, vol. i,
pp. 411 ff, *Liber Pontificalis*, ed. Duchesne, vol. i, p. 260, Ph. Hughes,
History of the Church, vol. ii, pp. 75 f, and Duchesne, *L'Eglise au
VIme Siècle*, pp. 152-69.

according to Cardinal Zabarella, lays down that it should be the Emperor who, in cases of a disputed election, should summon the General Council.[1] The precedent of the quarrel between Symmachus and Laurentius justifies, in the opinion of Zabarella, this generalization. For the Gothic king Theodoric, himself an Arian,[2] summoned a council to decide which of the two claimants was the rightful occupant of the papal chair ; moreover, it was the king himself who made the decision in favour of Symmachus (499). It is upon this precedent that Zabarella rests his now famous opinion on the Emperor's authority.[3]

In elaborating his argument the cardinal says that if, in this struggle, it was the concern of the king to establish peace in the Roman city, how much more should it now be his concern to establish peace within the whole world ? The rule of two popes is ruinous for the world and Christianity itself ; and the readers are reminded of the utterance in the gospel : *Omne regnum in se divisum desolabitur.* That it is precisely the Emperor who is charged with this duty follows from his being the *advocatus et defensor ecclesiae.* As to the legal basis proper, Zabarella finds this in *Dist.* 65, c.9 : here it is laid down that it is the people themselves who have to summon the neighbouring bishops for special purposes, if the properly instituted bishop neglects his duty of summoning his colleagues.[4] Here,

---

[1] " Quando autem sunt plures, qui contendunt de papatu, sicut nunc, debet congregari concilium ad sollicitudinem imperatoris, dicto § hinc," *loc. cit.* ; the reference is to *Dist.* 17, c. 6, secunda pars (Gratian).

[2] See Ph. Hughes, *op. cit.*, p. 75.

[3] In his political views Zabarella was a thorough-going papalist. This emerges plainly from his commentaries on the *Decretals*, I. 6. 34, nos. 2–9, where he shows himself a staunch anti-imperialist. The pope is spiritual as well as temporal overlord ; on the strength of his plenitude of power he is expected to interfere with the temporal affairs of the empire—" ad papam spectat de imperio se intermiscere ", no. 8.

[4] The whole passage runs like this : " Si forte in provincia unum tantum contigerit remanere episcopum, superstes episcopus convocet episcopos vicinae provinciae, et cum eis ordinet comprovinciales sibi episcopos. Quod si facere neglexerit, populi conveniant episcopos provinciae vicinae . . ."

says Zabarella, is one in which the lay population is entitled to summon bishops for a special meeting. Now the Emperor is nothing but the (temporal) representative of the whole Christian people, since all imperial and supreme power has been transferred to him by the people.[1] The Emperor simply takes the place of the people mentioned in *Dist.* 65, c. 9, and, incidentally, in this way the circle of historical development appears to be closed : first the Emperor ; then the Pope ; then in special cases the people ; and, lastly, the Emperor again.[2] Moreover, the Schism, according to Zabarella, plainly concerns the faith and, here again, canon law states that the Emperor may take part in councils, not in order to boast of his might, but to avow his faith publicly.[3] Therefore, the Emperor actually is part of the council. Although Zabarella refers us here to dicta of some famous canonists, such as Innocent IV and the Archdeacon, who were supposed to support him in this, we are unable to confirm the correctness of the cardinal's quotations : that is to say, the actual references are correct, but the ideas expressed by these two canonists can be adduced only if they are stretched widely enough.[4] On the other hand, the glossator, Joannes Teutonicus, appears, if anything, unfriendly to the expansion of the

[1]*Loc. cit.*: reference is made to Dig. 1, 2, 2, and C. i, 17, 1, 7, where the representative function of the Emperor is clearly expressed. This idea was not entirely unknown in the Middle Ages ; St. Thomas Aquinas especially adhered to the idea of the ruler (prince) as a representative of the people, see *Summa Theologica*, II. i, qu. 90, art. 3, when he speaks of the legislator and says : " Lex proprie primo et principaliter respicit ordinem ad bonum commune. Ordinare autem aliquid in bonum commune est vel totius multitudinis vel alicuius gerentis vicem totius multitudinis. Et ideo condere legem vel pertinet ad totam multitudinem vel pertinet ad personam publicam, quae totius multitudinis curam habet." Ockham, too, adhered to a similar conception, see his *Dialogus*, pars iii, tract. ii, lib. 3, cap. 7 and 12 (*vice omnium*).

[2]" Loco ipsorum ergo populorum habet congregare concilium, et sic ω revolvabit ad α, quia extremitas retrahitur ad principiam . . . revertimur ad jus pristinum," p. 691, that is, if the historical aspect had been correct.

[3]*Dist.* 96, c, 2.

[4]Zabarella also refers to the gloss of Laurentius, which I was unable to consult.

Emperor's powers in the ecclesiastical field. Commenting upon *Dist.* 17, c. 6, § *hinc*, Joannes said that the bishops (in the case of Symmachus), though they obeyed the citation of the king, were not bound to appear in the synod.[1] But in Zabarella's commentary on the *Clementines* there is expressed an opinion that comes very near to that which he maintains in the tract. Speaking of fear during a papal election, Zabarella asks who is to decide whether fear was justifiable ? The gloss, he says, asked the same question without answering it. Cautiously Zabarella says that it is for the Emperor, by virtue of the powers which are conferred upon him by *Dist.* 51, c. 3.[2] Although it is highly doubtful whether the interpretation by Zabarella of *Dist.* 51, c. 3 is correct, he could nevertheless have found strong support for his " imperial " theory in the writings of the extreme papal publicist, Augustinus Triumphus. In his *De Potestate Ecclesiastica* Augustinus ascribed to the Emperor the role of a " defender and advocate of the Church " and, furthermore, declared that the General Council—the " collegium universalis ecclesiae "—represented the Church and that the General Council may be convoked by the Emperor.[3]

The cardinal himself seems somehow to feel that he is standing on insecure ground when, in a somewhat apologetic

[1]" Isti episcopi venerunt ad citationem regis, non quod venire tenerentur, sed ut revocarent eum ab errore suo."

[2]*In Clementinas Commentaria*, Venice, 1602, *Clem.* i, 3, 2, § Porro, fol. 18, no. 5: " Quaero, si dubitatur, an metus sit justus, quis cognoscat de justitia metus ? Glossa eandem quaestionem format et non solvit. Videtur dicendum, quod ipse dominus temporalis cognoscit per potestatem sibi traditam per. c. praeterea, quod tenet Lau. et Gen." It should be observed that *Dist.* 51, c. 3, certainly does not speak of any conferment of powers on the Emperor. " Lau " is bound to be Laurentius, who wrote his *Apparatus ad Decretales* between 1208 and 1212, according to Gierke, *Deutsches Genossenschaftsrecht*, vol. iii, p. 239. I was unable to establish the identity of the glossator " Gen ".

[3]See Augustinus Triumphus, *De Potestate Ecclesiastica*, written about 1308, Romae, 1583, I, quaestio III, art. 2, qu. IV, art. 1 seq., qu. VI, art. 6 and qu. XXIII, art. 4, etc. Because this treatise belonged to the publicist, and not the canonist, literature, Zabarella probably did not consider it a work of any value for his purpose.

manner, he says that extraordinary situations demand extraordinary measures : and to allow that there are two popes at the head of Christendom would be a palpable violation of a fundamental article of faith, as the Bull *Unam Sanctam* has so explicitly and emphatically laid it down.[1] And the proposal that the Emperor should be the convening authority though perhaps at first startling, appears to Zabarella not so unorthodox : he sees, of course, quite plainly that some jurisdictional powers may be attributed to the Emperor, if he is called upon to convoke a General Council. But, says the cardinal, this too is not contrary to the law, for there are a number of instances in which the secular authority assumes jurisdictional powers over ecclesiastical persons and institutions.[2] The objection, therefore, that the Emperor is only a layman who should not meddle in ecclesiastical affairs, can consequently be dismissed as invalid.[3] For special reasons the Emperor or the secular authority has jurisdictional powers, as, for instance, in feudal litigations, which must be decided, even if the litigants are clerics, by the secular judge—a legal provision that is contained in the *Decretals* II, 2, 7, and in the

[1] He also refers to C. vii, q. i, c. 12, p. 692.

[2] This was a very delicate and controversial point in medieval lore. Generally speaking, the secular and ecclesiastical judges wanted an enlargement of their respective spheres of jurisdiction, each at the expense of the other. I have attempted to give some examples of this controversy in *The Medieval Idea of Law*, pp. 79–90, 136–8, but a clear demarcation of the authority of either judge and, consequently, of whether civil or canon law should be applied, has, so far as can at present be ascertained, not been achieved.

[3] " Nec quempiam moveat, quod imperator est laicus, ut ex hoc putet inconveniens . . .", p. 692 (B).

On the importance of this tract, see Scholz, *Unbekannte kirchenpolitische Streitschriften aus der Zeit Ludwigs des Bayern*, Rome, 1914, vol. ii, p. 481. According to Marsiglio it is the *legislator humanus* who is permanently charged with convening the general council, see *Defensor Pacis*, Dictio Secunda, c. 21, but the basis of his views is totally different from that of Zabarella ; Marsiglio rarely refers to canon law (see C. W. Previté-Orton, " The authors cited in the Defensor Pacis ", in *Essays in History presented to R. L. Poole*, ed. H. W. C. Davis, pp. 405–20, at pp. 413–4) and mainly supports himself by taking his examples from the pseudo-Isidorian *Codex*.

Sext II, 15, 3 (§ Debet).[1] And in the present case we have a *ratio specialissima* for the intervention of the Emperor : as the *advocatus et defensor ecclesiae* it is his duty to see that the Catholic Faith does not suffer any longer, as would certainly be the case if the dual papacy were allowed to continue.[2] But, apart from the special legal provisions conferring jurisdictional powers on the secular authority, other instances also go to show that the Emperor enjoys a specially privileged position in ecclesiastical matters. Thus, according to Zabarella's interpretation of *Clem. I*, 3, 2 (§ Porro), the secular authority can exercise an indirect pressure during the election of a pope on those cardinals who leave the conclave without having elected a pontiff ; moreover, *Sext* I, 6, 3 (§ Verum) gives the secular authority the right to restrict the supply of food to the cardinals, if they have not elected a pope within the first three days of the conclave.[3] Though Cardinal Zabarella himself does not know how, in fact, pressure could be exercised on the cardinals[4] to re-enter the conclave, he sees in this theoretical provision the right of the secular authority to compel the electors in an indirect manner.[5]

Lastly, Cardinal Zabarella resorts to an extra-legal consideration. It is true, he says, that the pope alone is the legitimate

[1]Here it should be pointed out that the two passages referred to in the text do not lay down this principle in the categorical way in which Zabarella would like them to read : *unless* privilege or custom has decided otherwise, feudal litigations belong to the secular judge, says the passage in the *Sext ;* whilst that in the *Decretals* is still vaguer, merely saying that *if* the feudal litigation is not a matter of decision for the ecclesiastical judge (the bishop), it should then go before the secular judge. The general trend, however, seems to have been that such litigation should be decided by the secular authority, see Lucas de Penna, C. x, 43, 4 no. 40, and the law of the Sicilian King Charles II in *Constitutiones Regni Utriusque Siciliae*, Lugduni, 1568, p. 313, which law declares the secular judge alone competent.

[2]*Loc. cit.*

[3]This interpretation, though not novel, can be derived from the two passages referred to, especially from the decretal *Ubi periculum.*

[4]" Et quamquam expositores non aperiant ibi, quomodo possint cogi ad ingrediendum conclave . . ."

[5]" Dixi, quod postquam sunt in conclavi, compelluntur indirecte expedire electionem . . . coguntur per subtractionem victualium."

authority to summon a General Council, but can the letter of the law strictly be upheld if the pope obstinately refuses to convoke one ? One has only to imagine, declares Zabarella, what incalculable damage would be inflicted upon the faith and the Church if the latter were in the hands of an heretical pope. That heresy is an item to be judged by the General Council is self-evident, because a matter of faith is at stake, but what is to be done if the pope refuses to submit to a General Council or even to summon one ?[1] In the case of a refusal by the pope, the Church would be " ruled " by a heretic to the unspeakable detriment of the Catholic Faith. The only way out of this difficulty is the convocation of a General Council either by the cardinals themselves or by the Emperor, in virtue of his specially privileged position. Moreover, the pope himself could declare null and void *Dist.* 40, c. 6, which lays down that in matters of faith the General Council is the competent judge. Consequently, no pope could ever be brought to trial before a council. If, then, the pope could not do this directly, he might circumvent canon law by simply refusing to convoke a council. It would be *maximum absurdum* to say that God had left His Church without a government, for that is what a refusal of this kind would entail. It could then easily happen that the heretical pope would only create those clerics cardinals who held to his heretical opinions ; they, in their turn, would again elect someone who is a heretic. " Sic contingeret, quod scriptum est, qualis rector dominus, tales et habitantes."[2] In this way, unless God intervened, the whole Church could be led astray and into error, which, however, cannot be admitted " as the Church cannot not be."[3] And there is no more capable minister of God—in an emergency like the present one—than the Emperor, seeing that he is the defen-

---

[1] " Finge, sicut aliquando accidit, quod papa esset haereticus, quo casu certe ad concilium spectat judicare, 17 dist. § hinc etiam, 2 q. 7, § item . . ."

[2] P. 693 (A) ; he continues : " Nam id, quod dogmatizat princeps, facile amplectuntur subditi."

[3] " Posset ergo, nisi Deus aliter succurreret, tota ecclesia perduci ad errorem, quod tamen non esset fatendum, cum ecclesia non esset nulla, 24 q. i, c, a recta ", *ibid.*

der and advocate of the Church.[1] " One must therefore assume that good clerics and loyal believers and followers of the Church would accept this proposal, seeing that neither pope nor college of cardinals have fulfilled their duty in convoking a General Council."[2]

No doubt Zabarella's ideas about the convocation of the General Council by the Emperor, should all other means fail, may appear very startling, perhaps perturbing, to a modern mind. And Zabarella himself may have felt somewhat uneasy at his own idea when he dealt with the very plausible objection that the Emperor as a layman could not be in a position to summon the Church's prelates to a purely ecclesiastical meeting. But it needs not much imagination to perceive that a modern man, when reading of this proposal, is bound to view it with distaste. How could the head of the State, he may legitimately ask, be given such powers over all dignitaries of the Church—to decide the fate of a pope or even of two popes ? State and Church, so may his argument run, are two entirely independent societies ; neither should meddle in the affairs of the other. Hence, to put forward such a proposal is nothing else but to attempt the secularization of the Church, if not more.[3] Now, it is in this very antithesis of State and Church, thus posited by such a modern mind, that its lack of understanding and appreciation is rooted. For this antithesis simply did not exist in the Middle Ages : there was neither a " State " as a corporate personality, nor a " Church " in this same sense.[4] For the medieval thinker society was crystallized in the conception of the Holy Roman Empire : there were no two societies, Church and State, within that body. Both constituted the Empire, aptly called a *Respublica Christiana*. Pope and Emperor were not two heads of two

---

[1] " Non est autem alius magis idoneus Dei minister ad obviandum, ne hoc accidat, quam imperator, qui advocatus est et defensor ecclesiae, ut supra," p. 693 (B).

[2] *Loc. cit.*

[3] We assume that it was this, or some similar attitude, that has made some modern historians view Zabarella with coolness and aversion, especially Pastor, *History of the Popes*, vol. i, p. 187 f, and E. Carusi, *Encicl. Italiana*, vol. xxxv, p. 858.

[4] Cf. Gierke, *Deutsches Genossenschaftsrecht*, vol. iii, pp. 249-50.

different corporate bodies ; rather they were the heads of one and the same body, each charged with special duties, rights and prerogatives in his own sphere of governing the same body. All medieval political thought was possessed by the overriding idea of unity—and, incidentally, all the quarrels between popes and emperors were rooted in this, that the one charged the other with preventing the longed for (and hardly ever achieved) unity—and this idea found its clearest expression in the dual headship of pope and emperor, the one administering to the spiritual, the other to the temporal, affairs of the same body politic.

With due deference to Maitland[1] we cannot agree with him that " these two bodies (Church and State) are distinct."[2] That is a modern view of the political structure of the Middle Ages which is not borne out by medieval reality. The interpretation of medieval political thought by J. N. Figgis comes much nearer to the truth and to the medieval reality when, in a memorable passage, he says that quarrels between pope and emperor were quarrels between two brothers.[3] But Figgis does not go far enough. The coronation of the " King of the Romans " as Emperor of the Holy Roman Empire by the pope is perhaps the most concrete manifestation of the idea that a Christian should, in the field of temporality, rule a Christian people : the examination and approbation of the emperor by the pope before coronation was merely a safeguard to prevent the temporal rulership of the Christian people from falling into the hands of a heretic or otherwise unsuitable person. The act of coronation did not mean that the emperor was thereby constituted as the head of a body, the State, distinct from that of the Church. It did mean, however, that the pope as the spiritual overlord approved publicly and *qua* pope of the personality of the emperor as the temporal overlord over the same people whose spiritual

---

[1]F. W. Maitland, *Constitutional History of England*, ed. 1926, pp. 101–2.

[2]*Op. cit.*, p. 102 : " The State has its king or emperor, its laws, its legislative assemblies, its courts, its judges ; the Church has its pope, its prelates, its councils, its laws, its judges . . . the general conviction (in the Middle Ages) is that the two are independent."

[3]John Nevile Figgis, *Churches in the Modern State*, p. 199.

affairs lay with the pope.[1] *Imperium* and *Sacerdotium* are two facets of one and the same idea—the Holy Roman Empire. If we consider the position of the medieval emperor under such aspects, much of the startling and perturbing character, and of the adverse criticisms, of Zabarella's proposal is whittled away.

We have singled out only the leading ideas of Cardinal Zabarella, as he propounded them in his tract, commonly misunderstood and misinterpreted, where not entirely forgotten. There are many other ideas contained in the tract, but to reconstruct them all would lead us into fields which are no longer of topical interest. His proposals for ending the Schism would merit a special analysis, especially with regard to their bearing on the doctrinal structures of Gerson and d'Ailly.[2] We may perhaps just mention his ideas on the theory of *subtrattio*, that is, not only the simple withdrawal of allegiance from both popes by the faithful, but also resistance by every individual against the Church's government. This truly pernicious proposal, which was most clearly developed by Nicholas de Clémanges in the letter of the University of Paris to the French king,[3] is of course nothing else but the right of revolution : individual Catholics were urged to resist all orders issued by either pope. If this revolutionary doctrine had been followed the consequences would have been unpredictable. It was perhaps partly due to the moderating

---

[1]Whatever the theoretical controversies as regards the position of the pope and emperor—all parties had this in common, that both were considered *minister Dei :* the controversy only started with the question, Is the temporal authority derived from the spiritual (the view of the papalists), or is it derived directly from God, without an intermediary ?

[2]Reference is made to his " via cessionis ", p. 696 (A), his proposal of abstaining from proceeding to a new election after the death of one of the popes, p. 697 (B), the possibility of drawing lots (*Consilium* CL, fol. 92 no. 19, col. 2), and to his opinion on the legal position, if either pope or emperor were to hinder clerics from attending a general council, pp. 690, 694, 710 of the tract in Schard.

[3]*Epistola Universitatis Parisiensis ad Regem Francorum directa super Schismate Sedando*, written on 8th June, 1394, and partly printed in Bulaeus, *Historia Univ. Parisiensis*, vol. iv, p. 687. Nicholas became a licentiate at Paris in 1380.

influence of Zabarella that this doctrine did not spread any further. In short, the cardinal condemns the theory of *subtractio*, and maintains that if a right of disobedience and resistance should exist, it then belongs to the cardinals : private individuals have no right to revolt against authority.[1] In another passage he doubts whether even the cardinals have this right of resistance : the only step he advised them to take was to appeal to a general council, so that the matter could be there thrashed out.[2] There seems to be a genuine dislike on the part of Zabarella for anything approaching so-called self-help by the citizens, in the sense that they could take the law into their own hands : if the faithful of either obedience believe in the justness of their cause, they will be saved : " Omnes enim ex utraque parte salvantur, dum tamen non errant scienter."[3]

The picture of Zabarella's character emerges in its full light in his commentaries on the *Decretals* and the *Clementines*, no less than in the *Consilia* and in his famous tract on the Schism. It is the character of a man who, on the one hand, deeply felt the disaster and tragedy that had befallen the Church, and who, on the other hand, was convinced that the way out of this disaster, and the only remedy to heal the Schism, was the application of the law and of legal doctrine. His position as a prince of the Church made it his duty to

[1] " Non licet privatis per seditionem ab obedientia desistere ", p. 700 (B).

[2] Speaking of the beginning of the Schism, he says, p. 695 (B) : "Ex quo fuit (Urbanus VI) in possessione papatus, non potuerunt cardinales se subtrahere ab obedientia et alium eligere, sed debebant prius facere de hoc discuti per concilium."

[3] P. 710 (B). Almost the same words can be found in his *Commentaria in Decretales*, Venice, 1602, i. 6. 6. fol. 106 *vo*, no. 13. In this commentary he refused to accept the plea of the cardinals that they were compelled to elect Urban VI. He enumerated here, in a long discussion of two folio columns, all the arguments which made him reject the argument of fear. But even if there had been fear on their part, that fear could not be pleaded any more after their own recognition of Urban as pope : " Ex his videtur purgatus metus, si quis intercessit." In no case could the cardinals be judges : " Non ergo ipsi, sed concilium habet judicare," referring to *Dist.* 79, c. 8.

contribute to the unification of the Church by propounding various proposals to that effect. If we cannot always follow him, or even if we are to consider some of his views as not in keeping with the dogmatic tradition and established Church doctrine, we cannot put the blame on Zabarella. It would be unfair to criticize a man by criteria not in existence in his own time : let us judge a man by contemporary standards, and not by those which only posterity has evolved. Zabarella was the typical product of an age that was nothing if not critical, an age whose far-reaching influence and whose implications for the development of European ideas on law and politics have not yet been fully grasped. In nearly every sphere of life the fourteenth century exhibited the traits of a crisis in which very few ideas could be said to be universally accepted ; the advance of the new entailed a challenging defence of the old, and both " new " and " old " were in a state of flux. That, under such circumstances, proposals and ideas were put forward which we are so easily inclined to dismiss as unorthodox, not to say damnable, can cause little surprise. It is indeed difficult to sense, in our materialistic twentieth century, how deep was the impact which the Schism had made upon men's souls. An extraordinary situation called for extraordinary remedies, Zabarella remarked. Believing as he did, and convinced as he was, that in the Schism the faith was imperilled by an issue that was nothing more than legal and constitutional—can we blame him for his interpretation of the law, and for his application of canonist doctrine to find a solution ? To him, as to everyone else in the fourteenth century, law was a direct manifestation of the divine idea of right. To interpret the law meant, for him, to apply the idea of justice to the concrete case. Rationalism, honesty of thought and a highly developed sense of justice—these are the facets of the man and of Cardinal Francis Zabarella which formed the subject of the funeral oration which the Florentine humanist Poggio delivered in one of the sessions of the Council of Constance :—

" Justitiae vero, virtutum omnium parentis, amantissimus fuit et servantissimus. Nihil ab eo inique dictum reperitur, nihil inique factum. Vixit ad praescriptum rationis, numquam deflexit ab aequitate, numquam progressus est longius quam honestas dictaret. Nec vero dubium est, quin si vixisset diutius, summo sacerdotio functus esset."

[1]See *Poggii Florentini Oratio in Funere Francisci Zabarellae, Patricii Patavini, eminentissimi J. U. interpretis, et S. R. E. Cardinalis Florentini, Habita in Concilio Constantiensi, anno* 1417, p. 17. This speech is also in von der Hardt, *Magnum Oecumenicum Concilium Constantiense,* Francofurti, 1697–1700, tom. i, pp. 537–8.

INDEX